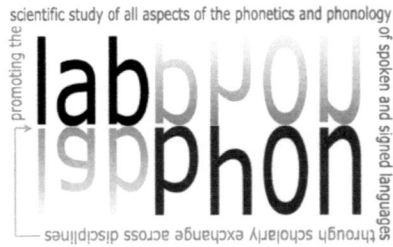

Studies in Laboratory Phonology

Chief Editor: Martine Grice
Editors: Doris Mücke, Taehong Cho

In this series:

1. Cangemi, Francesco. Prosodic detail in Neapolitan Italian.

2. Drager, Katie K. Linguistic variation, identity construction and cognition.

ISSN: 2363-5576

Linguistic variation, identity construction and cognition

Katie K. Drager

Katie K. Drager. 2015. *Linguistic variation, identity construction and cognition* (Studies in Laboratory Phonology 2). Berlin: Language Science Press.

This title can be downloaded at:
http://langsci-press.org/catalog/book/75
© 2015, Katie K. Drager
Published under the Creative Commons Attribution 4.0 Licence (CC BY 4.0):
http://creativecommons.org/licenses/by/4.0/
ISBN: 978-3-946234-24-1 (Digital)
   978-3-946234-25-8 (Hardcover)
   978-3-944675-56-5 (Softcover)
ISSN: 2363-5576

Cover and concept of design: Ulrike Harbort
Typesetting: Katie K. Drager, Sebastian Nordhoff, Felix Kopecky
Proofreading: Svetoslava Antonova-Baumann, Timo Buchholz, Andreea Calude, Hugo Cardoso, Christian Döhler, Martin Haspelmath, Andreas Hölzl, Maria Maldonado, Aviva Shimelman, Charlotte van Tongeren
Fonts: Linux Libertine, Arimo, DejaVu Sans Mono
Typesetting software: X∃LATEX

Language Science Press
Habelschwerdter Allee 45
14195 Berlin, Germany
langsci-press.org

Storage and cataloguing done by FU Berlin

Language Science Press has no responsibility for the persistence or accuracy of URLs for external or third-party Internet websites referred to in this publication, and does not guarantee that any content on such websites is, or will remain, accurate or appropriate. Information regarding prices, travel timetables and other factual information given in this work are correct at the time of first publication but Language Science Press does not guarantee the accuracy of such information thereafter.

To Mom and Dad

Contents

Acknowledgements		ix
Abbreviations		xi
1	**The separation of the social and the linguistic**	**1**
1.1	Introduction	1
1.2	The social, the linguistic, and the cognitive	4
1.3	Waves of variationist studies	7
	1.3.1 First Wave	9
	1.3.2 Second Wave	9
	1.3.3 Third Wave	11
1.4	Gradience and acoustic analysis	13
1.5	Experimental sociolinguistics	15
1.6	Laboratory phonology	17
	1.6.1 Token frequency	18
	1.6.2 Lemmas, lexemes, and phonetic detail	18
1.7	Multiple methodologies	19
2	**Social groups at Selwyn Girls' High**	**23**
2.1	Methodology	23
	2.1.1 Background	23
	2.1.2 The students	24
	2.1.3 Integrating myself into SGH	25
	2.1.4 The formal	26
	2.1.5 My role at SGH	28
	2.1.6 The myth of the neutral ethnographer	29
2.2	Selwyn Girls' High	31
2.3	Groups of friends	33
	2.3.1 CR groups	35
	2.3.2 NCR groups	44
	2.3.3 Outside of lunchtime	53
2.4	Salience and stance	54

Contents

- 2.5 A bit of self reflection 61
  - 2.5.1 The BBs 61
  - 2.5.2 The Trendy Alternatives 62
  - 2.5.3 The PCs 63
  - 2.5.4 The Real Teenagers 64
  - 2.5.5 The Relaxed Group 64
  - 2.5.6 The Pasifika Group 65
  - 2.5.7 The Goths 65
  - 2.5.8 The Christians and The Geeks 65
  - 2.5.9 The Sporty Girls 65
  - 2.5.10 Rochelle's Group 66
  - 2.5.11 Sonia's Group 66
  - 2.5.12 When research and friendship blend 66
  - 2.5.13 Shaping interpretations 68
- 2.6 Conclusion 70

3 *Like*: Frequency and phonetic realisations — 73
- 3.1 Methodology of interviews 73
- 3.2 Variation in use of *like* 75
  - 3.2.1 Use of quotative *like* at SGH 78
  - 3.2.2 Use of discourse particle *like* at SGH 84
- 3.3 Phonetic variation of *like* 86
  - 3.3.1 Methodology for acoustic phonetic analysis . 87
  - 3.3.2 Results 95
- 3.4 Discussion 105
  - 3.4.1 Frequency effects 106
  - 3.4.2 Special status of discursive tokens 109
  - 3.4.3 Changes in progress 112
  - 3.4.4 Prosody and phonetic variation 113
  - 3.4.5 Identity construction 113
  - 3.4.6 Reflection on influence from researcher ... 120
  - 3.4.7 Storage of phonetic detail in the mind 121

4 Variation in speech perception — 123
- 4.1 Experiment 1 127
  - 4.1.1 Methodology 127
  - 4.1.2 Results 130
- 4.2 Experiment 2 134
  - 4.2.1 Methodology 134

		4.2.2	Results	136
	4.3	Experiment 3		138
		4.3.1	Methodology	139
		4.3.2	Results	140
	4.4	Discussion		142
		4.4.1	Lack of social effects in function identification tasks	143
		4.4.2	Theoretical implications	144

5 Toward a cognitive model of stylistic variation in identity construction — 147
- 5.1 Summary of results . . . 147
  - 5.1.1 Maintaining and rejecting norms . . . 147
  - 5.1.2 Patterns in production . . . 148
  - 5.1.3 Patterns in perception . . . 148
- 5.2 Social theory . . . 150
  - 5.2.1 Phonetic information and identity construction . . . 150
- 5.3 Probabilistic linguistics . . . 151
  - 5.3.1 Bayesian model of syntactic parsing . . . 151
  - 5.3.2 Exemplar Theory . . . 153
- 5.4 Indexation of social information . . . 157
- 5.5 Conclusion . . . 163

6 Looking forward — 165
- 6.1 Speakers as style-creators . . . 166
- 6.2 Concluding remarks . . . 170

A Measures of familiarity — 175
- A.1 CR Groups . . . 175
  - A.1.1 The Sporty Girls . . . 175
  - A.1.2 The PCs . . . 176
  - A.1.3 Trendy Alternatives . . . 177
  - A.1.4 Rochelle's Group . . . 177
  - A.1.5 The BBs . . . 178
  - A.1.6 The Relaxed Group . . . 179
- A.2 NCR Groups . . . 180
  - A.2.1 The Pasifika Group . . . 180
  - A.2.2 The Goths . . . 180
  - A.2.3 The Real Teenagers . . . 181
  - A.2.4 The Christians . . . 181
  - A.2.5 Sonia's Group . . . 182

	A.2.6 The Geeks	182
	A.2.7 Cecily's Group	183
	A.2.8 Loners	183
B	**Production data**	**185**
C	**Stimuli for perception experiments**	**187**
D	**Perception experiment data**	**219**
References		**227**
Index		**238**
	Name index	238
	Subject index	242

Acknowledgements

This book is a slightly altered version of my Ph.D. dissertation, which I completed with the insightful and generous help from the wonderful mentors I had while at the University of Canterbury. First and foremost, I would like to thank Jen Hay. I can't begin to express how indebted I am to her. She is my mentor, my role model, and my good friend and it has been an incredible honour to work with her. Through knowing Jen, I have come to understand the kind of teacher, researcher, and mentor that I would like to be. I am also extremely grateful to Alex D'Arcy, my associate supervisor, for her valuable critiques of my work and her wonderfully caring and supportive nature. Additionally, I would like to thank Christian Langstrof, Anita Szakay, Elizabeth Gordon, Heidi Quinn, and Jeanette King. I would also like to thank Abby Walker, who I have had countless academic discussions with and who has been there for me on a personal level more times than I can count.

After completing the ethnographic portion of this study, I had the opportunity to spend time as a visiting student at two overseas universities: Stanford University and the University of Oxford. While at Stanford, I had the pleasure of working with Penny Eckert, with whom every discussion resulted in a new insight. I am also grateful to John Coleman for allowing me to work at the Oxford Phonetics Lab, where I completed the majority of the acoustic analysis that is presented in this book.

I am extremely appreciative of the helpful comments made by Margaret Maclagan, Felcity Cox, Jane Stuart-Smith, Lauren Hall-Lew, Laura Staum Casasanto, Rebecca Greene, Paul Foulkes, Benjamin Munson, ʻŌiwi Parker Jones, and Keith Johnson. I would also like to thank Gerry Docherty, who served as a reviewer for this book and whose comments and suggestions were especially valuable. I am also indebted to the many proofreaders who volunteered their time.

Thank you to Carolyn Morris, Martin Fuchs, and Norma Mendoza-Denton for providing support and advice regarding the ethnographic portion of the study. I would like to thank Robert Fromont for his (continued) development of ONZEMiner, some of which he developed specifically for the requirements of this work. And I would like to thank the University of Canterbury for funding this research through the University of Canterbury Targeted Scholarship.

Acknowledgements

I would like to thank my friends and family who have provided continual emotional support. Never once have I doubted the love and support of my parents, Chris and Charlene Drager, or my brother, Blake. And I'm not sure I would have been able to finish this work without the support of my friends, Emma Parnell and Alice Murphy. Thank you.

I would also like to thank Selwyn Girls' High for allowing me to conduct an ethnography at their school. And last, but certainly not least, I would like to express my sincere gratitude to the girls of Selwyn Girls' High, who have given me so much more than I was able to give to them.

Abbreviations

CR	Common Room
NCR	non-Common Room
SGH	Selwyn Girls' High
The BBs	The Blazer Brigade
The PCs	The Palms Crew

1 The separation of the social and the linguistic

> It's kind of like there's youth culture and then there's human beings and it's really nice to be like accepted as a human being.
>
> Katrina (The Relaxed Group).
> Interview, 18-10.

1.1 Introduction

High school can be a difficult period as it marks the transition between childhood and adulthood. Adolescents are expected to take on additional responsibilities but are not yet treated like adults or, as Katrina expressed feeling, not yet treated like human beings. This transitional period is marked by linguistic variation, as the teenagers "try on" different personae in an effort to construct their identities within the context of the changing perceptions of their identities.

Additionally, there is pressure from within the social make-up of the school, where an individual's style is often interpreted as a reflection of who she is (Pomerantz 2008: 2). While Pomerantz (2008) focused on clothing styles, this is true of other aspects of an individual's style, where style is defined as a "socially meaningful clustering of features, within and across linguistic levels and modalities" (Campbell-Kibler et al. 2006) and non-linguistic levels and modalities. High school students construct their identities in relation to each other (in addition to the world around them) and in doing so, they make use of a multitude of stylistic components, including ways of dressing, ways of walking, and ways of talking.

In this book, I examine the link between linguistic variation and identity in order to develop our understanding of the ways in which language and social information are stored in the mind and accessed during the production and perception of speech. Specifically, I examine the degree to which lemma-based phonetic

1 The separation of the social and the linguistic

variables are manipulated in the construction of social personae and I investigate the extent to which the relationship between social, phonetic, and lemma-based information influences speech processing. Within the context of data from an all girls' school, I argue that social theory needs to be incorporated into linguistic theory and in Chapter 5, I present a possible avenue in which to explore this unification of theories.

Along with Weinrich, Labov & Herzog (1968), I believe that a

> nativelike command of heterogeneous structures is not a matter of multidialectalism or "mere" performance, but is part of unilingual linguistic competence (Weinrich, Labov & Herzog 1968: 101).

Empirical evidence can bring to light the richness and complexity of this competence, resulting in a better understanding of linguistic patterns found at all levels of the grammar. Using empirical methods to inform a unified probabilistic model of identity construction, speech production, and speech perception, the research questions I explore here relate both to social theory and to how social information is stored in the mind and is indexed to linguistic representations. The specific questions to be addressed are:

1. Can lemmas that share a wordform have different realisations?

2. Do speakers manipulate their realisations of a lemma in the construction and expression of their identity?

3. What is the relationship between the phonetic realisation of a lexical item and how predictable that item is given who the speaker is?

4. How is this construction of personae related to other speakers who share a similar stance?

5. And what role does this phonetic, lemma, and social information play during speech processing?

In order to address these questions, I have employed the use of multiple methodologies within a single study, combining the qualitative method of ethnography with the quantitative methods of acoustic analysis and experimental design.

I spent a year at Selwyn Girls' High, the pseudonym for the all girls' high school in Christchurch, New Zealand where I chose to conduct an ethnographic investigation of identity construction. The girls shared details of their lives with me and allowed me to record their conversations. While there were a number of close-knit groups at the school, these groups could be categorised according to whether they embodied, created, and perpetuated the school's norms (forming what I refer to as Common Room groups) or whether they dismissed, rejected, or failed to conform to these norms (forming what I refer to as non-Common Room groups). The qualitative findings from the ethnography are presented in Chapter 2.

The linguistic analysis focuses on the word *like*, a word with a number of different functions including the quotative (*and Mum's **like** "turn that stupid thing off"*), the lexical verb (*I don't really **like** her that much*), and the discourse particle (*Lily was **like** checking out my brother*). In Chapter 3, I discuss the frequency with which different girls and groups at the school used these different functions and I present results from acoustic analysis conducted on tokens of *like* from the girls' speech. I discuss the results within the context of theories of identity construction and consider the possibility that colloquial words can serve as loci for socially-meaningful phonetic variation. The work presented in Chapter 3 can be found in article-form in Drager (2011a).

In Chapter 4, I present the method and results from three perception experiments that I conducted at the school, which are also presented in Drager (2010). The experiments were designed with the aim of determining whether perceivers could use phonetic cues in the signal to identify a word (here, a particular function of *like*) and whether they could extract social information attributed to a speaker when exposed to only short clips of speech that contain phonetic and lemma-based information.

In Chapter 5, I discuss the results within the context of two linguistic models: one that relies on Bayesian statistics (Jurafsky 1996; Narayanan & Jurafsky 2002) and an exemplar model of speech production and perception, where complete acoustically-detailed representations of encountered utterances are stored in the mind (Johnson 1997; Pisoni 1997; Pierrehumbert 2001). I then argue for the need to incorporate theories of identity construction into linguistic models and I propose a model in which to explore this unification. In the concluding chapter, I discuss some developments in the field since writing my dissertation.

In order to inform the presentation of methods and results in the following chapters, the remainder of this chapter reviews relevant literature, focusing on the development of social theory within linguistics, recent insights into the storage of sociophonetic relationships in the mind, and other work which demonstrates the probabilistic nature of linguistic variation. This book is an adaptation of my Ph.D. dissertation (Drager 2009b). Therefore, much of the background literature I discuss is reflective of the field at that time though I have added some discussion of more recent work, when needed. Additionally, I have added a concluding chapter that discusses an avenue for future exploration of work along these lines.

1.2 The social, the linguistic, and the cognitive

> I have resisted the term *sociolinguistics* for many years, since it implies that there can be a successful linguistic theory or practice which is not social.
>
> Labov (1972a: xix)

Despite the fact that language use occurs in a social realm, sociolinguistic findings are rarely incorporated into formal linguistic models; socially-conditioned linguistic variation has been treated as an epiphenomenon to grammatical and phonological variation. This tendency had its beginnings over a century ago with Saussure's distinction between *langue* (the knowledge of a language's structure that is shared across the speakers of that language) and *parole* (the actual language used by an individual in their everyday life) (de Saussure 1983 [1916]). Saussure believed that *langue*, with its regularity and structure, should be the focus of linguistic study and that *parole* was too erratic and variable to be of scholarly interest. Half a century later, Chomsky (1965: 4) built on this with the distinction between *competence* (a speaker-hearer's knowledge of his or her language) and *performance* (actual language use in everyday life), later making the differentiation between I-language (internalised language) and E-language (externalised language) (Chomsky 1986: 20-22). The focus of structural linguistic theory has been *langue*, competence, and I-language, treating language as invariant and linguistic categories as absolute. Methodologies used to investigate internalised linguistic structure typically include eliciting data from a native speaker of a particular language or relying on the intuitions of the researcher. Surveys are also sometimes conducted, while other studies use texts to determine whether certain structures are grammatical.

In attempting to answer the question of *how language works*, it is imperative that social effects on linguistic structure be investigated. This cannot occur only by studying the homogeneous linguistic knowledge of an "ideal" speaker-hearer,

1.2 The social, the linguistic, and the cognitive

nor can it occur only by investigating the relationship between linguistic variation and broad social categories. Language is both social and individualistic; the construction of a symbol's meaning is a social enterprise and how this information is stored and used by a speaker-hearer is determined both by the unique experiences of that individual and by the experiences shared with others from the same community. In an investigation of identity, researchers must study both the community and the individual, ultimately examining the relationship between them (Wenger 1998: 146). Similarly, language does not belong only to an individual or only to the society to which that individual belongs; language exists within and across both. Linguistic variation that in Saussure's time was considered too messy to be investigated is now known to correlate with a number of factors, including social characteristics of the speaker and the formality of the situation (Labov 1972a), token frequency (the number of times a speaker has encountered a word) (Bybee 2002), and how predictable a word is given its position in a sentence (Jurafsky, Bell & Girand 2002). Furthermore, there is evidence that this information is stored and affects speech processing (Strand 1999; Jurafsky 2003). Variation is not somehow systematic "noise" that is filtered out; it is stored and used during the perception and production of speech.

Sociolinguists have made *parole*, performance, and E-language the focus of their investigation, examining the large amount of variation across different speakers and within the speech of a single individual. While there is a great deal of variation, much of it is predictable based on social characteristics of the speaker, the persona that the speaker is constructing in a given situation, and the various stances a speaker takes during an interaction. The variation is not only predictable but meaningful; it is a component of linguistic knowledge. Researchers examining this variation argue that a speaker's communicative competence is reflected in their behaviour (Hymes 1972). Therefore, examining this behaviour (i.e. actual language in use) provides insight into how language is stored in the mind and accessed during speech production and perception.

Empirical methods of linguistic study allow researchers to "avoid the inevitable obscurity of texts, the self-consciousness of formal elicitations, and the self-deception of introspection" (Labov 1972a: xix). Empirical methods provide a means of examining speakers' behaviour with the intention of identifying patterns among the variation. Traditionally in the investigation of sociophonetic patterns, these methods involve the quantitative analysis of variables from sociolinguistic interviews (see §3.1), but a growing number of studies use experimental methodologies (see §1.5). Both methods help demonstrate how linguistic variation is dependent on both social and linguistic information.

1 The separation of the social and the linguistic

Outside of sociolinguistics, there is a growing body of work by researchers who use empirical methods to examine language in use (Bod, Hay & Jannedy 2003). Like sociolinguists, they have made gradient "messy" variation the focus of their research and have shed new light on the nature of the variation. This work provides strong evidence that language (at all levels of the grammar) is probabilistic; there is a great deal of variation in language and it is predictable if treated stochastically.[1]

Insights into how language is stored and accessed during production and perception can be gained by investigating:

1. how language is used in everyday life across different speakers, by individual speakers, and at all levels of the grammar; and

2. how perceivers are influenced by trends from production based on both linguistic and non-linguistic information.

Patterns in the production and perception of speech, regardless of whether they are conditioned by linguistic or social factors, can tell us something about a speaker's linguistic competence, blurring the traditional boundaries between competence and performance, *langue* and *parole*.

In this chapter, I present research that has informed the work presented in this book. Because I used a number of methods (ethnography, acoustic analysis, and experimental design) and I address a number of theoretical issues (the role of gradience, speaker-specific probability of producing a word, accessing the lemma versus the wordform, and the construction of an individual's identity), this requires stepping through a vast amount of work from traditionally distinct linguistic subfields. I begin by discussing the progression of social theory through the waves of variationist studies. I then describe results from sociophonetic work that uses acoustic analysis and I discuss how this challenges some key assumptions made by popular linguistic theories. Next I present findings from speech perception experiments that investigate the relationship between linguistic and non-linguistic information. At this point, the discussion digresses from work in sociophonetics and focuses on two questions of interest that (at the time of writing my dissertation) had largely not been addressed in the sociolinguistic literature, namely the degree to which token frequency influences phonetic realisations and the degree to which different words that share a wordform can have different realisations.

---

[1] I would not argue that the study of language based on intuitions has no place in linguistics. However, I do believe that this method can only come part-way in answering the multitude of questions that ultimately address how language works.

1.3 Waves of variationist studies

Different speakers produce different realisations from one another and at least some of this variation is correlated with the speakers' social characteristics. Here I step through what Eckert (2005b) refers to as the First, Second, and Third Waves of variation studies.

Research in the First Wave treats social variables as indexed directly to broad social categories, such as age, gender, and socioeconomic status. Research in the Second Wave examines variation that is correlated with locally constructed social categories and research in the Third Wave treats linguistic variables as indexed both to a speaker's style and to a speaker's stance, "a socially recognised disposition" (Ochs 1990: 2).

In addition to different views about the nature of indexation between linguistic and social factors, particular methodologies are associated with each wave. In order to elicit data, researchers working in the First Wave use either quick and anonymous questions or standard sociolinguistic interviews; the researcher need not be highly familiar with the subjects to determine a correlation between a broad social category and a linguistic variable. Research in the First Wave focuses on participants who are assumed to be linguistically typical of a predetermined social category (Milroy 1987: 35).

In contrast, work in the Second Wave uses qualitative methodologies to determine locally constructed social categories that are meaningful to the speakers. For work in the Second Wave, "the unit of study is the *pre-existing social group*, rather than the individual as the representative of a more abstract social category" (Milroy (1987: 35), italics in original). A key tool for work in the Second Wave has been ethnography, a methodology adopted from anthropology that uses participant observation and qualitative analysis to describe a culture or group. It is useful for sociolinguists because linguistic variation is only one symbolic tool individuals can use to express their identities; there are a multitude of other symbols at work at any given time, each potentially unique within a given culture or community.[2] In order to interpret the meaning behind the linguistic symbols, one must understand the context in which that symbol has meaning (Saville-Troike 1982: 22). This is demonstrated by Labov's (1963) work on Martha's Vineyard, where speakers adopted local phonetic realisations associated with covert prestige (prestige associated with locally-based models) rather than those associated with overt prestige (prestige associated with externally-based models, often spo-

---

[2] Here, the word *symbol* refers to a linguistic or non-linguistic "social object used for communication to self or for communication to others and to self" (Charon 1995: 42).

1 The separation of the social and the linguistic

ken by an influential group). Crucial to understanding this choice in variants was an understanding of the emotions and opinions of the people on the island. The inhabitants of the island had negative feelings toward the mainlanders who visited the island every summer. Rather than adopting the prestige forms produced by the visitors, a number of Martha's Vineyeard's inhabitants adopted variants produced by the local fishermen.

Another method used for research in the Second Wave is Lesley Milroy's *snowball* technique, where the researcher uses the social networks within a community to recruit new participants (Milroy & Gordon 2003: 32). Though primarily a method of subject recruitment, the snowball technique can be used to study the speakers' social networks as an analytical construct as opposed to focusing on a social category. This method can facilitate qualitative analysis because of its focus on friendship ties; the researcher has access to more information about the speaker than would be gleaned from an interview with someone whose connections within a community were unknown. This method is unlike ethnography in that it does not necessarily involve extensive observation of individual speakers. While a fieldworker may choose to become more involved with a community of networks, this involvement is a key component of an ethnographic approach.

In order to investigate the relationship between linguistic variants and a speaker's style, work in the Third Wave employs qualitative methodologies like those used in the Second Wave. Style is made up of smaller components, such as the use of a certain word or a particular realisation of a vowel and these components are socially-meaningful; the styles and their meanings are co-dependent and constantly shifting. As the stylistic components are manipulated in different ways to construct an individual's style, they take on new meanings. An individual's style does not stem only from the manipulation of linguistic variants but also relies on non-linguistic factors, such as wearing certain clothes, walking a particular way, or adopting a specific posture. The combination of all of these factors, linguistic and non-linguistic, determine an individual's style. Therefore it is necessary for researchers working in the Third Wave to utilise qualitative methodologies such as ethnography to observe these styles, the styles' linguistic and non-linguistic components, and the components' constantly shifting meanings.

The names of each wave refer to the progression of social theory within sociolinguistics rather than to a strict linearity on a temporal scale. For example, although Labov's (1963) study on Martha's Vineyard predates his (1966) study in New York, the New York study is considered First Wave while the Martha's Vineyard project is a key example of work in the Second Wave. In fact, the vast majority of work conducted today continues to be in the vein of the First Wave, its appeal no doubt stemming from the ability to gain insights in less time and with less emotional involvement than that imposed by methodologies used in the Second and Third Waves.[3] In the following sections I step through examples of work conducted in the First, Second, and Third Waves of variation studies.

1.3.1 First Wave

Beginning with his seminal work on sociophonetic variation in both Martha's Vineyard and New York (Labov 1963, 1966), Labov has been the single most influential researcher in the field of sociolinguistics. In New York, Labov (1966) surveyed retail workers at three different department stores that each had target clientele from different socioeconomic groups. He demonstrated how realisations of /r/ in the phrase *fourth floor* patterned depending on the expected socioeconomic status of the addressee. Since then, a multitude of studies have arisen displaying trends in other languages and dialects, the majority of which have focused on phonetic variation that patterns with a group's social category (e.g., Trudgill (1972); Romaine (1978); Wolfram (1974).

The vast majority of sociophonetic work conducted on New Zealand English has been (and continues to be) in the vein of the First Wave. Some examples on New Zealand English (NZE) include work by Maclagan, Gordon & Lewis (1999), Hay & Maclagan (2010), Daly & Warren (2001), and Starks & Reffell (2006).

1.3.2 Second Wave

Work in the First Wave demonstrates how linguistic variables are correlated with a speaker's social characteristics; the indexation between them is treated as direct. Through adopting an ethnographic approach, work in the Second Wave expands on the observation that linguistic variation is related to a speaker's social characteristics by focusing on the motivation behind the variation: why do certain groups adopt certain variants and avoid others? While, for example, Trudgill (1972) reflected on the possible motivations, these interpretations did not stem from observation of, or interaction with, the speakers themselves; they were based on observations of society more generally. In addition to providing a means of observing the meanings behind the variation, ethnography allows researchers to avoid using predetermined social categories, instead investigating

---

[3] Ethnography and other methodologies that require repeated interactions between a subject and a researcher take a great deal of time and they can be emotionally exhausting. "For the fieldworker such [Second Wave] studies are extremely demanding in energy, persistence, time and emotional involvement" (Milroy 1987: 79).

1 The separation of the social and the linguistic

social categories that are created by, and relevant to, the speakers themselves. In addition to Labov's work on Martha's Vineyard, studies in the Second Wave include work by Holmquist (1985), Eckert (2000), and Milroy & Milroy (1978).

Of these studies, the one which has most influenced the work presented here was conducted by Eckert (1989; 2000). Employing an ethnographic approach at Belten High, a high school in a Detroit suburb, Eckert (1989; 2000) found that phonetic realisations in an individual's speech patterned with whether that individual was categorised as a Jock or a Burnout, categories that were not based on social groups (tight groups of friends who, if asked, would name each other as part of a group) but on social network clusters (affiliations between individuals, not all of whom considered each other friends, but who nonetheless shared practices) (Eckert 2005b: 11). Students were highly aware of these polarised categories and they applied the labels to males and females and to themselves and others. Where the Jocks took part in school activities and behaved largely as was expected by the school, the Burnouts rejected the school's expectations and were viewed as rebellious in the eyes of the school, smoking cigarettes and going "cruising" (driving in a car with friends without a predetermined destination). While the Jocks accepted the school's norms and strove for upward mobility, the Burnouts rejected the norms and valued cooperative peer networks. Eckert examined a number of variables that were undergoing change as part of the Northern Cities Shift (Labov, Yaeger & Steiner 1972). Although the change was most advanced in the city, it was evident in the speech of some Belten High students. Eckert found that, in addition to a correlation between phonetic realisation and being a Jock or a Burnout, the phonetic variables were related to each group's distinct construction and expression of femininity and masculinity. For example, Burnouts were more likely than Jocks to raise the nucleus of the diphthong /ai/ (as in *price*). But within each group, males and females behaved differently; Burnout girls produced a greater number of innovative variants than Burnout boys and Jock boys produced a greater number than Jock girls. Eckert argues that in developing patterns of behaviour, people orient to their own gender group within the context of the larger networks with which they are involved (Eckert 2000: 122-123). While traditional notions of femininity may have applied to Jock girls, they did not apply to Burnout girls; individuals in the different networks adopted socially-meaningful variables that expressed their membership as a Jock or a Burnout within the context of their own gender group.

Through obtaining an understanding of the local relations, values, and ideologies of a community, studies in the Second Wave gain insight into why phonetic variables are correlated with social group membership. But one key to understanding the variations remained: understanding the motivations of an individual. Do individuals orient to broad and local social groups (e.g., female and Jock), or are individuals' social goals more malleable and varied than these categories would imply?

1.3.3 Third Wave

Where studies in the First and Second Waves view sociolinguistic variables as indexed to a social group, studies in the Third Wave treat stylistic practice as fundamental. Studies in the Third Wave examine how linguistic variants contribute to an individual's collection of styles and the construction of their social personae; they focus on social meaning where social meaning is not defined through membership in a social group but through the individual's stance and the expression of who they are. Variables and social categories are indexed indirectly through their direct relationship with style. This insight helps to explain how what the individual does in their everyday conversations (micro) manifests as socially-conditioned at the group level (macro).

Central to the Third Wave has been the investigation of a community of practice, a term coined by Lave & Wenger (1991) which Eckert and McConnel-Ginet define as "an aggregate of people who, united by a common enterprise, develop and share ways of doing things, ways of talking, beliefs, and values - in short, practices" (Eckert & McConnell-Ginet 1999: 186). Wenger (1998) states that to be a community of practice, a group must be involved in mutual engagement, a joint enterprise, and a shared repertoire of practices. It is through these that a community of practice negotiates the meaning of the practices themselves, drawing on and connecting meaning to what people know and do not know (Wenger 1998: 73-85). Linguistic variables are adopted and rejected on the basis of this social knowledge, making communities of practice promising groups in which to observe socially-conditioned phonetic variation:

> The individual constructs an identity — a sense of place in the social world — in balancing participation in a variety of communities of practice, and in forms of participation in each of those communities. And key to this entire process of construction is stylistic practice. (Eckert 2005b: 17)

Thus, speakers create their own distinctive personae through combining linguistic variables (e.g., phonetic variants, lexical items, and syntactic constructions) and non-linguistic factors (e.g., clothing, make-up, and ways of walking) and these personae are located within a larger social order. Viewing her work at Belten High within the context of the Third Wave, Eckert (2005b) described how

1 The separation of the social and the linguistic

the Jocks and Burnouts were in fact indexing stances through their use of both linguistic variables (e.g., the diphthong /ai/) and non-linguistic factors (e.g., cruising). Jocks were school-oriented and aimed for upward social mobility; Burnouts were neighbourhood-oriented and valued solidarity. Whereas the Jocks viewed the Burnouts as irresponsible and antisocial, the Burnouts viewed the Jocks as disloyal and status-oriented. The stances of these two communities of practice were diametrically opposed, and the observed patterns for the phonetic variables reflected this.

Among younger students, Eckert (1996b) identified linguistic variants that co-varied with non-linguistic cues such as nail polish, lip gloss, hair style, and new ways of walking. All of these cues served a symbolic means. Through adopting a socially-meaningful variant (e.g., backed /æ/ before a nasal) and taking part in certain activities (e.g., wearing nail polish), the girls each constructed an individual style that was to define their social persona. Other studies in the Third Wave include work by Mendoza-Denton (2008), Zhang (2005), and Podesva (2011).

Studies in the Third Wave demonstrate how speakers manipulate linguistic and non-linguistic factors in creating and exhibiting their style. Whereas studies in the First and Second Waves treat linguistic variables as indexed to either broad or local social categories, studies in the Third Wave investigate the social meaning of variables and how these variables contribute to an individual's persona.

Much of the work regarded as Third Wave includes techniques used in the First and Second Waves, including the investigation of covariation between linguistic variables and social categories observed in a speech community. The work presented in this book employs multiple approaches; the role of the individual is discussed in Section 3.4.5.1 and the relationship between a linguistic variable and a speaker's social grouping is discussed in Section 3.3.2. While investigating stance and style is important to aid in the understanding of why many speakers use linguistic variants associated with a larger social group to which they belong, it does not make the examination of the relationship between variants and larger groups irrelevant. In fact, I would argue that macro-level (e.g., First Wave) variation informs style-making just as style-making is the vehicle through which macro-level variation arises.

Work in all three waves displays how phonetic variation is not merely "noise" but is meaningful and is a part of a speaker's communicative competence, the competence required by a speaker in order to communicate effectively (Hymes 1972). In order to be manipulated in such a systematic manner, the relationships must be stored in speakers' minds and accessed during speech production. Like linguistically-conditioned variation, socially-conditioned variation contributes to linguistic structure and is a reflection of a speaker's (not necessarily conscious) knowledge about language. But if this information is stored, it might also be expected to influence speech processing. In Section 1.5, I discuss results from experimental work demonstrating that an individual's knowledge of sociophonetic trends from production does in fact influence speech perception. In the next section, I discuss studies that have used acoustic analysis to investigate a speaker's linguistic competence of nuanced variables.

1.4 Gradience and acoustic analysis

Most formal phonological theories, such as those based on features or constraints, were not developed with gradience in mind. Some researchers working in these theories (e.g., Boersma 1997) have sought to incorporate methods of accounting for the probabilistic distribution of phonological variables. Still, few formal linguistic models can handle gradient phonetic data despite the fact that phonetic variables are not clear-cut categories but points along a multi-dimensional continuum. These dimensions include segment duration, vowel quality differences related to formant frequencies, the frequency range of aperiodic energy for fricated segments, and voice-quality features such as glottalisation and nasalisation; all of these can contribute to the overall quality of a token. In contrast with auditory analysis which necessarily treats variants as points in auditory/acoustic space, acoustic analysis allows investigation of gradient variables, such as duration, as well as variables where differences between the realisations are extremely subtle and therefore difficult to conduct auditory analysis on.

Sociophonetic work which has used laboratory techniques to examine variation (e.g., Labov 2001; 2007) has overwhelmingly focused on vowels, most often measuring the midpoint in the first and second formants (F1 and F2). When plotted on an F1-F2 graph, the measurements provide an idea of the height and backness of a token for a particular speaker relative to other variants produced by that speaker (Peterson & Barney 1952: 182-184). Labov (2001: 466-497) plotted variables this way to demonstrate how different factors influence sounds undergoing change. Although acoustic analysis is more time-consuming than auditory analysis, it more accurately reflects the distribution of variables in acoustic space and demonstrates how phonetic variation is both systematic and gradient.

Consonants can also differ depending on a combination of phonological and social factors. Most sociophonetic studies examining consonantal variation use auditory analysis. But as with vowels, some of the differences in realisations are nuanced, lending themselves to investigation by laboratory methods. Sociophonetic research that has conducted acoustic analysis on consonants includes work by Hay & Maclagan (2010), Docherty & Foulkes (1999), and Foulkes, Docherty & Watt (2005).

Hay & Maclagan (2010) investigated the relationship between /r/ intrusion and social factors. They found that male speakers and New Zealanders from lower socioeconomic backgrounds were more likely to produce intrusive /r/ than females and New Zealanders from higher socioeconomic backgrounds. They also investigated the amount of constriction of the /r/, where a lower F3 value is impressionistically more /r/-like. Investigating only those tokens that were identified as having intrusive /r/, they found that participants from lower socioeconomic groups were more likely to produce the /r/ with a lower F3. The likelihood of intrusive /r/ depends on the social characteristics of the speaker and so does the degree of the constriction when producing the /r/.

In addition to examining gradience, acoustic analysis provides a way to investigate highly nuanced phonetic variation. Docherty & Foulkes (1999) uncovered phonologically and socially-conditioned variation among realisations of pre-pausal and intervocalic /t/, variation that was so subtle that it had been overlooked by researchers conducting auditory analysis on similar tokens. They also found that children as young as two already exhibit the socially-conditioned variation in /t/ realisation (Foulkes, Docherty & Watt 2005). These findings provide evidence that individuals adopt socially-meaningful variables, even when differences between variants are extremely nuanced and difficult to perceive. This raises questions regarding the nature of the phonetic information that is stored in the mind: how detailed is it?

The work discussed in this section demonstrates the benefits of using acoustic analysis in sociophonetic investigations of both vowels and consonants. The results have important theoretical implications, providing support for probabilistic models of speech production and evidence that stored representations of phonetic information are acoustically detailed. They also raise questions about the relationship between an individual's production and perception: how is it possible that speakers produce socially-appropriate variants when differences between the variants are difficult to perceive without the aid of voice-analysis software? In the following section, I discuss work that aims to shed light on this question through the examination of the relationship between phonetic information and social characteristics in speech perception.

1.5 Experimental sociolinguistics

Perception studies have yielded insights into how phonetic variation is stored in the mind through exploring the effects of non-linguistic information on speech processing. The research described in this section provides evidence that the social characteristics attributed to the speaker can influence how phones are perceived. This suggests that phonetic representations are indexed to non-linguistic information and that this non-linguistic information is accessed during speech processing (Strand 1999; Campbell-Kibler 2007; Drager 2011b). Additionally, given the subtle phonetic differences between variants, the results provide evidence that the phonetic representation contains rich detail that previously was assumed to be filtered out during speech perception, storing only an abstracted form in the mental representation.

For example, the focus of the aperiodic energy of the alveolar fricative /s/ is higher than for the palatal fricative /ʃ/ within the speech of a single individual. The acoustic boundary between /s/ and /ʃ/ tends to be higher for females than males. This means that it is possible for a token of /s/ produced by a male to have its turbulence focused in a similar frequency range as a female's token of /ʃ/. In an experiment where video clips of men and women were matched with gender-ambiguous tokens from a /s/ - /ʃ/ continuum, Strand (1999; 2000) found that participants were more likely to perceive a token as /ʃ/ if shown a video of a female. In other words, the same fricative was perceived differently depending on the face with which it was paired. These results provide evidence that perceivers attribute social characteristics to a speaker and then use this information to help identify sounds produced by that speaker.

There is evidence that the perception of phonetic variables can also be affected by other social characteristics attributed to the speaker, including dialect area (Niedzielski 1999; Hay, Nolan & Drager 2006), socioeconomic status (Hay, Warren & Drager 2006), age (Hay, Warren & Drager 2006; Drager 2006; 2011b), and ethnicity (Casasanto 2010). The centring diphthongs /iə/ and /eə/, as in the words *near* and *square*, are undergoing a merger in NZE. This change has been led by members of lower socioeconomic groups; while some New Zealanders maintain the distinction, the diphthongs are merged in the speech of many New Zealanders who are young and/or members of lower socioeconomic groups. Using photographs to manipulate the perceived socioeconomic status and age of speakers in a perception experiment, Hay, Warren & Drager (2006) found that participants' accuracy at identifying distinct tokens of the diphthongs depended on the social characteristics of the person in the photograph. Likewise, Drager (2011b) found that the age of the person in a photograph could influence perception of variants undergoing a chain shift in progress. Results from both of these studies provide further evidence that individuals access stored social information attributed to a speaker during speech perception and that this social information can affect how sounds are perceived.

In both Detroit and Canada, speakers produce variants of the diphthong /au/, as in the word *mouth*, with a raised nucleus. Speakers from Detroit associate this variant with Canadians and are not aware that they also produce raised variants. Niedzielski (1999) conducted an experiment where participants were asked to match a vowel from natural speech to one from a synthesised vowel continuum ranging from raised variants to standard American English variants. She found that participants were more likely to respond with a raised token from the continuum if they were in the condition where *Canada* appeared at the top of the response sheet than if they were in the condition where *Michigan* was at the top of the response sheet. Niedzielski argues that participants shifted in their perception due to their expectations regarding the speaker's dialect area. In New Zealand, Hay, Nolan & Drager (2006) found similar results in an experiment that was based on Niedzielski's paradigm and manipulated whether 'New Zealand' or 'Australia' was written at the top of the answersheet. In contrast to the variable in Niedzielski's study, the target vowel /ɪ/ was one with different realisations in the two dialects. While participants in the Australian condition were more likely to respond with an Australian token from the continuum than were participants in the New Zealand condition, all but one of the participants indicated that they in fact knew that the voice was a New Zealander. Hay, Nolan & Drager (2006) argue that instead of expectations regarding a speaker's dialect area affecting performance on the task, the mere mention of another dialect area was enough to orient perception toward that dialect.

The experiments outlined above investigate the extent to which speech perception can be affected by social characteristics that are either attributed to a speaker or triggered from exposure to a related stimulus. Another area of inquiry provided by experimental methodologies is an investigation of the degree to which phonetic cues in the stimulus and the participants' previous experience affect what social characteristics are attributed to the speaker.

For example, Clopper & Pisoni (2004) conducted an experiment in which they played participants clips of speech produced by speakers from different parts of the US and participants were asked to indicate the regional origin of the speakers. They found that participants who had not lived in a dialect area were less accurate at identifying the dialect than participants who had lived there. In other words, accuracy on the task depended on the participants' prior exposure to the different dialects.

Campbell-Kibler (2007) conducted a relevant and influential study in which she played groups of participants clips of speech and asked them to comment on the speakers (e.g., *What can you tell me about Jason? Where do you think he's from?*). There were two experimental conditions. The clips of speech used in the conditions were identical except that word-final nasals were spliced so that in one condition the alveolar nasal [n] occurred in a word (e.g., *fishin'* in the *-in* guise) and in the other condition the velar nasal [ŋ] occurred in that word (e.g., *fishing* in the *-ing* guise). Although all other aspects of the utterances were identical, speakers were more likely to be rated as educated and articulate when in the *-ing* guise than when in the *-in* guise. But the variable did not affect the perception of social characteristics equally for all voices; participants were more likely to identify one speaker in particular as gay, especially when in the *-ing* guise. These results provide evidence that even slight shifts in phonetic realisations can influence what social characteristics are attributed to a speaker and that interpretations of speaker identity are based on a combination of multiple phonetic cues that are present in the signal; the meaning of a single variable can change when other socially-meaningful phonetic cues are inherent in the signal.

Taken together, results from sociophonetic perception experiments provide evidence that non-linguistic information attributed to a speaker is accessed during perception and can affect how sounds are perceived. In the following section, I discuss recent work investigating the relationship between phonetic variation, token frequency, and the lemma.

1.6 Laboratory phonology

In addition to exploring the link between phonetic variants and identity construction, the work presented in this book investigates current questions of interest within the scope of what is sometimes referred to as experimental or laboratory phonology. Laboratory phonology uses empirically-based methods to test and develop linguistic models of speech production and perception. Though phonetics and phonology remain a central focus of researchers working in this field, much of the work investigates how these prelexical levels influence the production and perception of other aspects of the grammar, including syntax (Hay & Bresnan 2006) and the lexicon (Bybee 2002; Gahl 2008). This book explores questions surrounding the frequency of a lexical item and the relationship between phonetic information and the lemma during speech processing.

1 The separation of the social and the linguistic

1.6.1 Token frequency

Researchers have noted a relationship between phonetic reduction and token frequency (Bybee 2001; Zipf 1929) and there is some empirical evidence that such a relationship does indeed exist (Aylett & Turk 2004; Baker & Bradlow 2009; Bell et al. 2009). There is also evidence that more frequent words are more likely to contain centralised vowels (Aylett & Turk 2006; Munson & Solomon 2004), which – if centralisation is viewed as phonetic reduction – also supports this argument. Bybee (2002) argues that reductive phonetic change exhibits lexical diffusion (the sound change occurs in some words before others) and that the most frequent lexical items are the first to undergo change. She outlines an array of work exemplifying how intervocalic /ð/ deletion in Spanish as well as t/d deletion and vowel reduction and deletion in English are linked to word frequency; reduction and deletion are more likely to occur in high frequency words than in low frequency words.[4] There is also evidence that a speaker's vowel space is influenced by token frequency (Munson 2007) and that, in tonal languages, there is a relationship between token frequency and the overall F0 and tone dispersion within that word (Zhao & Jurafsky 2007).[5] Like the sociophonetic work described earlier, this work on the effects of token frequency demonstrates how language is probabilistic rather than categorical; the "messiness" of *parole* is far more structured than was previously believed.

1.6.2 Lemmas, lexemes, and phonetic detail

The level at which frequency-based information is stored is not yet clear. Previous research differentiates between a lemma (a syntactically/semantically defined entry) and a lexeme (a wordform entry that specifies, for example, segmental information) (Bock 1995). There is evidence that phonetic variation not only occurs across words with different wordforms but that polysemes and "homophones", such as *time* and *thyme*, can have different realisations and these realisations can be predicted by the lemma's frequency (Gahl 2008; Jurafsky, Bell & Girand 2002). While some of the variation attributed to token frequency may instead be a function of how predictable a word is given its position in a sentence

---

[4] Bybee (2002) treats words that are observed in corpus data fewer than 35 times per million words as low-frequency.

[5] One of the few sociophonetic studies to include token frequency in the analysis was conducted by Hay, Jannedy & Mendoza-Denton (1999), who found that both lexical frequency and the ethnicity of the referee (the person being discussed) predicted /ai/ monophthongisation in the speech of the television personality, Oprah Winfrey. The social effect of the referee was stronger than the effect of token frequency.

(Jurafsky, Bell & Girand 2002), Gahl (2008) found that, over and above effects from contextual predictability, words of homophone pairs can differ in regard to their durations: the more frequent word in the pair is more reduced. This suggests that the lemma (in addition to the lexeme) is a locus of token frequency information.

If social factors are shown to influence the realisations of different words that share a wordform, it would suggest that either phonetic information is indexed to the lemma or that the lemmas do not share a single lexeme-based level of representation and the phonetic detail is indexed to their separate lexeme representations. If lemma-level representations are indexed to an additional representation where phonetic information is available, that information is inaccessible during a tip-of-the-tongue moment. In this book, I do not attempt to tease apart these two possibilities and use *lemma-based variation* for both.

1.7 Multiple methodologies

The work presented in this book draws on insights gained from the research discussed in this chapter, combining the various methods and research questions within a single study with the aim of unifying all results within a model of speech production and perception. Ethnography, speech perception experiments, and acoustic analysis were used in order to take advantage of the benefits of each. Through ethnography, I was able to become familiar with the speakers and come to understand their individual styles and stances. Through conducting acoustic analysis on their speech, I was able to investigate subtle differences in realisations of tokens. And through conducting speech perception experiments with participants who were the same individuals who took part in the ethnographic portion of the study, I was able to test the effect of phonetic cues on the attribution of social information during speech perception. Additionally, the qualitative data collected during the ethnographic portion of the study helped to interpret the results from the perception experiments, further exemplifying the benefits of employing multiple methodologies.

The work in this book also investigates questions of interest outside the scope of sociolinguistics. For example, the frequency counts in all of the work described in Section 1.6.1 were based on text-based corpora or spoken corpora from a multitude of different speakers and identical token frequency counts and lemma probabilities were used to examine effects across all speakers. However, the cognitive mechanisms to which these effects are attributed also predict an effect of speaker-specific token frequency and speaker-specific lemma-probability; if an

1 The separation of the social and the linguistic

individual speaker uses a lexical item more often in a given context, reductive phonetic changes such as those outlined by Bybee (2002) should be most advanced in that lexical item for that individual speaker. This hypothesis is tested in the production results described in Chapter 3. Likewise, the lemma-based phonetic variation described by Gahl (2008) raises the question of whether perceivers can distinguish between auditory tokens of lemmas that share a wordform. The experiments presented in Chapter 4 address this question. Ultimately, the work in this book investigates identity construction, gradience, lemma probabilities, and the relationship between phonetic and lemma-based information. The findings are used to inform the model of speech production, perception and identity construction discussed in Chapter 5.

In the following chapter, I describe Selwyn Girls' High through a description of my experiences from the year I spent there. As the work described in Section 1.3 demonstrates, speakers' social characteristics and styles are complex as is the correlation between these styles and the phonetic variables produced. I ask that readers take the time while reading Chapter 2 to reflect on what life at Selwyn Girls' High was like and to recognise that while most of the girls belong to certain groups, each girl is a unique individual. Through investigating individuals and how they construct their identities and through investigating variation not only in their production but also in their perception of variables, I aim to provide further evidence that the observed variation and the indexical meanings are fundamental aspects of what constitutes a speaker's linguistic competence.

The ethnographic portion of this study was conducted at Selwyn Girls' High (SGH) in 2006 with the aim of becoming familiar with individuals at the school, determining what, if any, social categories were relevant for the girls, and identifying different styles and stances that were present at the school. I was especially interested in how different individuals constructed their social identities through the manipulation of both linguistic and non-linguistic variables. As will be discussed in Chapter 3, some phonetic variation at the school appears to be linked to the girls' active construction of their social personae.

In the following chapter I describe different experiences I had while at Selwyn Girls' High. Although I write from my point of view (and, in fact, start the narrative from my point of view), I have tried to focus the attention on the students rather than myself so that the reader may appreciate the richness of their lives and understand those aspects of life that the girls considered important. These are real people, with real frustrations and real excitement. But as explained by Narayan, we as ethnographers "do not speak from a position outside 'their' worlds, but are implicated in them" Narayan (1993: 676). Any results are only "true" insofar as they are understood in relation to ourselves being implemented within the reality of the speech community we are trying to describe. Additionally, findings should be interpreted within the context of our biased observations. We are not objective; our presence and previous biases are inseparable from ourselves. Therefore, I have tried to remind the reader throughout the text that this is only my story, my "truth", of the situation at Selwyn Girls' High and I apologise to the girls for presenting them in a way that reflects at best only a part of who they are. Still, though it fails to describe the girls entirely, I hope it reflects a part of each of them, however incompletely.

2 Social groups at Selwyn Girls' High

2.1 Methodology

2.1.1 Background

I was raised in Southern California, an ocean apart from the students of Selwyn Girls' High. Prior to joining them, my education experience in New Zealand was limited to the university and despite talking to several New Zealanders about what it had been like when they went to high school, I still did not have a clear idea of what to expect. In her ethnography on New Zealand teenagers, Gray (1988) focused on what was important to adolescents (e.g., friends and family) and not on the construction of their social groups or their identity. I was unsure of how to proceed and uncertain about what I might find. I knew most students at most schools wore uniforms. I knew that I might not find an equivalent of the Jocks and Burnouts observed by Eckert (1989) and I entered the school thinking it possible that I may not find any distinct groups at all.[1]

Selwyn Girls' High seemed the ideal school to conduct my analysis: It was an all girls' school with students from a range of socioeconomic backgrounds. I wanted to work in an all girls' school to observe adolescents' construction of identity in the absence of members of the opposite sex. Previous work has focused on identity construction within the context of the heterosexual marketplace (Eckert 1996b). Though the marketplace certainly still comes into play with girls from an all girls' school, they do not necessarily construct their school identities in the same way that girls at co-ed schools do.

Schools in New Zealand are assigned a decile depending on how many of its students come from low socio-economic communities. Decile 1 schools are the 10% of schools in New Zealand with the highest proportion of students from low socio-economic communites and decile 10 schools are the 10% with the lowest proportion of students from low socio-economic communities.[2] At the time of

---

[1] One colleague from New Zealand suggested that I might observe a hierarchy of "coolness" as opposed to distinct groups of students.

[2] Deciles are assigned so that schools with a high percentage of students from low socio-economic communities can receive more government funding.

the study, SGH had a decile of 6, which reflects the range of socio-economic backgrounds among its 1200 students. SGH was a public school and students came from very distinct parts of the city as well as from surrounding rural areas. This mixture of students from different backgrounds appealed to me. Given the ubiquity of class-based sociophonetic findings (e.g., Labov (1966), Trudgill (1972), observing an absence of socially-meaningful linguistic variation in this context would be surprising and given the aims of the project, observing variation that was socially-meaningful could be enlightening. Therefore, I felt confident that I would have some sociolinguistically interesting finding, whatever the outcome.

2.1.2 The students

I focused on the girls in their 13th and final year of school. In New Zealand, high school runs from Year 9 to Year 13.[3] Most Year 13 students turn 18 during the course of the year.

High school in New Zealand is not compulsory for students over 16. Though it is discouraged by teachers and many parents, students can choose to "sign out" of school and it does not have the same social stigma as in North America.

I was interested in the Year 13 girls in particular because they would have established friendship groups and reputations and they would (theoretically) already have a clear interpretation of other girls' expressions of identity. I was also interested in this year because they were about to embark on a new chapter of their lives. Because it could potentially help inform the social make-up of the groups and the linguistic variation observed at the school, I wanted to find out how the girls were planning for their future beyond high school.

Girls in Year 13 were the only students at SGH who were not required to wear uniform. When I first arrived and was not yet familiar with the girls, this helped me to distinguish them from the more junior girls.

The names used to refer to the girls and the school are pseudonyms. I gave girls the opportunity to choose their own names, though Rose, Pascal, Charlie, Patricia, and Clementine were the only girls who chose to do so. Most girls asked me to choose one for them and I tried to choose names that were an inside joke between me and them (e.g., Angel), were relevant to a story they had told me (e.g., Esther), or were the names of people they reminded me of (e.g., Christina). However, there were times when I simply needed to come up with a name and used whatever name came to mind and in these cases I chose a name that was appropriate to her cultural background (e.g., Marama, who is Māori).

---

[3] In the past, 'years' were referred to as 'forms', where 7th form was the equivalent of Year 13.

2.1 Methodology

2.1.3 Integrating myself into SGH

I spent the entirety of the school year at Selwyn Girls' High, four days a week, most often for the length of the school day. Much of that time was spent interacting with the girls, as the timetable was set up so that at least one group of students was in Study at any given time.[4] Study was a period set aside to give students time to do homework, though it was more often used to discuss people and events. The interactions were a mixture of helping each other with schoolwork, helping each other with personal problems, and gossiping about other people. The girls allowed many of these conversations to be recorded.

Although the style was casual and I was not always a major contributor to the conversation, times when the recorder was on are referred to as "interviews". Before beginning recording, I asked the girls permission to record.[5] The methodology of the interviews is described in more detail in Section 3.1.

The atmosphere of Study depended on the group, though the girls in most periods were talkative. When the chatter got too loud, teachers came in and asked everyone to speak more quietly. The girls often kept their books open on the desk in case a teacher came in (they wanted to at least appear to be working) and, during conversation, they sometimes worked on school projects.

Students were expected to remain in the designated classroom for the duration of their Study period, with the exception of going to the library or joining me to go elsewhere for a recorded interview. Although they were expected to sign their names on a roll call list at a non-standardised time, many girls found ways around this requirement, such as getting another girl to sign for them. Upon leaving the room, some girls went to a different classroom or to the common room, a space set aside specifically for the Year 13 students. Other girls went to the library, either to work at the desks or to watch DVDs provided by the school, and still others went to the art room to work on projects. On sunny days, some girls chose to sit outside, while others left school altogether. I followed the girls to these different locations and they seemed happy to have me along as they said

---

[4] In an assembly at the beginning of the school year and on the consent form that each girl signed before an interview, they were informed that I was conducting an ethnographic and linguistic study with Year 13 students at the school and that the aim of the project was to determine how they portrayed their identities through the use of language, clothing, activities, and other means. At the end of they year, I presented some preliminary findings at an assembly.

[5] In some cases, girls shared sensitive information with me while I was recording. While none of the information is incriminating, it is not information I would feel comfortable sharing with a general audience. Portions of interviews that contain sensitive information have not been transcribed and tokens from these sections were not extracted for the phonetic analysis presented in Chapter 3.

I gave them a valid excuse if questioned by a teacher about being outside the Study room.

I always joined a group if invited explicitly. During the first two weeks of school, two groups, The BBs and The Relaxed Group, told me that I was welcome to sit with them anytime. Because I wanted to become familiar with a number of girls, I tried to sit with a different group during lunch than the one I had sat with during morning break and I tried not to sit with the same group two days in a row. Interestingly, being seen sitting with different groups did not seem to cause problems in my relationships with any of the girls. For example, if The Real Teenagers walked by while I was sitting with The PCs during lunch, they would greet me and ignore the girls I was sitting with. When talking with The Real Teenagers later in the day, the interaction seemed no different than before the brief interaction during lunch. The girls knew that I was interested in talking with girls from a variety of groups and they accepted it. This was an aspect of school life where my role as a researcher (and as a non-student) exempted me from one of the social rules at the school: Don't Be a Traitor.[6]

This was a rule readily enforced by in-group members.[7] There were only a handful of girls who would sit with groups other than their own and they were largely fringe members who were not fully accepted by either of the groups.[8] When most girls chose to sit with another group, it became a permanent change, as they were immediately treated unfavourably by their former group.[9]

2.1.4 The formal

In addition to spending time at the school, I took part in some out-of-school activities. For example, I attended Sport's Day at a pool on the other side of town. I went to the champagne breakfast of The BBs and I went shopping with Lily of The Trendy Alternatives. Girls and I would talk while waiting for, or riding on, the bus. I was invited to parties (by The Real Teenagers, Rochelle's Group, and The Relaxed Group), but I chose not to attend.

---

[6] I have capitalized the names of the unspoken school rules. I suspect that many of these rules could be found in school settings other than Selwyn Girls' High.
[7] The different groups are discussed in Section 2.3.
[8] Group integration is considered as a factor when examining phonetic variation at the individual level in Section 3.4.5.
[9] As discussed in Section 2.4, some girls, such as Rachel, claimed that they felt free to sit with any group. However, core girls like Rachel did not sit with another group unless they were changing groups or their group was good friends with another group (e.g., A girl from The Sporty Girls could sit with The PCs but not The Pasifika Group). Rachel's claim is what Katrina referred to as the tendency to "deny cliques", which is also discussed in Section 2.4.

One event I attended that most girls took part in was the Year 13 formal. The formal was held at the end of the first semester and it was the main topic of conversation for all groups during the preceding months. Whether they thought it was going to be fun or not, each group had strong opinions about the formal and discussed it frequently. In fact, several girls only stayed in school so that they could attend the formal and they signed out several days afterward. Girls who were involved in the planning (mainly The BBs, The PCs, and The Trendy Alternatives) discussed where they should have it, what music should be played, and how much it should cost. All girls discussed what they would wear; Marama (The Pasifika Group) made her own dress, and Onya (The Real Teenagers) secured her rental gown over a month in advance. Girls in groups who were not involved in the planning had opinions about the formal and they expressed some frustration that those in charge of planning seemed to ignore their suggestions.

Girls began to ask me whether I was planning to attend. I was reluctant to join them because I worried that it would make them feel observed or self-conscious on a night that was clearly very important to them. Without prompting, girls from a variety of distinct groups encouraged me to attend. In the end I accepted and brought a date, thinking that if I brought an aspect of my personal life into the world of SGH, it would help relations with the girls.

The formal itself provided a rich backdrop against which to observe the different groups of individuals. Andrea and Natasha (The BBs) greeted everyone as they arrived, taking tickets and helping guide guests toward the photographer. Katrina (The Relaxed Group) had an argument with her mother just before the formal and her friends were more focused on cheering her up than they were concerned about having fun themselves. Joanna (The PCs) spent the entire night on the dancefloor, bursting with energy from the party pills she had swallowed earlier.[10] Instead of a date, Claudia (The Real Teenagers) brought a friend who had signed out of school the year before so couldn't have attended otherwise. Because former SGH students were not allowed to attend the formal, Claudia hid her bewigged friend under the table, much to the amusement of the other girls in her group. Lily (The Trendy Alternatives) chose to spend the night with me and my date rather than with her group. This choice helped to emphasise just how distant she felt from the other girls (see Section 2.3.1).

In addition to the opportunity of observing the girls away from the school grounds, the formal provided a means of gaining a shared memory with the

---

[10] Party pills are a legal stimulant in New Zealand. According to the Urban Dictionary (www.urbandictionary.com accessed 2008 − 07 − 31) their main ingredient is benzylpiperazine (BZP) and they give users feelings of alertness, euphoria, and a general sense of well being.

girls, thereby adding to the rapport I had already started to gain. I spent the night talking and dancing and afterward, the girls were able to tell me about the experience from their point of view in more detail because we had a shared jumping off point on which to build.

One common post-formal topic of conversation was the pre-parties, which each group held separately. For example, while most of the groups met for "pre-drinks", The BBs met for "pre-juice" though Jane explained that she did not actually drink any juice but ate grapes instead. I also heard a great deal about the afterparty, an organised event that was prohibited by the school and was attended by many of the girls.[11] The girls complained about how the boys at the afterparty were disrespectful and gave unwelcome pinches and gropes and everyone shared their version of how Daphne (The PCs) was escorted home by her parents after vomiting and passing out in the toilets.

2.1.5 My role at SGH

During their morning and lunch breaks, the girls and I would eat and talk and I would watch and listen. These breaks provided additional opportunities to learn about the girls' personal lives and to begin to understand their joys and frustrations. They told me about their struggles at home. I learned about their loves, lovers, and parties. We listened to music on their iPods. They taught me about how clothing, hair, and make-up varied across the different groups at the school, and where each group sat during lunch.

How much I took part in conversations depended on how much they seemed interested in including me. Primarily, I was the listener. When they asked me questions, I answered honestly. I wanted them to know that they could trust me and that I was happy to share my experiences with them in exchange for their willingness to share with me. When they addressed me, they often asked about the United States and what it was like there: Were high schools really like they were in the movies? The girls were also curious about my love life: Who was I with? Was he hot?! And as the year progressed, girls who planned to go to university asked me about my favourite classes and what lectures were like. To these girls I became a link to the world that they were about to join: university.

At SGH, I found myself becoming more and more a part of the girls' reality, just as they were becoming a part of mine. I tried to reflect continuously on how they placed me, based on my clothing, my opinions, and my accent. I was not a student. I was not a teacher. And I was certainly not a neutral, objective observer.

---

[11] Girls who attended the afterparty were in CR groups, a category that is discussed in Section 2.3.

2.1.6 The myth of the neutral ethnographer

Upon first entering the school, I faced a number of challenges and was unsure of how to proceed. Not only was I an outsider to the school but an outsider to New Zealand culture. I also worried about finding a balance between building rapport with the girls and maintaining a professional relationship with the school. As a novice, I continually questioned myself: When is it appropriate to begin recording? Who do I approach first? What do I wear, how do I act, and where do I start? One of my greatest concerns was how I could remain neutral among the different groups of girls, knowing that speakers accommodate their speech depending on who they are speaking to and who is present (Giles & Powesland 1975; Bell 1984; Giles, Coupland & Coupland 1991). Because one of my key aims was to compare phonetic variants produced by different girls, surely my goal was to remain as neutral as possible, effectively treating myself as a control across the different exchanges.

Yet, ethnographers are never neutral. For example, girls in different groups asked different questions and therefore knew about different aspects of my life. Through our different shared experiences as well as their individual stereotypes and prior experiences with people they deemed similar to me, the interpretation of my identity is bound to have varied between the different girls. Furthermore, different aspects of my identity were highlighted at different times. "Which facet of our subjectivity we choose or are forced to accept as a defining identity can change, depending on the context and the prevailing vectors of power" (Narayan 1993: 676). One's identity and placement within a community is continually shifting, not only across different groups but also in interactions with a single individual (Narayan 1993: 680). Mani (1990) describes how she shifts between her different identities. She attributes the shift to her identification with more than one ethnicity, being what she calls a "hybrid", but all of us are hybrids with our multiplicity of identities, identities we may choose to highlight or mask in different situations. In cases where there was a conflict between student and teacher, I tried to side myself with the student (placing myself in a friend/student role), but other situations would surface where I relied more heavily on my status as an outsider (emphasising my role as a researcher). For example, Year 13 girls were not required to wear uniforms and my choice of clothing on any given day was only slightly more formal than clothes worn by the majority of the girls. In fact several of the girls owned items of clothing that were identical to ones I wore. As a result, teachers who I had not yet met sometimes mistook me for a student. There was one Study Period where a teacher was occasionally present. One day, this teacher reprimanded me for talking. I politely explained that I was a researcher from the university and was asking the students, Kelly and Clementine, if they would be interested in doing an interview. I made it clear that I had permission to do so. During my explanation, I felt myself shift the emphasis from pseudo-student (slouching in my seat and whispering to the girls) to my role as a researcher (sitting up straight and challenging the teacher's accusation). I performed my role as researcher not only through the semantic content of my explanation, but through the manner in which I spoke and the posture in which I presented myself. I was polite, but I was also professional. Upon leaving the room with the girls for the interview, we burst out laughing: Whoa, look at you, Miss University Researcher! And then they quickly shifted to sharing their thoughts on the recent school formal.

Accepting the inevitability that I would project aspects of my personality and identity whether I wanted to or not, I decided it best to express myself freely through, for example, clothes, jewellery, and opinions. I tried to be aware of how I expressed myself at different times, both as a way of interpreting the girls' behaviour and in order to provide a more honest portrayal of my experiences at SGH.

The combination of trying to "be myself" while gaining the rapport of girls in disparate groups meant that my identity was not constant across the different groups. For example, I smiled more when I was sitting with The Geeks and I expressed more concern when listening to Rochelle's Group. I responded emotionally to each situation as I would whether or not I were an ethnographer and the situations varied from group to group. However, the expression of my identity shifted less than I initially expected because with all groups I found myself in the role of the quiet listener. I was happy with this role because it gave me an opportunity to get to know the girls: their opinions and views, and their worries and joys. The girls also seemed happy to have me in this role as I provided them with an eager, attentive audience. They could tell that I was genuinely interested in what they had to say and in time, they learned that I would not share secrets with their parents or with the school.

I also found that the social perception of my identity was not always under my control. Girls or teachers sometimes made comments that served to place me either inside or outside the school community, or that emphasised my status as American. For example, Camden (Rochelle's Group) placed me inside the student community when she expressed surprise (and annoyance) that the school or I would deem it inappropriate for me to get drunk with her. And girls placed me outside the school community through emphasising our difference in age; a number of girls mid-conversation commented that they knew someone my age or that they were surprised I was "that old". One very outgoing girl, Naomi, approached me on the first day of school and asked if I was a new seventh former. Several days later, Naomi approached me again and asked my age, the answer to which she found so amusing that she decided to share it, proclaiming loudly for all to hear, "Can you believe it? She's twenty-six!" So much for remaining neutral. This non-neutrality meant that there were different levels of familiarity between me and different girls and this could lead to differences in the choice of variants used (Cukor-Avila & Bailey 2001). However, sharing aspects of my life from outside the school had benefits as well, as it provided me with a higher level of familiarity in general than I would have been able to achieve otherwise. It is imperative that a researcher reflects on one's own position at different points throughout the research and, in the written text, acknowledges the ever-changing projections and interpretations of one's identity.[12]

2.2 Selwyn Girls' High

On a warm autumn day, I sat reading on the grass under the shade of a large tree, waiting for morning break. I normally followed girls to class, but I relied entirely on their invitations and on this day I had failed to get invited.

After a time, small groups of girls began to appear, dotting the quad with uniforms. The bell rang, and a flood of girls swarmed the lawn.

I watched as the different groups of girls arranged themselves in different areas on and around the grass. Most formed oblong circles so that each girl could see all of the others and they expanded their circles as needed when others came over to join them. It was only the first week of school, yet the girls already appeared to know where to look for their friends.

I was quite content with my detachment from the action, as I was still learning who was friends with whom. This way I was free to observe the clear division of groups from a distance. Before even half of the girls had settled and begun to eat their lunches (it was often the case that lunches were not saved until lunch but eaten during the morning break), Naomi called out to me. I had talked with Naomi several times and was already growing quite fond of her. She was outgoing and, as a result, was one of the first girls I met at the school. I felt comfortable approaching her from the beginning. She yelled at me from across the grass to

---

[12] The linguistic analysis presented in Chapter 3 controls for this because speech from girls with whom I was variously familiar was analysed for both CR and NCR groups. A girl's speech patterns were consistent with her constellation of stance rather than with how close I was with her.

come sit with her and her friends. When I came over she informed me that I shouldn't sit by myself or people might think I'm a loser. I had assumed that my age combined with my status as a researcher would exempt me from students expecting that I would conform to their social norms; I was wrong.

The girls were trying to interpret my identity and assign meaning to my role as an ethnographer so that they could determine what information they could share with me and how much they could trust me. Understandably, they were not sure what to make of me; I was not a teacher who ate lunch separately, wore my "nanna's clothes" and scowled when they talked about sex and drinking, but neither was I a fellow student who attended class regularly, partied with them and shared intimate details of my love life. In order to understand my role in their social world, they needed to negotiate my role with me and determine who I was to them.

I wanted to be accepted by the girls so that they would be willing to share their thoughts and opinions with me, so when Naomi called out to me, I quickly left my distanced position under the tree and joined her and her friends. In this instance at least, Naomi was aligning me with the students, expressing that the same social rules to which the students adhere were also applicable to me. This particular rule was one of the most prominent ones I observed at the school: Don't Be Seen Alone.

By suggesting that I conform to her expectations, Naomi was effectively asserting a kind of 'symbolic violence' (Rabinow 1977: 130) with her power to control the ethnographer's behaviour to fit a pattern that she and the other students could interpret and understand. My apparent failure to have understood this rule caused a temporary breakdown in the students' understanding of me, which was at least partially remedied by my quick acceptance of and adherence to the rule.

Expectations on the side of the students caused me to behave in particular ways, such as always choosing to sit with a group during break time. The students and I cooperated in the endeavor to lessen the distance between me and them, between Self and Other. As Kondo describes, "for my informants, it was clear that coping with this anomalous creature was difficult, for here was someone who looked almost like a real human being, but who simply failed to perform according to expectation" (Kondo 1986: 76).

In the adult world, the Losers Sit Alone Rule no longer applies or at least sitting alone does not carry the same amount of social stigma that is found in the adolescent world. My failure to adhere to the rule was quickly recognised and I was explicitly directed to behave in accordance with it. These negotiations between me and the students continued throughout the year, but they were most noticeable toward the beginning of my time at SGH, before I conformed to some of their expectations (e.g., I should sit with a group during lunch) and they accepted some of my inescapable idiosyncrasies (e.g., carrying clunky recording equipment).

The students' expectation that I would sit with a group during lunch helps to illuminate the relevance of group membership among the girls. It emphasises the importance of each girl's chosen sitting area and the awareness the girls had of where and with whom other girls sat. That the students' social rule would apply to me, an outsider, demonstrates how prominent it was in their lives. The rules were self-governed and self-defined, yet the girls themselves could not escape them. Having friends was considered crucial.[13] The girls were, in part, defined by others in terms of their friends.[14] Where a girl chose to eat lunch was more than a mere eating place. It was an expression of who she was friends with. It was an expression of who she was.

2.3 Groups of friends

The girls were self-organised into different groups, which varied from very large groups of thirty to paired individuals and two loners. Several of the larger groups were a result of past mergers, where two smaller groups had joined forces. In some cases, the merging of previously distinct groups was the result of recognising similar interests between them. In other cases, it was due to the perceived necessity of maintaining the group's size, as several of the groups were continually losing members as girls signed out. As Pixie explained, the seating arrangement within the merged groups made evident who had belonged to each of the previously distinct groups. Although as many as twenty-five members of her group, The PCs, might have been sitting in a circle on the grass, particular individuals, such as Marilyn and Joanna, faced slightly toward the centre of their own separate circle, an indication that they were, to some degree, still separate from the others.

Not including the smaller subgroups as distinct entities, I regularly interacted with girls from 11 of the different groups at the school. There were another two groups and two loners who I discuss briefly here though I interacted with them to a lesser degree in the interest of gaining greater familiarity with fewer indi-

---

[13] There were two loners in Year 13. Most girls avoided being seen alone.
[14] Among other things, girls were also defined by others in terms of what they wore, whether they partied, whether they played sport, and how friendly they were to girls outside their group.

viduals. The groups with whom I was more familiar were: The PCs, The BBs, The Pasifika group, The Christians, The Goths, The Geeks, The Trendy Alternatives, The Relaxed Group, Rochelle's Group, The Sporty Girls, and The Real Teenagers. Those who I knew to a lesser degree were: Sonia's Group, Cecily's Group, and the two loners, Charlie and Polly.

The group labels used here are in some cases based on something a group member said during an interview (The Relaxed Group). In other cases, the label is a term used by other girls to refer to a particular group (The Geeks). It may seem odd that I have chosen the label used by girls outside the group rather than by a girl who belongs to the group. However, a number of girls from different CR groups described themselves as "normal" and I saw no way to decide which groups would have a claim on this label. Furthermore, I hoped to shed light not only on the identity that a group was trying to project, but on other girls' interpretations of that group's expressions of identity.

Like the Jocks and Burnouts, these groups each formed a community of practice (Eckert 2005b). The girls in each of the groups at SGH negotiated the meanings of different aspects of style and individual girls in a group constructed their own unique personae within the context of that group (e.g., the leader, the listener, the drama queen). These personae are located within the larger social orders of their groups and the school.

Upon being asked what groups were at Selwyn Girls' High, the girls pointed to an area of grass in the quad or an enclave of a building and asked whether I knew the group that ate there. They then named the group or a member of it. Girls knew where the other groups ate and when a member of a group was not aware of a change of lunch plans, it led to a mad rush of texts in an attempt to locate her friends. This is not surprising given that choice of lunch locale carries social meaning in high schools. For example, in her sociolinguistic ethnography of a high school in Northern California, Mendoza-Denton (2008) observed lunchtime segregation: groups who ate lunch in the cafeteria versus groups who ate lunch in the inner quad. As at SGH, the groups each adopted a space they considered their own, boundaries that

> served as isoglosses that divided students in every detail, from the seemingly inconsequential such as clothing and hairstyles to distinctions that would certainly endure over the course of the students' lives: courses taken, grade point averages, and public perceptions. (Mendoza-Denton 2008: 27)

On cold and rainy days, the girls left the outdoors in favour of drier sitting areas. Some groups chose to sit in the common room. It contained a microwave, a stereo, and beanbags. The common room (CR) was the only space at the school set aside specifically for Year 13 students, but only some groups used it (CR groups). Groups who chose not to use it (NCR groups) complained that it smelled bad and instead they went to a classroom or left school.[15]

Girls who ate lunch in the common room still sat in their separate groups, though they occasionally interacted to ask about a song on the radio, sell chocolate for a charity, or make suggestions for the formal. Many of the girls in the separate groups had classes or Study together and they were sometimes mentioned by girls in other CR groups. Girls who did not eat lunch in the common room were rarely discussed by the common room girls. One exception was when there was sufficient conflict, such as when Kim (The PCs) mistakenly believed that Marama (The Pasifika Group) had stolen her mobile phone.

On sunny days, CR groups sat in the grassy quad in front of the school, on the concrete in front of the main building, or by the parking lot next to the quad. A map of the school and the different eating areas of all of the Year 13 girls is shown in Figure 2.1. Some of the NCR groups sat near the quad, though only Cecily's group sat on the grass. The Christians usually ate in a classroom in Building B and The Geeks chose to sit on the opposite side of the main building from the quad. When they stayed on campus, The Real Teenagers sat between the quad and the parking lot at the edge of the school grounds, an area sometimes also used by The PCs if the grass was wet. Sonia's group ate to the side of the main building (Building A). Girls in The Pasifika group left school most days during lunch, often going only a few doors down to smoke cigarettes in a driveway.

Table 2.1 displays the division of the groups into the Common Room (CR) groups and the Non-Common Room (NCR) groups.[16] These groups will be discussed in more detail shortly.

2.3.1 CR groups

The differences between CR groups were more subtle than those found between the NCR groups. In general, girls in CR groups took part in school activities and

---

[15] The room sometimes smelled of instant noodles and other food. Though the smell was not particularly pleasant, I interpreted the claim that the room smelled bad as an excuse for why they didn't use the room rather than an actual description of the room's smell. It is also possible that the claim was a direct insult to the CR girls, but that was not my impression at the time.

[16] During the Study period, The Pasifika Group often used the common room when no one else was there. However, they refrained from using the room when it was full of CR girls (e.g., during lunchtime) and they did not adopt the norms of the CR girls. Therefore, these girls have been identified as NCR girls.

2 Social groups at Selwyn Girls' High

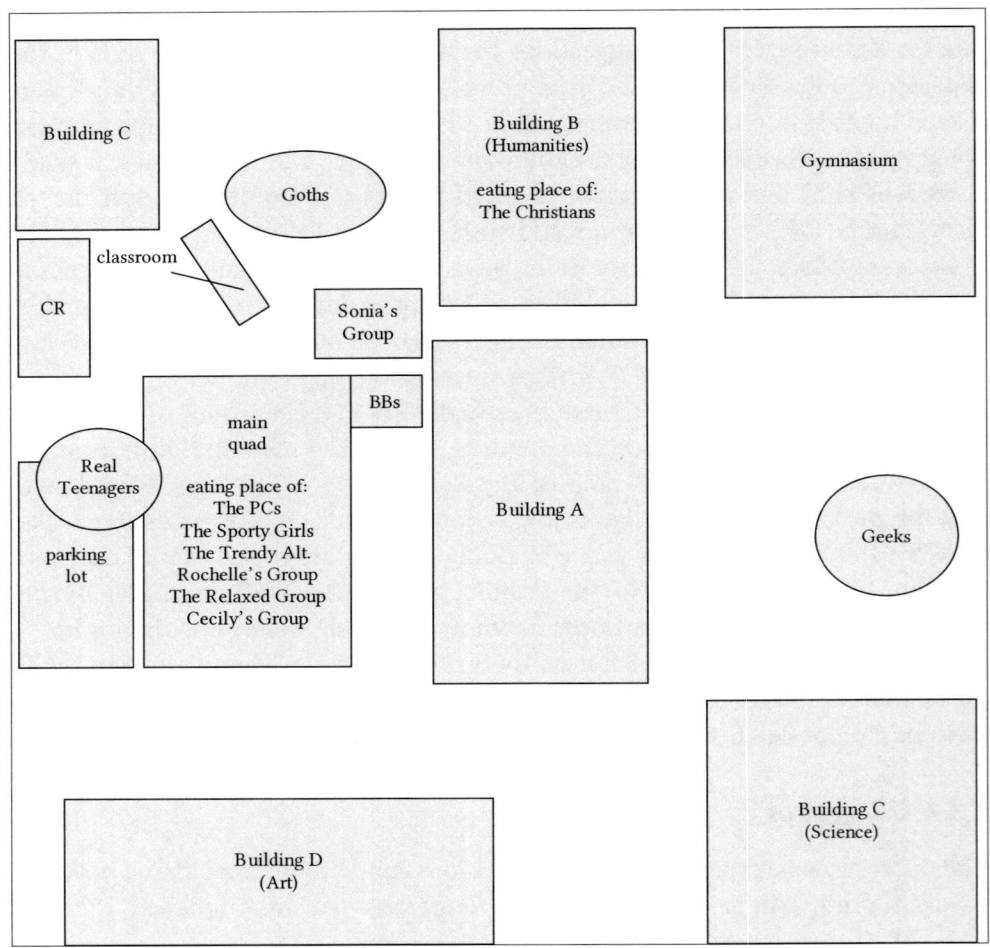

Figure 2.1: Map of SGH

Table 2.1: Common Room (CR) and Non-Common Room (NCR) Groups, in the order in which they are discussed

CR	NCR
The PCs	The Pasifika Group
The Sporty Girls	The Goths
The BBs	The Real Teenagers
The Trendy Alternatives	The Christians
Relaxed Group	The Geeks
Rochelle's Group	Cecily's Group
	Sonia's Group
	Loners

played sport. They represented a mainstream Pākehā (New Zealand European) sense of style. Being prude or dressing differently than the other CR girls was not considered acceptable. They wanted to be liked and they wanted to be admired. CR girls conformed to each other in what they liked and what they did, thereby setting the norms of the school. In some sense, they controlled, or at least embodied, the expectations of the school and of mainstream Pākehā society.

In the following sections, I describe the different groups who ate lunch in the CR. For a complete list of names of girls in each group, please refer to Appendix A. Throughout the chapter, I refer to particular girls as the central/main member, a core member, or a fringe member. This is based on my observations of the groups and the information gleaned from conversations, such as which girls were named when describing both their own or another group. They were not labels used by the girls but are meant to give the reader an idea of the social make-up of each group.

2.3.1.1 The PCs

In addition to observing the groups, I asked the girls about what different groups there were at the school. When questioned, they almost always first mentioned The PCs. The term "PC" refers to The Palms Crew, The Palms being a popular mall in Christchurch that the girls frequented. Girls from other groups admitted that they also sometimes shopped at The Palms, but the group had been labelled in junior years when The PCs were the only group who hung out at the mall.

Non-PCs explained that in order to be a PC, a girl had to be good-looking. As an outsider to the school, it seemed less that The PCs were inherently more beautiful than girls in other groups, and more that they wore the season's latest fashions from Christchurch's trendiest shops. While all PCs wore trendy clothes outside of school, only some members of The PCs straightened their hair and wore make-up and trendy clothes to school. The PCs who did not follow this trend went to the other extreme, wearing old track pants with holes and sometimes not brushing their hair. One of these girls, Kendra, explained that she didn't see the point of trying to look cute at school because there was no one she was trying to impress. Outside of school, however, she adopted the trendier styles of the other PCs.

Talking with Glenda (The BBs) and Ursula (a foreign exchange student who had joined The BBs), it became clear that The PCs were popular, not in the sense that they were the most liked, but in the sense that other girls looked up to them as the definers of what is and what is not fashionable. The PCs were also sometimes referred to as The Plastics, a reference to characters in the Lindsey Lohan movie Mean Girls because they were known to be "fake"[17] and to talk about each other behind each other's backs. When Ursula first came to SGH, she ate lunch with The PCs, but she switched groups because she said their conversations made her feel uncomfortable. Both Glenda and Ursula were quick to add that, while as a group they did not particularly like The PCs, each of The PCs was nice on an individual level. I wondered whether this was related to the Losers Sit Alone rule: individual PCs being nice when interacting one-on-one because they did not want to be seen alone. Whether or not this is true, The PCs were not the most well-liked group at SGH, but they were certainly the most popular.

Neither Cleo nor Kim (The PCs) were especially forthcoming with me and both eventually refused to take part in further interviews. Kendra, however, encouraged me to spend time with her group, explaining that I would get crazier stories from them than from any of the others. She was not entirely incorrect. Members of this group threw large, exclusive parties and they openly discussed sex, alcohol, and party pills. Noelle, June, and Joanna did fairly well in school, but the majority of The PCs viewed school as a social arena rather than a learning centre. In fact, by the end of the year, Marilyn, Amber, Larissa, Kendra, and Minnie had dropped out. The PCs who stayed until the end of the year expressed a mixture of excitement and sadness when graduating; they worried there would never come

---

[17] According to Urban Dictionary (urbandictionary.com), *fake* is a term used to describe a person, usually a girl, who "acts too nice to be real in order to lure in pathetic dopes and use/betray them, frequently crushing the victim's soul in the process." For more detail, see work by Stacy Lewis, who has conducted a linguistic analysis of "mock fake" speech: speakers imitating girls who are fake (Lewis 2009).

a time when everyone in their group was together again. As Tracy lamented, "I think I need another year" (Tracy, The PCs, Interview, 22-10.)

2.3.1.2 The Sporty Girls

The Sporty Girls were active in the school, though many of them had been more involved in previous years. Though distinct groups at the beginning of the year, contact between The PCs and The Sporty Girls increased as the year progressed. There were two groups within The Sporty Girls who were especially close: Stella, Candice, Rachel, Elise, and Naomi; and Stella, Patricia, Ruby, and Betty. Stella is listed in both groups because she appeared to be the uniting member between them. Patricia's closest friends went to other schools, but at SGH her closest friends were Stella and Ruby. Kanani joined the group at the beginning of the year. She was the only girl in the study who switched from a NCR group to a CR group.[18]

Girls in the group viewed themselves as friendly, "normal", and "in between". The label, *Sporty*, was not something used by the girls in the group to refer to themselves. Though some of them wore athletic clothes to school, sports were not necessarily how they identified. In fact, Patricia did not play sport at all and, along with Betty and Ruby, wore some of the trendiest clothes of all the girls. *Sporty* was a label used to refer to this group by girls in other groups, most likely as a result of the clothing worn by Candice, Stella, and Rachel. At the beginning of the year, Naomi also wore athletic clothes, but by the end of the year she had switched entirely to wearing trendy clothes and make-up.

2.3.1.3 The BBs

(1) Pam and Odette (The BBs). Fieldnotes, 06-04.

> Pam: the PCs may be cooler than us
>
> Odette: but we'll go further in life

Although girls in their final year at Selwyn Girls' High were no longer required to wear a uniform, some members of The BBs continued to wear theirs, thereby

---

[18] In terms of the production patterns that are presented in Chapter 3, Kanani behaved more similarly to the NCR girls than the CR girls. Though I have not yet examined other features of her speech systematically, she appeared to use a mixture of phonetic features utilised by girls in both groups.

acquiring the label "the Blazer Brigade". This was a friendly group of girls who were good students and who participated in a large number of school activities. At the beginning of the year there were two distinct groups, one of which was referred to as The BBs and the other of which was referred to as Pam's group. Upon recognising that they were really very similar, they began to spend more time together and, by the end of the year, had merged into one group. I use the term "BBs" to refer to the ultimate, larger group.

Most BBs were friendly with girls from a number of groups, particularly those who also ate lunch in the common room. They were talkative in class and were involved in school activities. They went to parties and several of them were sexually active. They were more subdued than The PCs in how they partied and they were less inclined to discuss details of parties with me.

The BBs viewed themselves as "normal". As shown in Example 1 above and Example 2 below, The BBs viewed themselves as somewhere in between the other groups. They were good students, but they did not view themselves as geeks.

(2) Andrea (The BBs). Interview, 31-07.

> Andrea: we're not like super cool
> but we're not . like . super nerdy
>
> [laughter]
>
> if that if that's that doesn't sound too mean

They were school-oriented and felt a responsibility to be good role models for younger girls. They were friendly toward girls in other groups and Andrea claimed that they got along with other groups better than anyone else did. The BBs who did not wear their uniform wore casual clothes, such as jeans and a t-shirt, and most of the girls planned to attend university.

2.3.1.4 The Trendy Alternatives

The Trendy Alternatives were artsy girls who took the latest trends and put a twist on them. The girls effectively treated Justine as the leader of the group and she was freely able (and willing) to interrupt the conversation and determine its direction.

Justine described university-bound students from other groups as "the people that wanna do something with their lives" (Justine, The Trendy Alternatives,

Interview, 03-05), but she did not feel the need to succumb to society's expectations of attending university directly after high school. Though some girls in The Trendy Alternatives were not particularly interested in school (e.g., Justine and Jewel), they planned to go to university after the age of twenty, at which point universities in New Zealand do not have entrance requirements. Other girls in this group were more school-orientated (e.g., Pascal) and went straight to university after high school.

Although this group often ate lunch in the common room, they rarely spoke to girls from other groups. Kelly and Clementine were exceptions. Although they did not sit with other groups (and were therefore not viewed as traitors), they sometimes interacted briefly with The BBs. Kelly was well-liked by girls in other groups. Lily, who expressed feeling like an outsider to her own group, was also friends with Rose (The Relaxed Group) and Kanani (The Sporty Girls), but she quickly left their side if someone from her own group walked into the room. Justine was on the committee that was planning the formal, as were a number of other CR girls. She had a clash with several girls from other groups over the venue for the formal. She was accused of being too outspoken on the subject and was reluctant to argue with them because she did not want to appear "outspoken about being accused of being outspoken" (Justine, The Trendy Alternatives, Fieldnotes, 13-04).

2.3.1.5 The Relaxed Group

Rose and Megan were the two central members of The Relaxed Group.[19] They were best friends and they had been since primary school. The group was also made up of Barbara, Katrina, Lorna, and Anita. Anita transfered to SGH at the beginning of the year. I met her just before the school's powhiri, a traditional Māori welcome ceremony which served to welcome new guests to the school grounds. She had just been approached by Rose and Megan, who, upon seeing me trying to figure out where I was meant to go, suggested that Anita and I stick together. Although shy and understandably confused by my role as a researcher rather than a student or teacher, Anita befriended me immediately. She also joined the group of the very first girls she met at the school. This was a group with whom I also felt comfortable and I often sought them out. Rose became one of the girls with whom I was closest and we have continued to stay in touch, nearly ten years since my first day at SGH.

---

[19] Girls referred to this group as "Rose's Group".

While most of the girls in this group agreed that having fun was what life was all about, Katrina had a different outlook. She expressed frustration at being a teenager and she felt a great deal of pressure from her parents and the school, lessening her enjoyment of the life that her friends seemed to cherish. The other girls felt responsible to look after Katrina. This sense of responsibility was so strong that it tarnished the fun of the formal. Katrina did not want to attend, but her friends insisted that she come. She had a fight with her Mum just before the formal started and she spent the night distant and upset, sitting at the table with me rather than with her friends, and remaining there with my date when girls grabbed me to go dancing. Rose was emotional that night, worrying over Katrina. In general, Katrina was disappointed in Year 13, which she had been assured would be the best year of high school. She was not impressed with high school and felt ready for the next chapter of her life.[20]

When I asked Megan and Anita what made their group different from other groups, they explained that they were more relaxed and cared less about image than some of the other groups. They explained how they could wear jewellery or a belt if they wanted to feel cute one day but that they did not feel pressure to do so if they were not in the mood. Girls from this group wore little make-up to school and their style of clothing was the least trendy of all the girls who ate lunch in the CR. Barbara and Katrina played sport and Rose and Megan became increasingly interested in parties as the year progressed. Lorna was a fringe member and was also good friends with Rochelle's Group.

2.3.1.6 Rochelle's Group

At one point in the year I was struggling with my own personal relationship woes and girls in a variety of groups were exceptionally sensitive to my emotional state, for which I was (and continue to be) extremely grateful. One group in particular offered to listen and provide support because, as Camden explained, "We know drama" (Fieldnotes, 26-10). And indeed, these girls did. From break-ups to break-ins, these girls almost seemed to thrive on their struggles and the mutual fondness they gained through sharing their stories with each other.[21]

---

[20] Katrina was much happier once she went to university. She has made good friends and she now admits that in high school she would have liked to have been better friends with The Goths but worried at the time that it would cause problems with girls in The Relaxed Group.

[21] Because of this drama, I have referred to this group elsewhere as the Drama Queens (Drager 2008). I am not entirely happy with this label: It was not one used by any of the girls and they do not fit my stereotype of drama queens. Therefore, I felt it was misleading and have refrained from using the term here.

This group was a CR group, but apart from Lorna's friendship with girls in The Relaxed Group, they did not get along with CR girls from other groups. From my point of view, it seemed as though they intentionally instigated confrontations with other girls. Camden (Rochelle's Group) and Lily (The Trendy Alternatives) openly talked badly about one another and Lorna (Relaxed Group/Rochelle's Group) rolled her eyes if one of The BBs approached to ask her opinion on a Year 13 matter. Mindy, however, was quiet and friendly both in and outside of class and Rochelle made an effort to be friendly and to smooth things over with other groups. Perhaps it was she, the leader, who maintained their status as a CR group. She was the only one in her group who embodied the CR girls' trait of wanting to be liked and wanting to be admired.

Interestingly, these girls performed drama differently from other people I know. Rather than talking up their news as though it was full of juicy details, these girls downplayed their drama. My impression was that they wanted me to believe that they had so much drama in their lives that something that I might consider drama-worthy was hardly worth mentioning. For example, one day when I was talking with both Camden and Rochelle, Camden told me that she thought she was pregnant and that the father was neither nice to her nor wanted to be in a relationship with her.[22] Rochelle, an incredible optimist on a number of occasions, stated with a sigh that she wanted to go ice skating and Camden agreed that ice skating would be fun. They were not avoiding the topic of pregnancy; both girls were quite open about sharing this type of information with me. The nonchalant manner in which the information had been provided and the quick change of subject to something entirely unrelated and, in my opinion, much less dramatic, left the impression that dramatic events were so commonplace in the lives of these girls that it hardly needed mentioning. That Camden explicitly made a claim on drama ("we know drama") indicates that this was in fact the defining characteristic of this group and reflected how they viewed themselves.

2.3.1.7 CR groups as a constellation

The CR girls' claim on the common room was no coincidence. The common room was a piece of prime real estate and they felt entitled to use it. Through actions such as writing on the whiteboard and posting photos of their friends on the wall, they not only used the room but made sure everyone knew that it was theirs. They believed, or at least claimed to believe, that everyone was friends with everyone else. If everyone was friends, there was no need to negotiate who was entitled to use a shared space like the common room.

---

[22] She later found out that she was not pregnant.

Together, the groups who ate lunch in the common room formed a constellation of practices, a term used by Wenger (1998) to refer to groups who were too broad and diverse to be considered communities of practice but who shared interconnected practices nonetheless. "The term *constellation* refers to a grouping of stellar objects that are seen as a configuration even though they may not be particularly close to one another, of the same kind, or of the same size" (Wenger 1998: 127). He explains that constellations of practices are more abstract than communities of practice. They need not be named nor do the individuals need to be aware that they form any kind of grouping. Though between CR groups there was a web of interconnected practices, they did not form the tightly woven bonds of a community of practice as described by Wenger. The CR girls were not the only constellation of practices at the school. The whole of Year 13 was a constellation of practices and, in fact, the whole of Selwyn Girls' High was as well. Constellations of practices can take a number of forms and can be observed at multiple levels of categorisation.

The CR girls also formed what I refer to as a *constellation of stance*, an aggregate of individuals or groups of individuals who commonly take shared stances toward other individuals, concepts, and constructs. It is this that sets them apart within the constellation of the school. Here, I take stance to mean "a socially recognised disposition" (Ochs 1990: 2). CR girls expressed similar views of themselves and similar attitudes toward these views (e.g., the view that they were "normal" and that "normal" was a positive attribute, that upward social mobility was a positive attribute and that people who did not aim for it were not going to go far in life). Through doing so, they form a constellation of stance and they shared a number of interconnected practices (e.g., planning the formal, playing sport, and going to parties), thereby forming a constellation of practices. The reason behind distinguishing between these different types of constellations will be clearer in the following section which discusses the NCR girls: While the NCR girls formed a constellation of stance, they did not form a constellation of practices that was separate from that which they also shared with the CR girls.

2.3.2 NCR groups

Despite the CR girls' claims, not everyone at SGH was friends with everyone else. There were girls who were not accepted into CR groups but who, for the most part, did not want to be. Though the groups shared little in common with one another, NCR groups actively rejected the behavioural norms set by the CR girls, and, in doing so, unwittingly shared a common stance.

Of course, the different NCR groups each established their own sets of norms. For example, girls in The Real Teenagers were expected to party and girls in The Geeks were expected to try hard in school. But the number of members in each of the groups was simply not high enough to overturn the school's norms set by the CR girls. In other words, while there were norms for each of the NCR groups, they were not the norms of the school.

2.3.2.1 The Pasifika Group

All members of The Pasifika Group were Māori or Pacific Islander (PI).[23] While there were Māori girls in other groups, ethnicity was not a topic they introduced into our conversations.[24] Girls in The Pasifika Group, on the other hand, immediately identified themselves in terms of their ethnicity and expressed pride in their culture as well as frustration at the lack of ethnic diversity among the students and teachers at SGH and in Christchurch in general. They were particularly frustrated that the school did not seem to address their need for a more ethnically diverse faculty. There was no Pacific Island teacher and they felt misunderstood by the single Māori teacher at the school. The school's failure to hire non-Pākehā teachers may well be due to a shortage of such teachers, but it left the girls feeling unsupported, as exemplified in Example 3.

(3) Masina, Alana and Lela (Pasifika Group). Interview, 20-09.

> Masina: 'cause I seen it happen quite a lot of times
> but I mean a lot of parents have come in school .
> um . to complain about it but they just .
>
> Alana: don't take . any notice of it
>
> KD : really?
>
> Lela : yeah it's "oh yeah I don't care"
>
> Masina: they don't take us seriously

---

[23] Pacific Islander is a term used to refer to people with ancestry from Polynesia, Micronesia, and Melanesia. In New Zealand, it is does not usually include indigenous New Zealand Māori.

[24] One exception was Kanani, who was proud of her Polynesian roots but distanced herself from The Pasifika Group after switching to The Sporty Girls. Girls in The Pasifika Group were no longer friendly to her and she constructed her own sense of style (both linguistic and non-linguistic) that was reminiscent of both Pacific Island style and a style consonant with that of her new group.

2 Social groups at Selwyn Girls' High

As demonstrated in Example 4, Masina and her friends felt as though they were treated differently, not by the other girls, but by the school itself.

(4) Masina (Pasifika Group). Interview, 20-09.

> Masina: but . yeah . um I mean they seem .
> like they've had issues with . us brown people um .
> not attending school and stuff
> and they just knock . all of us off .
> like . all that like . one after one they h-
> they're just like . completely give up on us
> instead of giving us the support that we need to stay in school

They attributed the difference to the colour of their skin, explaining that most of their group had already left school and that they believed that teachers had "written off" those who remained. They also viewed themselves as different from the majority of girls, stating that they needed different kinds of support than other girls and wishing that there was a faculty member who understood where they were coming from culturally. They felt that while the school treated them differently, it did not treat them differently in a constructive way.

The Pasifika Group had very little interaction with Year 13 girls from other groups. They did not eat lunch in the common room and they kept to themselves during class. One of their good friends, Ripeka, was very involved in the school, both with sport and with kapahaka (traditional Māori performing arts) and she had friends in other groups. Unfortunately, I was not able to record an interview with Ripeka.

Although girls in The Pasifika Group had little interaction with girls from other groups in their year, they interacted regularly with more junior girls (who were also Māori or PI), which was not something done by girls in most other groups.

2.3.2.2 The Goths

Only one member of The Goths, Santra, wore black clothes and dyed her hair black, but girls in other groups referred to the entire group as The Goths.[25] All of the girls in this group described themselves as "weird" and they at least claimed not to care about what other people thought about them. They were intelligent

---

[25] Goths are a youth subculture that see beauty in the dark side of life. They tend to wear black clothes, heavy eyeliner, and medieval-inspired clothing.

girls who were enthusiastic students but who also questioned the school's ability to teach them life's most important lessons. They were knowledgeable about world events and had strong opinions about societal issues. Santra, Vanessa, Meredith, and Marissa were the original members of the group. In Year 12, The Goths were joined by Tania (previously of The Relaxed Group) and in Year 13, by Bianca, who seen less and less frequently with The Geeks as the year progressed.

The Goths had a particular area of the school grounds that they considered their own. It was separated by large plants from the courtyard where most of the other groups hung out and it contained a small wooden deck and a large rock. The Goths ate there even when the weather was very cold and on rainy days they moved under the enclave of a building nearby. This group had eaten lunch in this area since the beginning of high school. They were very territorial and girls from other groups rarely challenged their claim. However, there was one lunchtime where The Goths had to assert their authority. They arrived to the area later than usual and some younger girls were sitting on the deck. Rather than approaching them and telling them to leave, The Goths surrounded the deck and exclaimed in loud voices, "Don't you hate it when people sit in their [sic] spot" (Santra, The Goths, Interview, 03-05). The younger girls gathered their things and left, glaring and mumbling in angry voices under their breath. Girls in The Goths tended to be friendly, but the area where they ate was a part of how they constructed their identity. They felt they had a claim on the place and they were willing to chance confrontation in order to preserve that claim.

2.3.2.3 The Real Teenagers

Some groups trusted me immediately. I was a researcher and university student. My presence had been approved by the school principal and this legitimised me in the eyes of some students (e.g., The BBs). In contrast, it required more work to gain a rapport with The Real Teenagers and after over a month at the school, I began to lose hope that I ever would. One day, however, the opportunity arose.

"No entry". The sign on the door was in clear view and it had not been there the day before. I did not know any way to the classroom other than through that door or through a maze of already-full classrooms. I had not seen Onya walk through the door, but I knew she had. Alex was walking toward it.[26] She opened the door and moved aside the chairs meant to block the entrance, beck-

---

[26] At the time, Alex and Onya were good friends. However, once Isabelle switched groups, Alex switched back to Cecily's Group, informing me that it was her "real group" while Onya stood listening nearby. Onya (The Real Teenagers) and Cecily (Cecily's Group) did not get along though they had friends in common including Alex as well as others who did not go to SGH.

oning for me to follow. I hesitated a moment, unsure of whether I should follow this group of rather rebellious girls whose favour I had been attempting to gain (unsuccessfully), or follow my inclination to obey school authority. My desire to abide by the school rules was strong, perhaps a habitual remnant leftover from my own school days, or perhaps out of fear of losing the privilege of conducting research at SGH. The door, having been left unattended while I stood watching it, was just about to close, when suddenly I grabbed it and walked in. While I was maneuvering around the chairs that blocked my way into the hall, the teacher (whose class I had hoped to attend) emerged from her classroom. She glowered and reprimanded me. I felt ashamed and humiliated. Alex came to my defense, at which point the teacher began to aim some of the accusations at her. Alex and I both remained silent, neither of us informing the teacher who, besides myself, had walked through that door.

The shame I felt during the teacher's scolding surprised me. The reprimand itself was not what was surprising; I knew that I had disobeyed the rules and that I deserved to pay the consequences. I was surprised by my shame.

But if shame was my payment, my reward was rapport. From that day forward, this group of girls welcomed me to join them and they openly shared details of their personal lives to a level I had not anticipated. It was then that I appreciated the value of gaining rapport, even when achieved through somewhat uncomfortable means, as exhibited by Geertz when he was finally able to gain rapport with Balinese locals after siding with them during a government break-up of an illegal cockfight (Geertz 1973). Like Geertz, I had to face the temporary disfavour of an authority figure, but in turn I was able to gain the trust of those with whom I had previously had none.

The Real Teenagers were a group of rebellious girls who partied hard and, as they saw it, lived life to the fullest. One of the core members, Onya, gave an overview of their conversation topics: sex, drugs, and rock 'n' roll. The Real Teenagers claimed that they didn't care what others thought about them, but the explicit nature of the conversations and the volume at which they spoke while within listening distance of other girls suggested otherwise: They were out to shock. When in class two of The BBs said that they wished their lives were as exciting as The Real Teenagers', Alex and Onya laughed. They enjoyed their status as the crazy party girls and they were pleased when the other girls acknowledged it.

Most girls at SGH referred to this group as Onya's group; the "Real Teenagers" was not a name used by girls at the school. Toward the beginning of the year, Isabelle (formerly of The Goths) decided to switch groups. Example 5 displays a conversation between Meredith, Vanessa (The Goths) and me.

(5) Meredith and Vanessa (The Goths). Interview, 03-09.

> KD: how come Isabelle switched groups?
>
> Meredith: to become a teenager
>
> Vanessa: that was her words
> to become a teenager
>
> KD: what's that mean?
>
> Meredith: the group she's now with
> they go out and they get pissed like . every like .
> a couple times every weekend
> oh they just do stupid things
>
> Vanessa: they have sex a lot
>
> Meredith: yeah have sex a lot they just .
> they're like the real real real teenagers

The central members of The Real Teenagers were Onya, Claudia and Renee. Sarah was also a good friend, though she did not always get along with Onya. At the beginning of the year, Alex (Cecily's Group) and Onya spent a great deal of time together. However, Isabelle, rather than Alex, became Onya's close friend partway through the year when Isabelle started dating Onya's good friend, Luke. Sally (Cecily's Group) became good friends with Renee over the course of the year but was rarely seen with the rest of The Real Teenagers.

Though The Real Teenagers and The PCs shared a love for parties and a less than enthusiastic outlook toward academic subjects, the groups were different on a number of counts. The PCs had values associated with more mainstream New Zealand society. Many of the girls belonged to higher socioeconomic groups and PCs who did not live in prestigious suburbs (e.g., Fendalton or Sumner) didn't talk freely about the area where they lived. The PCs wore clothes from chain stores found at New Zealand malls. They wanted to be liked by girls in other groups and they smiled at girls who they talked badly about afterward. In contrast, The Real Teenagers rejected mainstream values in favour of a more artistic chaos: homemade skirts accented in ribbons and lace, worn with Doc Marten boots, fishnet stockings, and handmade accessories from the clothing boutique where Claudia worked. Though high heels were not allowed at school, Onya loudly clomped down the main corridor wearing heels in defiance. Many of the girls belonged to lower socioeconomic groups. Onya talked with pride about living in Aranui, the poorest and most stigmatised suburb in Christchurch, and Renee explained that she had only brought a banana for lunch because her father couldn't afford the groceries that week (at which point her friends divvied up their lunches and shared them with her). They wanted other girls to recognise their party lifestyle and they wanted to be admired, but not for their money or their parents' social status. And they displayed no desire to be liked; they made it perfectly clear to all when there was someone they did not care for.

2.3.2.4 The Christians

In stark contrast to The Real Teenagers were The Christians. This group was made up of two girls: Esther and Theresa. Esther and Theresa felt most comfortable among people who shared their beliefs and adhered to their expectations of right and wrong. Despite their general satisfaction with life, they felt separated and different from the other girls at the school. Both worked hard at school and expressed enjoyment of their adolescent years.

Theresa, who was not religious prior to meeting Esther, grew up in a small rural town in New Zealand and Esther spent her childhood in a small village in France. They became good friends after Esther invited Theresa to Easter Camp, a multi-day Christian camp with live music, games, and activities. At the time, Esther had only lived in the country for a short time and had not realised that there were non-Christians in New Zealand. She invited Theresa assuming she would already be familiar with the idea of Easter Camp. Theresa came out of curiosity and had a wonderful time surrounded by more people than she had ever seen. Esther and Theresa were best friends from then on.

Both Esther and Theresa dressed conservatively and said they would not feel comfortable wearing clothes, such as short skirts, that many of the other girls wore. Like girls in The Pasifika Group, they interacted very little with other girls in their year but had several friends from youth group who were in more junior years. Exceptions in Year 13 were two of The Goths with whom they occasionally interacted during Study, though only one of The Goths, Marissa, encouraged the friendship. Both Esther and Theresa were good students and had conservative values and they both viewed Christianity as the defining feature of their group. There were other Christians at the school, but it was viewed as a characteristic of an individual as opposed to the central component of the group's identity.

2.3 Groups of friends

2.3.2.5 The Geeks

The girls in this group did not fit my stereotype of "geek" at all. I viewed them as an eclectic group of individuals, each with their own distinct style. It was the most multi-national and multi-cultural group in Year 13. "The Geeks" was a label used by other girls to refer to this group; it was not something used by the members themselves. Although this was not a group commonly mentioned by girls in other groups, CR girls used the term "Geeks" when asked explicitly about the group.

The make-up of The Geeks, most of whom were good students, only formed in Year 13. Joy, who was originally from Australia, attended another school in Christchurch before coming to SGH in Year 12. In intermediate school[27], Mariah had been in a group with some of The BBs, but that group broke up when the unifying member moved to Australia. Valentina was new to SGH but quickly became a core member of the group. Aerial had a falling out with her former group (The Relaxed Group) the previous year and The Geeks befriended her. Bianca, a fringe member of The Geeks, also spent time with The Goths, and by the end of the school year was spending more time with The Goths than with The Geeks.

On warm days, most girls at SGH ate lunch on the sunny side of the school. The Geeks, however, ate lunch on the other side of the building from the main quad, as shown in the map in Figure 2.1. The only other groups who ate in this area were in younger years. Joy and Mariah, the two central members, tended to dominate the lunchtime conversation.

The styles worn by The Geeks varied more than those worn by girls in other groups. For example, Aerial and Valentina wore short skirts and sandals, while Joy wore track-pants; Aluna and Nisha wore long flowing skirts, Kristin wore punk clothes with studded wrist bands, while Mariah wore corduroys and blouses from secondhand shops. Though styles of apparel varied among The Geeks, girls from other groups saw fit to comment on their clothes, particularly those of Joy, Kristin, and Mariah. The other girls' expectations of what the girls in The Geeks should wear were not the norms of the school; The Geeks were expected to dress differently from the other girls. For example, one day Mariah came to school wearing a purple nose ring. The other girls were shocked, telling Mariah that it didn't suit her. Megan (The Relaxed Group), who was critical of Mariah's nose ring, had a lip ring herself and had commented on how she liked my nose piercing. It was not as though the girls did not accept piercings in general; they did

---

[27] Intermediate school is between primary and secondary school and is equivalent to junior high or middle school in countries such as the United States.

not accept that Mariah, a Geek, would pierce her nose. After nearly an hour of taunting, Mariah removed her nose ring, revealing that the nose ring was one that did not require a piercing and that her nose was not, in fact, pierced. The other girls teased her even more after realising that the piercing wasn't real and Mariah never wore the purple nose ring to school again.

2.3.2.6 Cecily's Group

Cecily's Group was a group of friendly and funny girls. They had an alternative sense of style and liked live music and art. The majority of girls in Cecily's Group took art classes and several of them played musical instruments. Their interests were diverse and Sally explained how they each had their own little niche within the group through these different interests. Sally was an artist, Pania was a surfer, and Lindsey was a Christian, but they all enjoyed doing things together and valued each other's friendship.

When I asked Sally whether she thought the school was very divided, she first claimed that most people at the school got along but then added that there was some level of judgment by at least some people, as shown in Example 6.

(6) Sally (Cecily's Group). Interview, 11-04.

> Sally: everyone just goes and has fun like
>
> KD: yeah
>
> Sally: I don't know .
> but maybe slightly judgmental sometimes I don't know
> there's some degree of judgment everywhere I suppose eh

As discussed in Section 2.4, the belief that everyone "just goes and has fun" is consistent with the stance of the CR girls, whereas acknowledging that some girls are judgmental is consistent with the beliefs of the NCR girls. This suggests that Sally's views were somewhere in between those of the CR girls and the NCR girls. In fact, the girls in Cecily's Group seemed to get along with girls in NCR groups, such as The Real Teenagers, as well as CR groups, like The BBs.

Members of Cecily's Group were good students, but they also partied and they genuinely seemed as though they didn't care to (or feel the need to) meet the social expectations of the CR girls. Cecily appeared to be the most central member and was usually the girl mentioned when other girls referred to this group. Because the girls in Cecily's group were very active at the school and had little free time, I had less of a chance to get to know them as well as I would have liked.

2.3 Groups of friends

2.3.2.7 Sonia's Group

Sonia's Group was not a group that was pointed out by the other girls.[28] I came to know two of the girls in this group, Holly and Sonia, through attending their Study period. Though neither of the girls were seen conversing or sitting with The PCs at school, Holly and Sonia saw some of The PCs on a bus trip one weekend, a drunken night where groups are bussed between out-of-the-way pubs in and around Christchurch. Thereafter, both Holly and Sonia talked about The PCs as though they were friends, leaving me with the impression that they looked up to The PCs. Given their acceptance of the CR norms, this group could potentially be classified as a CR group.[29] However, I have listed them here as a NCR group because they did not actually eat lunch in the common room.

2.3.2.8 NCR groups as a constellation

The groups labelled here as NCR were a mix of diverse groups with very distinct ideologies and lifestyles. By placing them in a single group (NCR), I do not mean to imply that there were similarities among them. The trait they shared was a rejection of the practices that were established as normal by the common room girls, forming a constellation of stance. "We not only produce our identities through the practices we engage in, but we also define ourselves through practices we do not engage in" (Wenger 1998: 164).

The NCR groups were separate, diverse groups with wildly different styles from one another, but crucially, they all viewed themselves as different from the other girls.

2.3.3 Outside of lunchtime

The CR-NCR distinction extended beyond the lunch hour. There was one Study group in particular that exemplified the divide. While most groups in a single Study period were made up of fewer than 20 students, there was one period where over 30 students had Study. Due to the larger number of students, two classrooms (as opposed to the usual single room) were provided and the students

---

[28] Sonia appeared to dominate conversations. Although I am not certain that she was actually the central member, I have used her name in the group's label.

[29] In the production analysis presented in Chapter 3, patterns in Holly's speech more closely resembled those found in the speech of the CR girls. However, I deemed it to be poor methodology to alter my qualitative analysis after this time, but I interpret Holly's use of both linguistic and non-linguistic factors associated with CR girls to be consistent with her eagerness to conform to the CR girls' norms. This is discussed further in Section 3.4.5.

were free to chose which of the two rooms they spent the period in. Without exception, girls in CR groups sat in one classroom and girls in NCR groups sat in the other. The NCR girls interacted minimally across the different groups, though occasionally Esther (The Christians) commented on conversations between different members of The Goths. The CR girls, on the other hand, sat on top of the desks and talked with one another throughout the Study period.

When running the perception experiments, I asked the CR girls in this Study period if they would like to take part. Maya suggested that I ask the girls in the other room, commenting that they would be happy to help and that she would help later if I still needed participants.[30] As I walked from one room to the other, I heard the CR girls laughing. I presumed that they were laughing at Maya's dismissal of my experiments, pawning the task off onto a group of girls with whom she did not care to interact. Alternatively, they may have been laughing because Maya told me what to do and I obeyed: I went to the "others", thereby acknowledging that they were the "freaks and geeks" who would take part in experiments and it was with them that I belonged.

There was no label used to describe the differences between girls in one room and girls in another, but this is not surprising: Constellations of practices often go unnamed (Wenger 1998: 128) and I suspect that constellations of stance are even less likely to be named. Despite this, Maya had inadvertently acknowledged the divide between the Year 13 groups.

2.4 Salience and stance

The Second Wave of variationist studies emphasises the importance of using an ethnographic methodology in order to uncover social groupings of a community that are relevant to the speakers within that community. There is always a danger of a researcher imposing their expectations and prejudices upon speakers, thereby failing to identify categories that are relevant to the individuals being studied. However, I believe that less salient groupings of speakers can also be relevant to sociolinguistic variation. Extending the meaning to the context of SGH, I use the term *relevance* to refer to how much a factor or group is "connected with, or pertinent to the matter at hand" ('Relevance' 2002), regardless of whether that factor or group is above or below the level of consciousness. I use the term *salience* to refer to a gradient level of importance or prominence of an item in relation to its neighbours; the more salient an item, the more the item

---

[30] Maya did later take part in the experiment.

stands out. Salience attracts attention, and greater attention leads to a higher liklihood of awareness.

Although girls at the school were acutely aware of the different, smaller groups (e.g., The PCs, The BBs, etc.), they were not aware of the constellations of stance: the CR-NCR distinction. This is not to say that the girls were unaware of where other groups ate lunch (though several CR girls had trouble naming NCR groups), but CR groups and NCR groups were not listed as belonging to a shared grouping. As mentioned earlier, Maya referred to the NCR girls in the other room and treated them differently to the CR girls she was surrounded by, but this was the closest anyone came to acknowledging this divide. No one used labels to refer to CR versus NCR groups and no one even mentioned the similarities across the different CR groups. The groupings "CR girls" and "NCR girls" were not salient categories at the school and I want to make it clear that I am not arguing that they were explicit categories at all: They were groupings of girls who shared similar stances to the school's norms of behaviour. CR girls shared the belief that they were "normal" and in doing so, they conformed to each other's norms, thereby setting and perpetuating the norms themselves. In contrast, girls labeled as "NCR girls" shared a stance that was something akin to different than the norm. They rebelled against the norms of the CR girls in different ways (e.g., Santra of The Goths wore all black; Esther and Theresa of The Christians refrained from drinking alcohol; Joy and Aerial of The Geeks sat at the front of the classroom; Marama and Angel of The Pasifika Group did not reject their cultural values in favour of the Pākehā values that were embraced by the CR girls). These acts of defiance of the norms served to construct their social personae. CR girls and NCR girls formed two separate constellations of stance. Consistent with work in the Third Wave, I argue that linguistic variables can be indexed to stances rather than to any category of "CR" or "NCR", thereby allowing linguistic variables to be correlated with abstract groupings of individuals (constellations) of which the speakers themselves are less aware. A linguistic analysis and a discussion of how it correlates with these positions of "normal" and "different" can be found in Chapter 3. Here, I discuss some of the stylistic choices made by CR and NCR girls and then I provide several examples of interactions with the girls that help to illustrate their different stances.

A group's choice of lunch locale symbolises the position taken by those girls who conformed to expectations and norms at the school and those who did not. The girls' choice of clothing, piercings, and activities supports this distinction. The CR girls most often wore clothes from chain shops found in malls throughout

New Zealand. In most groups there was at least one girl with a facial piercing, usually a lower lip, eyebrow, nose, or Monroe (a piercing that is placed off-centre in the upper lip and resembles a beauty mark). Across the different NCR groups, there was a much greater amount of variation in how they dressed. The Real Teenagers mixed their own homemade creations with designer ones, and some had multiple facial piercings (e.g., both nostrils and the back of the neck). In contrast, The Christians wore conservative clothing and had naked faces (i.e. no make-up or piercings). That girls from the different NCR groups did not dress similarly to one another is not surprising. The girls were defined as NCR girls not by what they were but by what they were not: CR. Instead of focusing on commonalities between them (of which there were few), I wish to highlight the multitude of identities and the manner in which they failed to conform to the behavioural norms established by the CR girls. As individuals, they each rejected the expectations of the majority of girls at the school. Each of the groups rejected the norms in different ways, but some of these acts, such as not eating lunch in the CR, were shared across the different groups. Therefore the common room was more than a mere eating place: It reflected the degree to which an individual conformed to the norms established at the school.

During interviews, CR girls most often commented on how everyone at SGH was friends and how there was not the clear division between groups that they associate with US high schools.[31] For example, when I asked Rachel what groups there were at the school, she responded,

(7) Rachel (The Sporty Girls). Interview, 13-04.

> Rachel: like there's . kind of like what everyone calls like The PCs and then like
> like little groups and stuff
> but then in a way everyone I feel s- kind of gets on with everyone else as well
> like I don't feel like it's that divided
> well that's how I feel like some people might think it's different
> but I kind of feel like I'm friends with everyone like like
>
> KD: that's cool
>
> Rachel: I don't feel like I don't have the right to t- go like
> go up to a group and sit down with them

---

[31] I suspect this was usually a comment made to me specifically as an American.

    hang out with them one lunchtime
    or anything like

Rachel downplays any divisions among the Year 13 girls at SGH, going so far as to suggest that she could sit with another group at lunchtime. Though she made this claim, I only ever saw her sit with her own group and with The PCs (a number of whom were friends with The Sporty Girls) during lunch.

When I asked Andrea (The BBs) the same question, she explained that the groups were not as separated as they had been in previous years. She named the different groups in the following order: her own group (The BBs), The PCs, The Trendy Alternatives, and Rochelle's Group, all of which were CR groups. Without being asked, Andrea explained why she had not named a single NCR group.

(8) Andrea (The BBs). Interview, 31-07.

    Andrea: there's probably other groups
    that I don't really know about

    [laughing]

    . 'cause like .
    I probably really only know the groups
    that sit out on this . part of the lawn

While there were several NCR groups who ate within sight of The BBs, Andrea did not mention them. Andrea only knew those groups that were highly visible at the school and those with whom her group shared a number of practices. She only knew (or, at least, only mentioned) the CR groups.

During a conversation in a Study period with both CR and NCR girls present, Katrina, a CR girl, mentioned the tendency to downplay different groups even though they existed. Bianca, a NCR girl, added that she appreciated the diversity of groups at the school.

(9) Katrina, Barbara (The Relaxed Group) and Bianca (The Geeks and The Goths). Interview, 18-09.

    Katrina: but we kind of deny cliques as well

Bianca: yeah

Barbara: yeah

Barbara: what did you call it? cliques?

Katrina: yeah

[laughter]

Katrina: that's what it is

Bianca: but I like variety 'cause it
I kinda do like variety in a
in like a school 'cause if you have everyone that looks the same
. you know it's kinda boring

In contrast to other CR girls, Katrina acknowledged that there were divides at the school. Interestingly, Katrina was a CR girl who, in interviews conducted after her graduation, has admitted that she would have liked to have been better friends with NCR girls. Yet it took a NCR girl, Bianca, to state that she appreciated the diversity of personality types at SGH. That a CR girl did not make this statement is no surprise: NCR girls valued being different whereas CR girls valued uniformity.

Though the CR girls did not state it explicitly, their claim on the only space set aside for their year reflects their status at the school. They were "normal". They were unified. The existence of cliques was denied. In a world where "everyone" got along, they saw no reason that they should not use the room. This tendency for CR girls to express feelings of unity is not to say that amiable relationships existed between all girls who ate lunch in the CR. In fact, there were a number of rifts between girls from different CR groups. However, disagreements tended to be between girls rather than against an entire group and many CR girls, when describing a group other than their own, mentioned one member of that group with whom they got along.

In contrast to the CR girls, NCR girls consistently expressed how they felt different from other girls at the school, how they were not like everyone else. While CR girls viewed the social make-up of the school as a cohesive, unified community, NCR girls felt separated from other girls at the school. In the exchange below, Esther (The Christians), expressed how she felt that she had been labeled by the other girls as somehow different.

2.4 Salience and stance

(10) Esther (The Christians). Interview, 20-09.

    Esther: I don't know how but I think I just like from Year 9 I just .
    got the label that I wasn't . the same
    I don't know like like it's weird 'cause

    KD: the the same as what?

    Esther: I li- as everyone else

She attributed the difference between her and other girls at the school to her status as a Christian and in the statement above, she appeared to put the power of labeling in the hands of other girls. However, later in the interaction it became evident that the division was at least partially a result of her feeling that she couldn't relate to girls in other groups.

(11) Esther and Theresa (The Christians). Interview, 20-09.

    Esther: I I think the difference is probably kah-

    [breathes in]

    we're both Christian

    Theresa: yeah

    Esther: yeah
    like it's kind of weird

    Theresa: it is quite weird

    Esther: yeah

    KD: what do you mean?

    Esther: like 'cause . we have different standards from everyone else
    'cause yeah the . in history and they're all talking about
    you know "oh I slept with so and so on the weekend" and and
    and I mean I still wanna be their friend but it it's just kind of weird 'cause
    you know .
    I don't . sleep with so and so on the weekend and yeah

Esther felt discomfort with some of the other girls' discussions. Rather than an external bias against Christians causing her distance from the other girls, her emotional response to the others' behaviour separated her from them. She would have liked to be friends with the other girls but it was hard to find common ground on which to connect. Wishing they could connect with the other girls is not to be confused with wishing they were more like the other girls: Both Theresa and Esther had a strong sense of identity and were proud of who they were.

A very different group, The Goths, also took pride in their differences and viewed them as a defining characteristic of their personalities. They, along with The Real Teenagers, claimed that they did not care what others thought of them or whether others approved of them. As shown in Example 12, being "normal" was not necessarily considered a positive attribute by all girls. Whereas CR groups like The Relaxed Group and The BBs described themselves as normal, NCR girls such as Vanessa and Isabelle did not want to have a claim on this label.

(12) Meredith, Vanessa (The Goths) and Isabelle (The Real Teenagers). Interview, 03-09.

> Meredith: we're not weird we're normal everyone else is weird
>
> [pause]
>
> Meredith: I'm happy being weird
>
> Isabelle: well that's good
>
> Vanessa: as I said before if you don't like me then piss off
>
> Meredith: I'd hate to be normal it'd be so boring
>
> Isabelle: I know what is normal anyway?

Meredith began by claiming that she and the other Goths were not weird. She acknowledged that there was a difference between her and "everyone else", but that the difference was due to everyone else being weird, not her. When met by silence from her friends, she not only retracted her statement, but clarified that being weird was, in fact, a good thing. Isabelle, a Real Teenager, affirmed Meredith's claim on weirdness. The Goths and The Real Teenagers did not claim to be "normal". Instead they claimed to be "weird", setting themselves apart from the "normal" CR girls.

The Pasifika girls also expressed feelings of difference. Marama and Lela agreed that they would prefer to attend a school with a higher percentage of Māori and Pacific Islander students. They were proud of who they were, but they did not feel like part of the school community. In Example 13, their friend, Masina, stated what she viewed as the characteristic that set her apart from other girls: her skin colour. She explained that this had a negative effect on her opinion of the school.

(13) Masina, Pasifika Group, 20-09.

> Masina: oh yeah I go to this school I'm so proud I go to this school but . personally like to be honest I don't like this school
>
> KD: really why?
>
> Masina: yeah . because like . well for a lot of reasons
> I mean . like um . being a different . k- colour . you know .

The school was not ethnically diverse and girls in The Pasifika Group felt that their culture and their skin colour made them different in the eyes of the school. Masina and her friends did not want to be like the other girls - they were rightfully proud of their culture and skin colour - but they would have liked it if there had been more students who shared these attributes. Each NCR group's view of how they were "different" was not the same, but they each established social identities that they viewed as different from the majority of girls at the school.

2.5 A bit of self reflection

I entered the school an outsider, but to what extent did I manage to get "in" with the different groups? This varied depending on the group and the individual. In this section, I discuss my impressions of how well I knew different girls in different groups. An overview of the different groups and my perception of how close I was with each of the girls is shown in Appendix A.

2.5.1 The BBs

The BBs immediately befriended me. Of all the girls, they reminded me most of my friends from high school and as a result I was more comfortable around them than some of the other groups. Though I felt The BBs were happy to be my friends, I did not have the feeling that they valued our relationship as much as some other girls seemed to. However, Jane claimed that she felt I was "just kinda like another girl" (Interview, 09-05), suggesting that perhaps from her point of view, I had been accepted.

During the second to last week of school, The BBs invited me along to their champagne breakfast which was to be held on the morning of the last day of school. Pam approached me and asked if I would like to join them and when I said I would, I realised a number of The BBs were watching to see how I would respond. They seemed pleased with my acceptance and they refused to take the money I tried to contribute.

Several of the groups had planned to have real champagne on the morning of graduation, but the school was successful in their intimidation tactics and most groups abstained, including The BBs, who had their breakfast near the front quad on school grounds. We drank sparkling juice in lieu of champagne and they brought a kiosk-like cooking trailer where they made eggs and sausages. But prior to the breakfast, we were met with a shock. In what the day before had been a perfectly green grassy quad covered in newly laid sod, there was a Christmas tree. It was not in a stand: It had been stuck into the ground so far that it could not be pulled out. The girls began to laugh, realising that it was a prank played by boys who I suspected were from an all boys' school nearby. The girls took photos with the tree and everyone commented on it while we ate. School officials arrived and, after some time, they were successful in removing the tree. Girls in other groups began to arrive and The BBs, having been first on the scene, became the expert witnesses. The school questioned the girls (as well as me) on who had put the tree there.[32] I did not know who had done it and the girls either did not know or did not tell; I thought it best if I did not ask.

That The BBs invited me to their champagne breakfast and included me in their photos suggests that perhaps there was some element of truth to Jane's statement. While I would not claim to be "just kinda like" one of them, we had established a relationship that was mutually enjoyable.

2.5.2 The Trendy Alternatives

The Trendy Alternatives were friendly and seemed curious about me, though I felt Justine and Jewel viewed me with some skepticism. Lily, Clementine, Christina, and Kelly were The Trendy Alternatives who I felt closest with. Lily and I sent texts back and forth throughout the year and we went shopping and met for coffee even after she signed out of school.

---

[32] The rumour was that the prank had cost the school upwards of $10,000 because damage had been done to the recently installed sprinkler system.

2.5.3 The PCs

A number of The PCs wanted nothing to do with me or, at best, viewed me as a vehicle in promoting their status as the most interesting, popular, and beautiful girls at the school. When I first entered the school, they talked with me enthusiastically, but after several months they seemed to have lost interest, perhaps when they realised that I was talking with all of the groups, even those who were considered geeks. I was beginning to feel distraught that I would lose rapport with them completely, but I also was not willing to give up my relationship with the other girls. I knew that without rapport, none of them would be interested in completing the perception experiment I planned to run. I hoped to collect responses from girls in as many groups as possible and, given their prominent status at the school, felt it particularly important that I included responses from The PCs.

I was then given an opportunity to turn a negative aspect of my personal life into a positive factor for my research. I was leaving my husband. It was terrible. I was sad and ashamed and though all of the girls knew that I was married, I was reluctant to tell any of them about the separation for several weeks. Then one day I shared what I was going through.

The first girls I told were some of the central members of The PCs and one of their friends from The Sporty Girls, a group who by this point in the year had combined with The PCs. We were in Study and I was sitting with Tracy (The PCs), Emma (The PCs), Juliet (The PCs), and Betty (The Sporty Girls). It was one of the hottest days of the year and we had pulled the beanbags from the CR out into the sun. They were talking and I suppose I was even quieter than usual; I was certainly more distracted. They asked me about my husband. I was honest and told them I had left him. I was near tears and failed to hide the quiver in my voice. They consoled me and assured me that I had done the right thing, reminding me that we only live once and that we need to do everything we can to make sure that we are as happy as possible. Their response was mature and genuinely comforting. Though I had not intended it to be a rapport-building conversation, such was the result. Through sharing my experience and feelings of pain and through their thoughtful comments and reassurances, we bonded. They began to invite me to record them more often and all four girls who had been present readily agreed to do the perception experiment and even convinced several of their friends to do it as well. I believe they sensed that what I had told them was a difficult topic and that my emotion was real. Their view of me changed: Where previously I had been merely a tool for other means or a nuisance to avoid, what I had become was closer to a "real" person and a friend.

2.5.4 The Real Teenagers

Although initially I had been worried about not gaining rapport with The Real Teenagers, they ultimately became girls who I was very familiar with. Since graduation, I have received unsolicited emails from Isabelle, Alex, and Sarah; Onya approached me at a café after graduation, just to chat and introduce me to a non-SGH friend. During the course of the year, Alex gave a number of drawings to me. The one she gave me for my birthday is shown in Figure 2.2. In orange, green, and blue highlighter pen, it reads: "To a very special varsity student... Have an ultra super funk (day after) Birthday... From the exceptionally awesome 7th form of SGH + Alex, cause shes cool, ancih."

Figure 2.2: Drawing that Alex gave me the day after my birthday

2.5.5 The Relaxed Group

The Relaxed Group was another group I came to know quite well. I was especially grateful for their presence on days when I was tired. I felt comfortable with them and accepted by them. Exchanges with them took less energy on my part. When I asked Megan and Anita if they would mind if I recorded them, they asked who I had already recorded. When I told them that I had already interviewed around 20 girls, they were shocked: Why wouldn't I ask them first? They didn't seem

2.5 A bit of self reflection

as though their feelings were hurt; they simply seemed surprised that, given how close we were, they had not been among the first to be interviewed. Since graduation, I have met with Rose and Katrina and I am also still in contact with Megan.

2.5.6 The Pasifika Group

I became more and more familiar with The Pasifika Group over time, especially with Marama. The girls in this group were especially interested in my California background: What was it like living near LA? Are the boys better looking than here? Have you ever met Snoop Dogg? I enjoyed our conversations and it was my impression that they did, too. Although they were always friendly, I certainly never succeeded in feeling "just like" another girl in the group. They shared sensitive information with me, but they also adopted a more formal speaking register when addressing me directly.

2.5.7 The Goths

The Goths were very open with me from the beginning. They were talkative and they were quick to help shape my perception of them. They invited me to join them during lunch or morning breaks and then would (in a friendly way) argue over who I would follow to class, explaining that I would learn more about life at SGH in one class over another. I felt as though I knew most of The Goths very well.

2.5.8 The Christians and The Geeks

I am not Christian and I never once felt that Theresa and Esther needed me to be in order to interact with them or to be seen with them. In fact, they did not seem interested in whether or not I was Christian; they never asked and they always cheerfully accepted when I wanted to join them. Similarly, The Geeks were always welcoming and I immediately felt accepted by them.

2.5.9 The Sporty Girls

I came to know The Sporty Girls early on. Though Naomi and Rachel were the first two I got to know, Kanani and I became the closest by the end of the year. I have met some of her family and we continue to stay in touch.

2.5.10 Rochelle's Group

I was very comfortable with Rochelle's Group and I believe they enjoyed my company as well. They asked me to come to parties and, of all the girls, they were the most persistent in insisting that I come to the formal. Part way through the year, they began to go to the school gym during lunch to work out instead of sitting in the CR or in their usual place on the lawn. I joined them in the gym on occasion, though I never had the proper clothes or shoes to join in on the workout. They continually invited me to parties and made sure that I never felt excluded from Year 13 events.

2.5.11 Sonia's Group

Of all of the groups presented here, I knew Sonia's group the least. I had the impression that they were not interested in me or what I was doing at the school. The phonetic analysis (Chapter 3) conducted on Holly's speech is based on a recording of a conversation between her and Sonia. I was in the room during the conversation, but I was not included in it.

2.5.12 When research and friendship blend

During the course of my work at SGH, there were several girls who were forced to deal with major life challenges such as eating disorders, pregnancy, miscarriage, and the death of parents and loved ones. To protect the individual girls, I will refrain from describing these in detail. Suffice it to say that the challenges faced by the girls of SGH were far from trivial and I found myself shifting between being a researcher and being a friend.

In conducting ethnography, the distinction between being a researcher and being a friend is sometimes blurred; in even a short amount of time, strong bonds can form (Milroy 1987: 79). Ethnographers become a part of the lives of the people they study, but some researchers may have qualms about getting too close to one's subjects: One does not want emotion to interfere with science. "Without science, we lose our credibility. Without humanity, we lose our ability to understand others" (Agar 1980: 13).

There were times when the girls tested the boundary between my roles as researcher and friend in places where I felt there should be one. For example, while walking to the supermarket one Study period with Renee, Alex, and Claudia (The Real Teenagers), Alex commented that I could buy them alcohol, as none of them were yet 18. I could see her watching for my reaction and I treated it as a joke and laughed. That was not a boundary that I was willing to cross and, despite testing it, I do not believe that Alex expected that I would.

There were other times when I dropped the identity of researcher entirely and acted strictly as a friend, like the day that Sage collapsed. I had met Rose's sister, Sage, on a few different occasions, such as when she asked Rose to borrow lunch money. Sage was two years younger than Rose and seemed shy and sweet, but Rose worried about her. Sage's two best friends had decided that they would no longer be friends with her after "borrowing" a large sum of money. Soon thereafter, she was jumped and beaten up at a party. Then one day I witnessed something at the school and, embarrassingly, I did not respond as I should have.

It was just before class began and I was talking with Maya (The BBs) outside her classroom, which was one of many lined along the hall. Uniformed students stood in clumps talking, holding books and bags. A junior girl was pulling at her hair and I could see that she was trying to cover up a hickey. Out of the corner of my eye, I saw someone fall. I didn't see who it was and my view was obscured by three younger girls. I assumed it was someone messing around. Maya saw the fall, too, but kept talking, also assuming that it was some kind of joke. It wasn't. After what seemed like an eternity (but was probably more like ten seconds) I realised that the girl was not getting up. I pointed and asked if she was ok, at which point the girls blocking my view moved out of the way, though they kept staring at the girl on the floor. She was convulsing in what looked like an epileptic fit. I recognised her: It was Sage. A teacher saw her at the same time and rushed to her side. I told someone to get Rose. Someone else ran to fetch the school nurse. I stood waiting, watching Sage convulsing and wishing that I had acted sooner, wishing that I could do something. The bell rang and classes began, but there we were, separate from it all. Sage had stopped convulsing, but she remained on the floor. The teacher asked if she knew her name, if she knew the date. Sage did not answer and looked around blankly.

When Rose arrived, she rushed to her sister's side. Rose talked to her softly and it looked as though Sage was answering. The nurse came in. She assured Rose that her sister would be fine and asked her to call their Mum. Rose and I went into a nearby classroom that was empty. She didn't want her sister to see her cry and didn't want her to know how worried she was. Rose called from my mobile phone, but her Mum didn't answer. Feeling scared and frustrated, she let her arms drop and threw her head back. I hugged her, assuring her that her sister would be fine. She cried and explained that her sister hadn't eaten and that the recent trauma combined with a lack of food may have caused her to faint. After several minutes, Rose began to calm down. She was able to reach her Mum and they went to the hospital for tests.

I remained with Maya and the other girls in the hall, feeling vulnerable and helpless. I felt impressively insignificant. We were all in shock and felt uncertain of how to continue our day. I left school wondering what I could have done differently to help Sage sooner and wishing I had gone to the hospital with Rose. I wanted her to know that if she needed the support, I was there as a friend and not as the researcher who followed her and her friends around with a recorder. I texted her, asking how she was doing and asking whether Sage was ok. I got a text from Rose that night saying that Sage was fine and thanking me for helping. How had I helped? I could have (and should have) done more, but all I did was give Rose a hug.

I suspect that researchers in my field will come under fire if they get "too close" to the people they study because emotions could interfere with research-related judgments. But when faced with a crying girl who needs a friend, I will give her a hug if that's the best I can do at the time. Removing the human element from the methodology of ethnography is wrong and artificial. How could I avoid being there for Rose as a friend? And why would I want to avoid it? She had shared her hardships and worries with me during the preceding months. Not only would it feel unnatural to dismiss our friendship on the basis of "science", it would be unethical.

2.5.13 Shaping interpretations

How much were my interpretations of life at Selwyn Girls' High affected by my closeness with the girls, my own high school experience, and my life prior to SGH in general? Although I tried to go in open-minded, everyone's previous experiences inform the interpretations of new situations. Mendoza-Denton (2008) states explicitly that

> what I present as a text was filtered through my sensibility, my interpretation as well as my equivocation. Even what I noticed and considered as "data points" were selected in my perception according to the sum of my prior experiences and my take on the situations encountered. (Mendoza-Denton 2008: 44)

> No ethnographer is a blank notepad just as no linguist is a tape recorder. (Mendoza-Denton 2008: 48)

It is the type of insight that would most easily be gleaned by an outsider who could view the entire situation (including me and my biases) from a different perspective. One effect of my personality that is obvious even to me is inherent in my interpretation of the incident with Rose's sister, Sage. The women in my family have a history of inheriting an irrational form of guilt from the women of the previous generation (which has the unfortunate effect of making the previous generation feel even more guilty). We take responsibility for the world's problems (e.g., children starving, greenhouse gases, the war in Iraq), not to mention problems in our personal lives, and feel guilty when we are unsuccessful in solving them. Sage's collapse was not my fault and many people would have responded the same way, yet I felt (and continue to feel) guilty that I did not do more to help. I recognise the lack of logic behind the guilt and I considered removing that aspect from the description of the incident from my dissertation and, later, this book. However, as it is, it is the honest portrayal of my interpretation of the situation. My inherited guilt combined with the close relationship that had developed between me and Rose served to shape how I viewed (and continue to view) what happened to her sister. I feel better acknowledging these effects and portraying my interpretation honestly rather than removing the emotions from the text. This way the reader can make up their own mind about how to interpret the situation without it being filtered through the reasoning of my self-conscious mind.

> On entering the community, an ethnographer carries more baggage than a tape recorder and a toothbrush, having grown up in a particular culture, acquiring many of its sometimes implicit assumptions about the nature of reality... The problem is not whether the ethnographer is biased; the problem is what kinds of biases exist - how do they enter into ethnographic work and how can their operation be documented. (Agar 1980: 41-2)

Interestingly, I also observed an influence in the opposite direction: I felt the memory of my own high school life shift during my time at SGH. In the past, I had claimed that there were no cliques or "popular girls" where I went to high school. After spending time at SGH, I realised that, like the CR girls, I had simply denied the reality of their existence. It took experiencing high school life as an outsider for me to recognise and acknowledge this aspect of my own high school life. This is not to say that my previous experiences did not help to shape my interpretations of the girls' socially constructed identities, but I was surprised to observe an effect in the opposite direction.

2.6 Conclusion

In sum, there were a number of groups at the school. The girls identified strongly with these groups and each girl found her own unique place within the group. Some of the groups (CR groups) valued conformity and viewed themselves as "normal" while other groups (NCR groups) valued diversity and viewed themselves as different from the other girls. These aggregates of groups formed two distinct constellations of stance. The following chapter investigates the degree to which phonetic variation at the school can be predicted by these different constellations. It also discusses the tendencies for particular girls to exhibit certain trends in the production of their speech and how these trends are consistent with non-linguistic expressions of their identities.

3 *Like*: Frequency and phonetic realisations

3.1 Methodology of interviews

In a standard sociolinguistic interview, an interviewer asks questions designed to elicit the "vernacular", which is essentially the range of speech styles used in informal situations when there is no interviewer present.[1] Questions, such as whether the interviewee has ever had a near-death experience, are used to shift the focus from *how* the narrative is said to the content of the narrative itself. Often followed by read passages and/or wordlists, the traditional Labovian style interview is a popular method to elicit speech, as it provides a means of lessening the effects of the Observer's Paradox. As speakers become more involved in the interaction, they become less focused on the fact that they are being recorded (Labov 1972a). I adopted an alternative approach for my interviews at Selwyn Girls' High for the following reasons:[2]

(1) Previous work has shown that greater familiarity with an outsider decreases the amount a speaker will accommodate, thereby reducing the effect of the Observer's Paradox (Cukor-Avila & Bailey 2001). I did not begin recording until I had spent two months at the school, so I was already familiar with the girls at the time of the interviews.

(2) The Observer's Paradox was lessened even further through conducting multiple recorded interviews with many of the individual girls. They became more comfortable with the recording equipment after multiple encounters.

---

[1] *Vernacular* has been defined a number of different ways, including Labov's original definition of the term as "the style in which the minimum attention is given to the monitoring of speech" (Labov 1972: 208). Milroy (1992) defines the term as "real language in use". I have put the term in quotation marks because I view speech styles as points along multidimensional continua and am dubious of the ability to identify and label some portion of these continua as the vernacular.

[2] I use the word *interview* to refer to a conversation that was recorded, even when it was not in a format traditionally used for interviews. This term is used to distinguish these conversations from interactions that were not recorded but were written in my fieldnotes.

3 Like: Frequency and phonetic realisations

(3) Speakers are less likely to accommodate to the speech of a researcher if family members or peers are present (Labov 1972b: 115). Most of the interviews I conducted were with at least two girls.

(4) As a way of maintaining naturalness, I gathered recordings of conversations between different girls rather than between me and them. In addition to preserving naturalness, I used this technique because I was interested in documenting what they talked about with each other as opposed to what they talked about with me.

I conducted two different types of interviews depending on the situation. One involved multiple interviewees and spontaneous conversation between them and the other was an unstructured one-on-one interview. I will step through these in more detail shortly. In both types of interviews, girls asked what I was interested in and whether I had any findings thus far. I used these questions as an opportunity to ask about the social make-up of the school and how they viewed their own identity.

I most frequently used the first type of interview, which involved approaching girls who were already in conversation and asking if I could record them. Sometimes the place of conversation was too noisy for a quality recording and I suggested moving the conversation to a quieter room. After shifting rooms, the girls would continue the conversation where they left off, though they usually included me in the conversation for at least a part of the interview.

This technique had drawbacks, as there were girls who I was interested in interviewing but who I had not seen interacting with a group small enough to be suitable for recording. With these girls, I conducted one-on-one interviews that involved questions and answers by both of us. As a result, the role I played in the conversations varied across the different types of interviews. While there were bound to be linguistic differences as a result of these different interview techniques, it did not significantly affect the sociophonetic analysis presented in Section 3.3; individual girls who took part in the two interview types produced similar variants of *like* across both.[3]

I had time on my side, so I invited all girls to ask me questions in addition to any I might ask. I did not want the interview to have an unbalanced distribution

---

[3] The type of interview was tested statistically as a predictor for realisation in model 2, which is presented in Section 3.3. It was not found to influence production on its own ($p = 0.93$), providing statistical evidence that the different token types were evenly distributed across the different interview types, nor was it found to be involved in an interaction with /k/ realisation ($p = 0.33$), providing evidence that the interaction between /k/ realisation and social group is not an artefact of interview type.

of power based on the interviewer-interviewee relationship and I chose instead to emphasise solidarity by highlighting our equality in the interactions. As a result, there are portions of some interviews where I talked extensively. Of course, this loose interview style would not suit researchers interested in eliciting the maximum amount of speech in the minimum amount of time. However, spending four days a week among the girls for an entire school year meant that I had enough contact time to use the most naturalistic context possible.

Recordings were made in various places on the school grounds (a classroom, the common room, or outside if it was sunny) using the AKG:C543BL table microphone and a Marantz solid state recorder (PMD670), which records directly onto a CompactFlash digital memory card.

3.2 Variation in use of *like*

A select number of recorded interviews with the girls were transcribed using the tool Transcriber (Barras et al. 2001), resulting in a transcribed corpus of over 15 hours of speech from 59 different girls.[4]

The analysis presented in this chapter focuses on the speech of 28 girls, 14 of whom were CR girls. All girls whose speech was analysed took part in the perception experiments presented in Chapter 4.[5] Of the 42 girls who took part in the perception experiment, the 14 CR and 14 NCR girls who had the most speech recorded in the interviews were analysed. This was done in order to identify a large enough number of tokens for each speaker on which to conduct the statistical analysis. The individual girls whose speech was analysed are shown in Appendix A. Table 3.1 displays the number of girls from each of the individual subgroups whose speech was analysed.

A great deal of variation can be found in the girls' speech. In the interest of investigating subtle differences in pronunciation across social groups as well as across different meanings of a single word, this chapter focuses on variation within the word *like*. The type of phonetic analysis that I conducted is time-consuming, particularly since I coded for a wide range of phonetic information. Given time constraints, it would not have been possible to examine these phonetic variables across a range of words without losing the theoretical insights gained from ex-

---

[4] Due to the sensitive nature of some interviews and the criteria set out by the Human Ethics Committee at the University of Canterbury, all recordings were transcribed by me.
[5] I focused on transcribing interviews with girls who had participated in the experiments so that I could compare patterns of phonetic variables in their production to patterns of their responses during perception.

3 Like: Frequency and phonetic realisations

Table 3.1: The number of speakers in each subgroup that were analysed

CR GROUP	SPEAKERS	NCR GROUP	SPEAKERS
The PCs	3	Pasifika Group	1
Sporty Girls	3	The Goths	5
Trendy Altern.	3	The Geeks	3
Rochelle's Group	1	Real Teenagers	2
Relaxed Group	3	Christians	2
The BBs	1	Sonia's Group	1
TOTAL	14		14

amining phonetic variation of lemmas that share an identical lexical form. These insights are discussed in Section 3.4.

The word *like* was chosen for analysis because several of the different meanings of *like* were highly frequent in all of the girls' speech. This made it possible to conduct a within-speaker analysis of the realisations produced in spontaneous speech. Additionally, I hypothesised that socially-conditioned phonetic variation could arise depending on the nature of the different functions of *like*: some of the functions are traditionally grammatical while others are discursive and are themselves layered with social meaning. Given that they were highly salient at the school and were ideologically linked with youth culture (and with certain individual girls at the school, in particular), *like* seemed like a promising lexeme to focus on. I was particularly interested to see whether different individuals and groups of speakers produced different realisations that varied - not only according to their social group - but also depending on the token's grammatical function. For example, might there be a difference between groups in the pronunciation of a discourse-pragmatic function of *like* (discussed below) that is not observed for the more grammatical functions (e.g., the lexical verb)?

Furthermore, I am interested in the relationship between the phonetic realisation of a word and the word's probability of occurrence. I hypothesized that the likelihood that a speaker will producs a certain word might influence that speaker's pronunciation of the word. Focusing on the word *like* allowed me to test this hypothesis (1) because I could control for word-internal phonological factors and (2) all of the girls produced tokens of *like* though they did so to varying degrees.

Although this chapter focuses on phonetic variation in the word *like*, there was a great deal of other phonetic variation in the recordings. This variation has not yet been analysed systematically. However, I intend to examine it in more depth in the future.

For the analysis of *like*, I used the different grammatical and discursive functions of *like* as outlined by D'Arcy (2007). Among its grammatical functions, *like* may be a lexical verb (14a) or an adverb (14b). These were the most frequent of the grammatical functions of *like* found in the SGH data. Other grammatical functions of *like* are the noun (14c), the conjunction (14d), and the suffix (14e). The examples listed here are from D'Arcy (2007).

(14) a. Lexical Verb: I don't really LIKE her that much.

   b. Adverb: It looks LIKE a snail; it just is a snail.

   c. Noun: He grew up with the LIKES… of all great fighters.

   d. Conjunction: It felt LIKE everything had dropped away.

   e. Suffix: I went (mumbling) or something like stroke-LIKE.

The word *like* also has discursive functions. It can serve as a discourse marker (15a), a discourse particle (15b), an approximative adverb (15c), or a quotative (15d). All of the discursive functions occur frequently in the speech of girls at SGH. The examples presented here are taken from interviews with the girls.

(15) a. Discourse marker: LIKE it real cracks me up. (Emma, The PCs, 26-10)

   b. Discourse particle: Lily was LIKE checking out my brother. (Kanani, The Sporty Girls, 24-07)

   c. Approximative adverb: I did that in LIKE two days. (Theresa, The Christians, 20-09)

   d. Quotative: and Mum's LIKE "turn that stupid thing off." (Marama, The Pasifika Group, 02-11)

The lexical verb, adverb, quotative, and discourse particle were chosen for analysis because they were highly frequent, meaning that there were sufficient data for statistical analysis of their phonetic realisations. While the discourse marker

3 Like: Frequency and phonetic realisations

is also highly frequent, it occurs at the beginning and end of phrases whereas the analysed functions of *like* most often occur phrase-medially.[6]

Quotative *like* can be used in a variety of different situations. For example, it can be used to report speech, thoughts, and gestures (Romaine & Lange 1991). The analysis presented here combines all of the different pragmatic functions of quotative *like* into a single category though it is possible that they could have different distributions or phonetic realisations.[7]

3.2.1 Use of quotative *like* at SGH

The frequency of use of the different types of *like* varied depending on the individual. Based only on girls whose speech was analysed, two calculations were made with the aim of approximating a speaker's likelihood of using quotative *like*. I decided to use two calculations because (a) frequency of use has been measured previously on the basis of both calculations and (b) I wanted to provide the most complete picture of the distribution of quotative *like* among the girls.

The first measure of frequency of use of the quotative was the average number of times a token of quotative *like* was produced for every hundred words produced by a speaker.[8] A raw count of the quotative would not be representative of frequency of use due to differences in interview length across different girls. Though frequency of use is usually normalised per one thousand words, a smaller corpus necessitates normalising per one hundred (Biber, Conrad & Reppen 1998: 264). The measure is shown, by increasing use of quotative *like*, in Table 3.2. Token frequency measures are usually based on corpora, such as CELEX, that contain millions of words, but this is not realistic for examining speaker-specific frequencies. In the current study, the already relatively small word count of the corpus was made even smaller through examining intraspeaker frequency of use. Therefore, the values presented in Table 3.2 should be viewed with some caution.

Also shown in Table 3.2 is the number of all other quotatives (i.e. quotatives that were not *like*) per hundred words produced. When comparing the two normalised frequency measures, it is evident that while some speakers, such as Patricia, had low counts of quotative *like* but produced few quotatives overall, other

---

[6] Included in the analysis were tokens of quotative *like* where the remainder of the sentence was a gesture.

[7] An analysis of the different pragmatic functions of quotative *like* revealed no function-based variation in these data, but this may be due to the relatively small number of tokens of each function.

[8] Word counts were generated automatically using ONZE Miner. Words with hyphens (e.g., *ex-boyfriend*) were counted as a single word.

3.2 Variation in use of like

Table 3.2: Values based on the first measure of frequency of use of quotative *like*: The number of tokens of quotative *like* per hundred words produced, ordered by increasing usage of quotative *like*. Also shown is the number of all other quotatives by hundred words produced.

GROUP	CR/NCR	TOTAL WORDS	QUOTATIVE *LIKE*	OTHER QUOTATIVES
Patricia	CR	4629	0.1080	0
Santra	NCR	6462	0.2786	0.2321
Marissa	NCR	1238	0.3231	0.1616
Marama	NCR	2783	0.3234	0.2515
Mariah	NCR	6126	0.3265	0.0490
Juliet	CR	1032	0.3876	0.2907
Christina	CR	1440	0.4167	0.0694
Tania	NCR	3945	0.4309	0
Katrina	CR	1572	0.5089	0.0636
Esther	NCR	4532	0.5296	0.0662
Vanessa	NCR	4728	0.5499	0.1904
Justine	CR	2022	0.5935	0
Barbara	CR	2867	0.6278	0.2442
Bianca	NCR	4197	0.6671	0.2144
Clementine	CR	3093	0.6790	0.1940
Emma	CR	3916	0.7916	0.0255
Jane	CR	1236	0.8900	0.0809
Theresa	NCR	1279	1.0164	0.2346
Sarah	NCR	2150	1.1163	0.0465
Rochelle	CR	1850	1.1351	0.1622
Meredith	NCR	6815	1.2032	0.1321
Isabelle	NCR	6776	1.5939	0.1476
Betty	CR	1040	1.6346	0.1923
Tracy	CR	1157	2.0743	0.1729
Kanani	CR	1769	2.0916	0.1696
Rose	CR	3653	2.4090	0.1369
Holly	NCR	2878	3.1619	0.0695
Joy	NCR	683	3.5139	0.1464
		TOTAL: 85868	MEAN: 1.0494	MEAN: 0.1337

speakers, such as Santra, produced a large number of quotatives but used other quotatives nearly as much as they used quotative *like*.

The second measure was the percentage of all quotatives that were quotative *like*, a calculation that follows the Principle of Accountability (Labov 1972a). Because not all speech acts (and therefore not all recorded interviews) necessitate the use of quotatives, this measure provides a means of comparing the use of quotative *like* across speakers within the context of other quotatives they might use instead; it is a reflection of how likely a speaker was to use quotative *like* rather than one of the alternatives available. Therefore, it is a measure of token probability, which is related to but also distinct from token frequency.

Bybee's (2002) interpretation of the relationship between token frequency and phonetic reduction depends on overall token counts. This means that in collecting counts of speaker-specific token frequency, a researcher would need to record all interactions in which a speaker is involved over an extended period of time. Interpreting the measures of frequency presented here in terms of their reflection of speaker-specific token frequency is problematic because (1) some speakers, in general, may be less likely to use reported speech than others, (2) some speakers, in general, may talk more than other speakers, and (3) the recordings may not be equally distributed across speakers for different types of speech acts. While the second measure can control for the latter of these concerns, it is less clear how to account for the first two. The first measure, however, does not control for any of these concerns. Therefore, the measures presented here are not analogous to token frequency, but instead are informative of the relative frequency of a token. The first is the frequency relative to the number of words produced in the interaction and reflects the probability that, regardless of the speech act, a token will be quotative *like*. The advantage of this measure is that not all girls may use the same amount of reported speech. However, this measure is problematic in that it assumes that the ratio of total speech to reported speech is equivalent to what would be observed across all interactions with the speakers, which is unlikely given the small number of interviews analysed. For this reason, this measure should be viewed with some caution. For the second measure, the frequencies are relative to the frequency of alternative quotatives that could be used. This reflects the probability that, if producing a quotative, the quotative will be *like*. This measure of probability assumes that the ratio of quotative *like* to the other quotatives used by a speaker reflects the ratio used by that speaker in interactions that were not recorded.

3.2 Variation in use of like

Table 3.3 shows the percentage of all quotatives produced by a speaker that were quotative *like*.[9] Quotative *like* was the most common quotative for all of these speakers, accounting for the majority of quotative tokens for all 28 girls. Nonetheless, there was some variation in its frequency of use. It was least frequent in the speech of Santra (Goths), Marama (Pasifika Group), and Juliet (PCs) and it was most frequent in the speech of Justine (Trendy Alternatives), Patricia (Sporty Girls), and Tania (Goths). This will be discussed further alongside discussion of the alternative quotatives sometimes used.

The two measures for the speaker-specific frequency of quotative *like* are statistically correlated (Spearman's rho = 0.46; p=0.01). This is expected given that both measures are based on the number of tokens of quotative *like* for each speaker. However, notice how for some speakers with a low number of overall quotatives (e.g., Patricia, Tania, and Justine) the two sets of values are very different in terms of how the girls are ranked in their respective frequencies of use. It is likely that this is a result of calculating the first measure over the relatively small amount of speech recorded for each speaker. This emphasises the importance of analysing quantitative data in terms of the context in which it is relevant when working with a small corpus.

In both measures, CR girls produced more tokens of quotative *like* than NCR girls, as shown in the boxplots in Figure 3.1. However, the difference between CR and NCR girls was not significant for either measure (Wilcoxon, p = 0.25, p = 0.8).

Table 3.4 shows the percentage of all of the different quotatives used by CR and NCR girls. The two tokens labelled as 'other' were one token of quotative *yell* produced by a Real Teenager and one token of quotative *scream* produced by a Goth.

Quotative *like* was the most frequent quotative in the speech of both CR and NCR girls. CR girls used a slightly higher percentage of quotative *like* than NCR girls. The quotatives *say*, *be all*, and *go* were more frequent in the speech of the NCR girls than in the speech of the CR girls. With the low number of tokens, it is difficult to tell whether the differences between CR and NCR girls is a result of more documented quotative tokens from the NCR girls or whether it is some-

---

[9] The null quotative (reported speech without the use of a quotative verb) is difficult to search for and was not included in the count. Though the null quotative can account for as much as 20% of quotatives in other dialects, such as Canadian English (Tagliamonte & Hudson 1999), during transcription it was noted that though the null quotative was observed, it was infrequent in the speech of the SGH girls. Furthermore, work in New Zealand has found low rates of the null quotative among females of a similar age to the girls in the current study (Buchstaller & D'Arcy 2009).

3 Like: Frequency and phonetic realisations

Table 3.3: Values based on the second measure of frequency of use of quotative *like*: The percentage of all quotatives produced by a speaker that were quotative *like*, ordered by increasing usage of *like*

SPEAKER	CR/NCR	TOTAL QUOTATIVES	% QUOTATIVE LIKE
Santra	NCR	33	54.55
Marama	NCR	16	56.25
Juliet	CR	7	57.14
Marissa	NCR	6	66.67
Barbara	CR	25	72.00
Vanessa	NCR	35	74.29
Bianca	NCR	37	75.68
Clementine	CR	27	77.78
Theresa	NCR	16	81.25
Christina	CR	7	85.71
Mariah	NCR	23	86.96
Rochelle	CR	24	87.50
Esther	NCR	27	88.89
Katrina	CR	9	88.89
Betty	CR	19	89.47
Meredith	NCR	91	90.11
Isabelle	NCR	118	91.53
Jane	CR	12	91.67
Tracy	CR	26	92.31
Kanani	CR	40	92.50
Rose	CR	93	94.62
Joy	NCR	25	96.00
Sarah	NCR	25	96.00
Emma	CR	32	96.88
Holly	NCR	93	97.85
Justine	CR	12	100
Patricia	CR	5	100
Tania	NCR	17	100
		TOTAL: 900	AVERAGE: 85.09

3.2 Variation in use of like

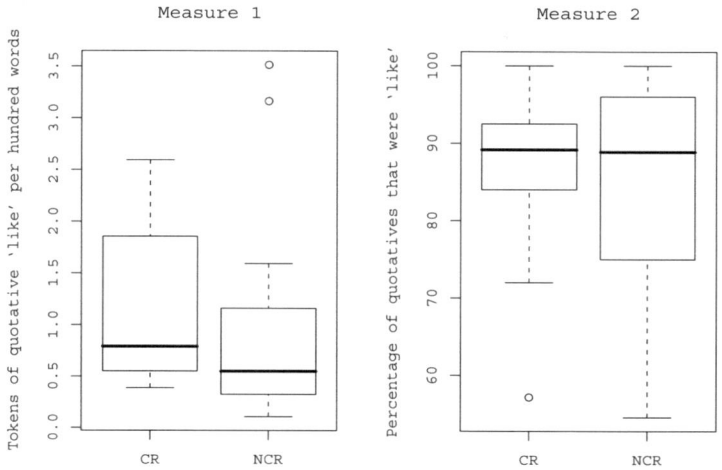

Figure 3.1: The frequency of use of quotative *like* by CR and NCR girls, based on the number of tokens per hundred words produced (Measure 1) and the percentage of all quotative that were *like* (Measure 2)

Table 3.4: The overall distribution of quotative verbs for CR and NCR groups

QUOTATIVE	CR		NCR	
	n	%	n	%
be like	379	90.67%	488	86.83%
say	28	6.70%	44	7.83%
be all	3	0.72%	15	2.67%
go	4	0.96%	10	1.78%
think	4	0.96%	3	0.53%
other	0	0.00%	2	0.36%
total	418		562	

83

thing more socially meaningful. Though *like* was still prevalent in their speech, it is possible that NCR girls chose to use quotatives other than *like* as an element in the construction of their identities. For example, Marama (Pasifika Group) was the speaker with the highest percentage of quotative *go* (with 4 tokens) and though there were only two documented tokens of descriptive quotatives, *scream* and *yell*, both were produced by NCR girls. In comparing the use of quotative *be all*, only three CR girls, Clementine (The Trendy Alternatives), Rose (The Relaxed Group), and Rochelle (Rochelle's Group), used it once each whereas a greater number of NCR girls used it and they used it more often: three tokens from Isabelle (The Real Teenagers), two from Meredith (The Goths), seven from Santra (The Goths), and one each from Mariah (The Geeks), Sarah (The Real Teenagers), and Tania (The Goths). Their use of alternative quotative verbs is consistent with their claims of being different from other girls at the school.

3.2.2 Use of discourse particle *like* at SGH

There was also variation in how often the girls used discourse particle *like*. A speaker's discourse particle frequency was calculated as the average number of tokens of the discourse particle produced by a speaker per hundred words of documented speech from that speaker. This is comparable to previous calculations based on tokens per thousand words that investigate how often people in different social categories (e.g., gender, age, and social class) use discursive functions of *like* (Anderson 2001: 287-299). Ordered from most frequent to least frequent users, the values from the SGH data are shown in Table 3.5. CR girls were significantly more likely to use the discourse particle than NCR girls (Wilcoxon, p=0.01).[10]

There is a loose correlation between the number of tokens of discourse particle *like* and the number of tokens of quotative *like* per hundred words produced (Spearman's rho = 0.38; p<0.05). This relationship is shown in Figure 3.2. For speakers with less than one token of quotative *like* per hundred words, there is a linear relationship between the frequency of use of quotative and discourse particle *like*. This is not the case for the speakers with a greater number of tokens of the quotative per hundred words produced. Though it would be desirable to calculate an alternative measure of discourse particle frequency based on contexts in which it could be used (such as that conducted by D'Arcy 2005), it is not possible here given time constraints.

---

[10] The frequencies presented here are considerably higher than those reported by Anderson from speakers of British English of a similar age (.0561 if re-normalised per hundred), and the difference would appear even greater if I had included token counts of all of the discursive functions as did Anderson.

3.2 Variation in use of like

Table 3.5: Values of speaker-specific frequency of discourse particle *like*: The number of tokens of discourse particle *like* per hundred words, ordered by increasing usage of discourse particle *like*

speaker	CR/NCR	word count	discourse particle
Marissa	NCR	1238	0.2423
Esther	NCR	4532	0.3089
Santra	NCR	6462	0.3405
Vanessa	NCR	4728	0.5500
Marama	NCR	2783	0.5749
Rochelle	CR	1850	0.5946
Sarah	NCR	2150	0.6512
Juliet	CR	1032	0.6783
Isabelle	NCR	6776	0.6789
Holly	NCR	2878	0.7992
Joy	NCR	683	0.8785
Patricia	CR	4629	0.9073
Kanani	CR	1769	0.9610
Christina	CR	1440	1.0417
Mariah	NCR	6126	1.0774
Katrina	CR	1572	1.1450
Justine	CR	2022	1.2859
Bianca	NCR	4197	1.3581
Barbara	CR	2867	1.3959
Betty	CR	1040	1.4423
Theresa	NCR	1279	1.6419
Jane	CR	1236	1.7799
Emma	CR	3916	1.8641
Tania	NCR	3945	1.9011
Tracy	CR	1157	1.9015
Clementine	CR	3093	2.1662
Rose	CR	3653	2.2174
Meredith	NCR	6815	2.6266
		total: 85868	mean: 1.1789

3 Like: Frequency and phonetic realisations

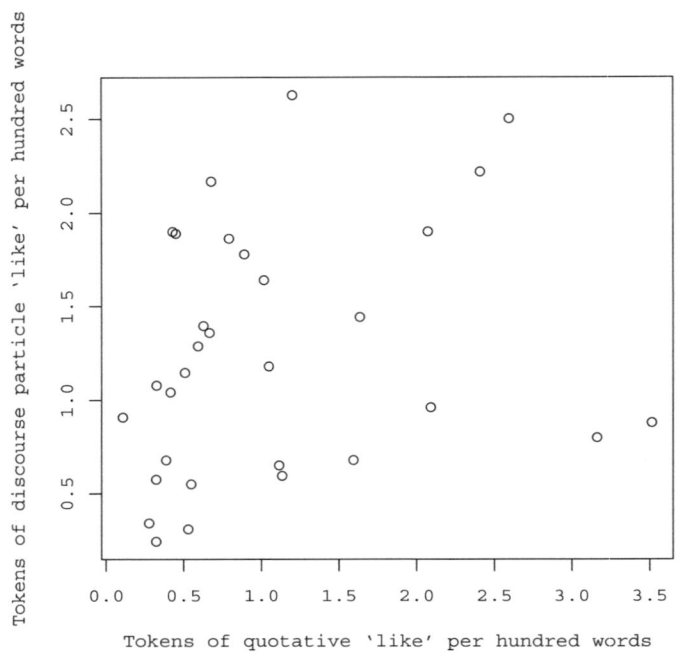

Figure 3.2: Plot of the number of tokens of quotative *like* and the number of tokens of discourse particle *like* per hundred words produced

3.3 Phonetic variation of *like*

There is variation among the girls' realizations of *like* in several respects: whether or not the /k/ is realised, the length and quality of the /l/, how diphthongal the vowel is, the vowel quality of the nucleus and offglide targets, the duration of the vowel, and the degree of glottalisation. All of these factors were analysed in order to determine whether there was any fine-grained phonetic variation that patterned systematically with (a) whether or not a speaker was a CR girl and (b) the different functions of *like*.

The CR-NCR distinction at SGH was noticed prior to beginning acoustic phonetic analysis. However, in order to determine whether this was an appropriate social distinction to include in the statistical analysis, I conducted a classification and regression tree (CART) analysis (see e.g., Breiman et al. 1984) predicting /k/ realisation before fitting the statistical model presented in Section 3.3.2. In-

Table 3.6: The distribution of analysed tokens of *like* for CR and NCR groups

	CR	NCR	TOTAL
quotative	119	120	239
discourse particle	160	132	292
grammatical (lexical verb)	48	56	104
grammatical (adverb)	49	51	100
grammatical (total)	97	107	204
total analysed	376	359	735

dividuals grouped according to whether or not they ate lunch in the CR, which suggested that the CR-NCR distinction was in fact an appropriate social category to include in the model.

3.3.1 Methodology for acoustic phonetic analysis

The various utterances of *like* from the interviews were extracted automatically from the corpus using ONZEMiner (Fromont & Hay 2007). Because of the particular functions chosen for analysis, the vast majority of tokens did not occur at phrase boundaries, did not carry primary stress, and were not the least stressed words in the sentence; only one token analysed occurred sentence-finally and carried primary stress.

I aimed to conduct acoustic analysis on 30 tokens of *like* for each girl. Whenever possible, these 30 tokens were made up of 10 tokens of quotative *like*, 10 tokens of the discourse particle, and 10 grammatical tokens. The grammatical tokens were made up of a combination of lexical verbs and adverbs depending on what was present in the data.[11] This, however, proved impossible for all girls due to low token numbers, and fewer than 30 tokens were analysed for some girls. For girls with more than 10 tokens of a particular function of *like*, the first 10 tokens extracted were analysed provided that they were unobscured by background noise. The token distribution is shown in Table 3.6.

---

[11] Preliminary analysis provided evidence that the lexical verb and the adverb were phonetically similar to one another for a given speaker in terms of /k/ presence and the degree of diphthongisation.

3 Like: Frequency and phonetic realisations

The final dataset included 104 tokens of the lexical verb and 100 tokens of the adverb, resulting in 204 tokens of traditionally grammatical functions. There were 239 tokens of the quotative and 292 tokens of the discourse particle in the final dataset. Of the 3159 tokens of *like* initially extracted for the speakers analysed, 735 tokens (or roughly 23% of the tokens extracted) were analysed using detailed acoustic analysis.[12] Tokens masked by noise or made ambiguous from false starts were not included in the analysis.

The unequal distribution and the low token numbers for some groups would pose a problem for an analysis of the smaller sub-groups (e.g., The Goths, The PCs). The analysis presented here focuses on differences at the CR/NCR level, though individual speaker differences are discussed in Section 3.4.5.1.

Phonetic features of the tokens were labelled in Praat textgrids (Boersma & Weenink 2005) in a way that allowed the analysis to be conducted both on gradient and discrete measures.[13] The boundaries between words were marked, as were the phoneme boundaries within the word *like* and the nucleus and offglide boundaries of the diphthong; gradient measures such as segment duration and formant values could be tested and gradient measures such as whether or not the /k/ was present (i.e. there were no boundaries marked for the /k/) could also be tested. Segmentation of this type is notoriously difficult because there are no clear acoustic boundaries between the segments (Ladefoged 2003: 142). For consistency, the following methodological decisions were made:

1. When preceded by a vowel, the first boundary of the /l/ was marked at the point where there was a noticeable dampening of the intensity in the waveform. When preceded by a fricative or a released stop, the boundary was marked at the point where there was a noticeable increase in the amount of periodic energy or, if absent, when there was a noticeable decrease in the amount of aperiodic energy in the signal as evidenced in the waveform. When preceded by a pause, the boundary was marked at the onset of voicing. When following a nasal, it was marked where there was a noticeable change in F2 or, due to an increase in tongue contact, a sudden dampening of amplitude as evidenced in the waveform.

2. The word boundary following the /k/ was marked after any evidence in the spectrogram and waveform of the /k/ release if the release was present.

---

[12] The percentage of tokens extracted that were analysed breaks down by function as follows: 30% of quotative *like* tokens extracted, 28% of discourse particle tokens extracted, 60% of lexical verb tokens extracted, 40% of adverb tokens extracted. If a greater number of tokens were analysed, it is possible that a larger number of factors would reach significance in an interaction with the social factor tested.

[13] A small subset of the data was checked for consistency by an independent phonetician.

3.3 Phonetic variation of *like*

Due to the difficulty of finding tokens of *like* where the entire token was unobscured by other noises (e.g., someone else talking), I prioritised finding tokens that were clear in other parts of the signal rather than the release. Therefore, I am not entirely confident about the segmentation following the release, so the duration of the release was not analysed. When the release was not present, the boundary was marked at the onset of the following segment. For example, if there was no closure period and the token was followed by a vowel other than /i/ or /ɪ/, formant transitions were used to identify the boundary. There were no tokens followed by /i/ that were analysed and for the eight tokens followed by /ɪ/, other cues were used. These cues included a transition in pitch and the point at which the vocal pulses are closer together after being further apart.

3. The boundary between the /l/ and the vowel was marked at a point where there was an increase in amplitude visible in the waveform. Because the amplitude was most often a gradual shift, the boundary was marked at the point just before a sharp rise in F1 toward the target of the following /ai/.

4. The boundary between the vowel and the /k/ was marked at the point of closure or, in the case of frication and zero closure, at the point where aperiodic energy began.

5. For tokens that were diphthongal (to any degree), the boundary between the nucleus and offglide was marked roughly at the half-way point in the transition between two steady states. For completely monophthongal tokens, the boundary was marked at the halfway point of the vocalic portion. This was done solely as a way to aid the automatic extraction of the labels; the durations of the nucleus and offglide were not analysed.

Also marked were the targets of the nucleus, offglide, /l/, and /k/. The target of the nucleus was marked at the point where F1 was highest and, if there were multiple points where F1 was high, where F2 was lowest. The target of the offglide was taken where F1 was lowest and F2 was highest but before a sudden drop in F1 that preceded the /k/ closure, if there was one. The /l/ target was taken midway between the influence of the preceding sound and the onset of the vowel at a point where F2 was visible.[14] The /k/ target was taken at the point of the offglide where F3 was lowest.

---

[14] This measure was initially intended to be used to calculate /l/ vocalisation. However, I was unhappy with this measurement (see e.g., Hall-Lew & Fix 2012). Additionally, I was surprised by the large number of tokens where /l/ was not present or where it was so short that F2 could not be reliably identified in the spectrogram. Therefore, the /l/ target was not analysed.

3 Like: Frequency and phonetic realisations

A three-way distinction of glottalisation of the vowel (not glottalised, mid-glottalisation, and full glottalisation) was also made. This was based on a judgment of the amount of irregularity in the intervals between the pulses of the vocal folds, as evidenced through both pulses in the waveform and striations in the spectrogram. The categories full and not glottalised were used when glottalisation (or the lack of it) was easily identifiable: a token was marked as not glottalised if there were evenly-spaced pulses in the token even when compared to the surrounding speech produced by the same speaker; a token was marked as fully glottalised if the intervals between pulses were considerably larger in some portion of the token than in another part of the token or the speech produced by that speaker surrounding the token.[15] The third category, mid-glottalisation, was used when assignment to one of the other two categories was not clear. In addition to tokens with creaky voice, tokens with glottal stops were marked as fully glottal, following work by Docherty and Foulkes who found that creaky voice was identified as a glottal stop during auditory analysis (Docherty & Foulkes 1999). Additionally, all tokens that may have been marked as containing a glottal stop had an increasing amount of glottalisation preceding the stop, making it difficult to distinguish these tokens from those with creaky voice at the end of the vocalic period and no glottal stop. Glottalisation in different parts of the token were not differentiated from one another.

Regarding the /k/, the boundaries between the vowel, closure, and release were marked. For tokens where there was no closure period but there was a release, the boundary was marked at the point where aperiodic energy began in the signal.[16] A /k/ was marked as dropped if it could not be heard during auditory analysis and one of the following applied:

1. The token was followed by a continuous segment (e.g., a vowel) and there was no period of closure or release.

2. The token was followed by a stop and there was no evidence of a velar closure (e.g., a velar stop); there was complete assimilation to the place of the following segment.[17] For the 84 tokens that were followed by a stop, the

---

[15] A distinction in the duration of the glottalised portion of the token was not made.

[16] The burst was not coded but would be an interesting avenue for future work.

[17] It is important to bear in mind that tokens where the /k/ was dropped and were followed by a stop were in the minority of the tokens analysed; 26 tokens were followed by a stop and labelled as having the /k/ not realised, compared with the 58 tokens that were followed by a stop and had the /k/ realised. Additionally, the 26 tokens followed by a stop where the /k/ was marked as dropped were not distributed across CR and NCR girls in a way that could be

3.3 Phonetic variation of like

transitions of F2 and the presence of a velar pinch (Harrington & Cassidy 1999: 89) were used to determine whether assimilation had taken place.

3. The token was followed by a pause and the formants from the token of *like* trail off gradually, as they do with pre-pausal vowels.

4. One of the above applied and the token was glottalised, in which case the token was marked as glottalised but not having the /k/ realised.

Although glottalisation and glottal stops are often treated as a particular realisation of /k/ (Lavoie 2002), it was marked separately from /k/ realisation for this study because glottalised tokens were sometimes produced with a clear closure and release of the /k/. Additionally, marking glottalisation and /k/ realisation allowed them to be tested both as separate factors or as a single variable once combined; treating them as a single factor during the phonetic analysis would only permit the latter.

To demonstrate how the textgrids were marked, examples are shown in Figures 3.3-3.8.

Tokens that were followed by a velar consonant were not included in the analysis. The preceding and following phonemes were marked in the textgrids, with an additional level distinguishing only between vowels, consonants, and pauses. Pauses were labelled as such when a phone did not immediately follow a token of *like*. Voiced continuants, such as /l/, were labelled as consonants. For counts of phonetic features in the raw data, refer to Appendix B.

After completion, the textgrids were converted into files that could be read by Emu (Cassidy 2007). In Emu, formant traces were corrected by hand. The formant values were extracted automatically along with other encoded information (e.g., segment duration and whether the token contained a released /k/) using a tailor-made library in the statistical software package, R (R Development Core Team 2007).

Target values of the nucleus and offglide were converted from Hertz to Bark using the equation posited by Traunmüller (1990) and the Euclidean distance of a token's vowel was calculated using these F1 and F2 values of the nucleus and offglide targets.[18] A completely monophthongal vowel would have a Euclidean

---

interpreted as the explanation for the results presented in this chapter; eight were tokens of the discourse particle and two were tokens of the quotative produced by CR girls and six were tokens of the discourse particle and one a token of the quotative produced by NCR girls.

[18] For formant values, the Bark scale was used instead of Hertz because it is a better reflection of how formants at the different frequencies are perceived by human listeners. For example, a shift in F1 is perceived as greater than a shift in F2 of the same amount in Hertz.

3 Like: Frequency and phonetic realisations

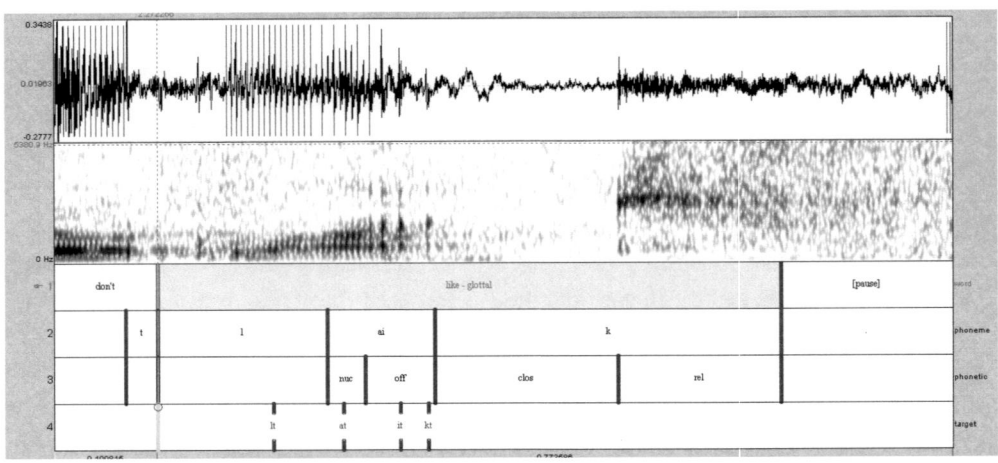

Figure 3.3: Lexical verb *like* from Santra (The Goths). /l/ present, diphthongal vowel, glottalised, /k/ released, preceded by stop, followed by pause

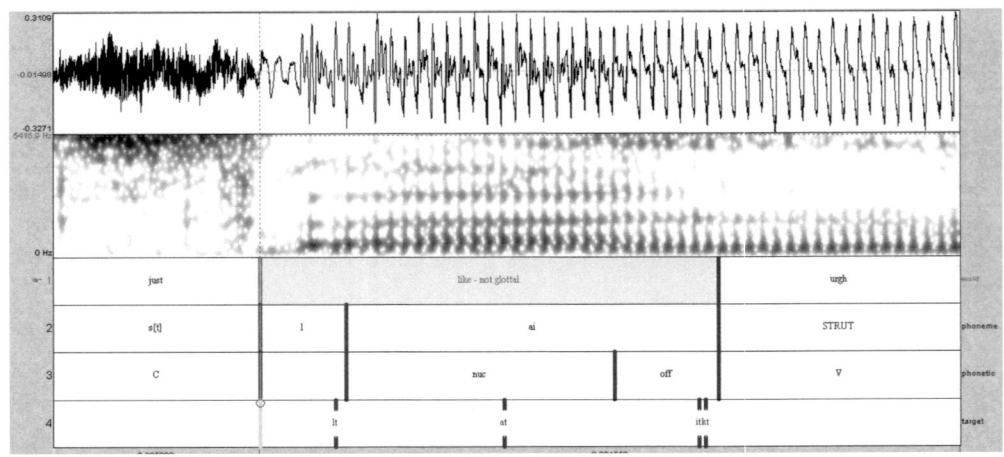

Figure 3.4: Quotative *like* from Patricia (Sporty Girls). /l/ present, diphthongal vowel, not glottalised, /k/ absent, preceded by fricative, followed by vowel

3.3 Phonetic variation of like

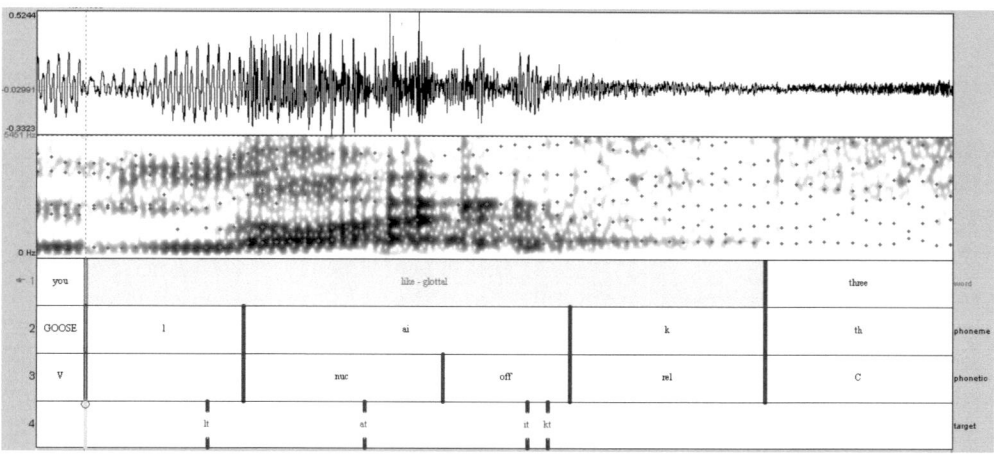

Figure 3.5: Adverbial *like* from Barbara (The Relaxed Group). /l/ present, diphthongal vowel, glottalised, fricated /k/, preceded by vowel, followed by fricative

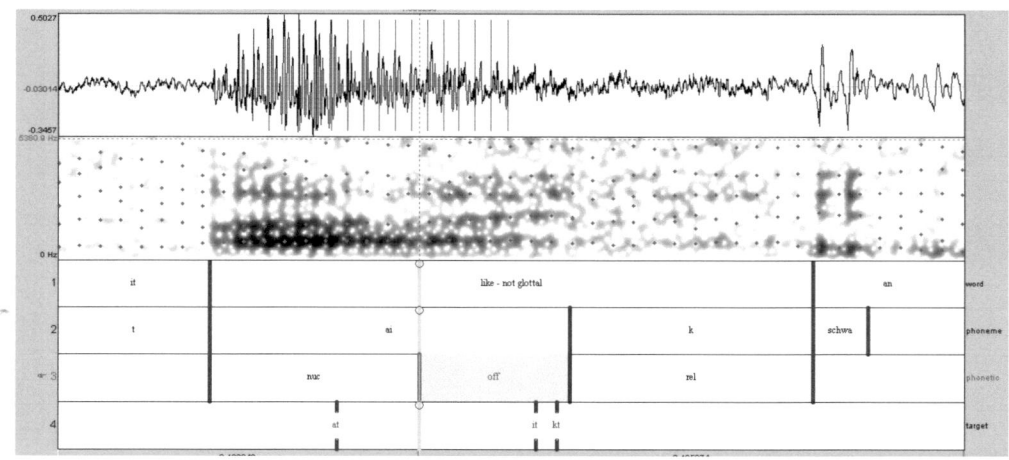

Figure 3.6: Adverbial *like* from Jane (The BBs). /l/ absent, diphthongal vowel, not glottalised, fricated /k/, preceded by stop, followed by vowel

3 Like: Frequency and phonetic realisations

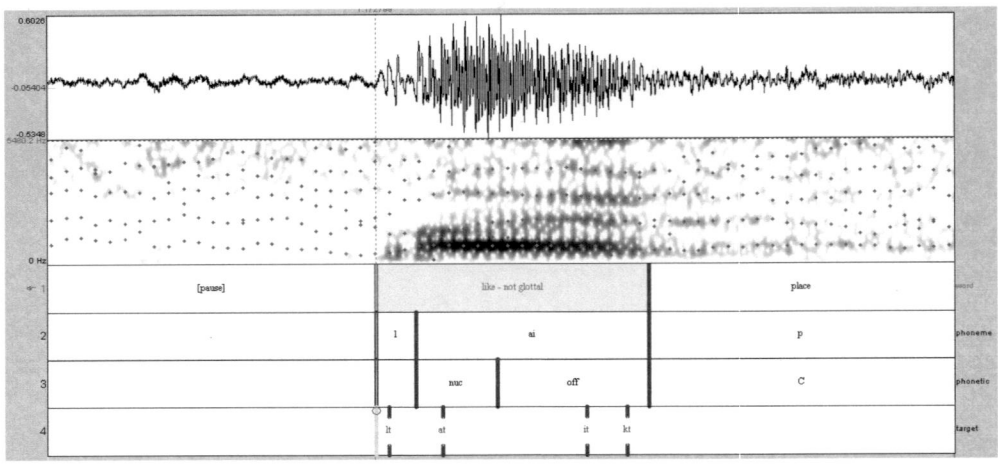

Figure 3.7: Discourse particle *like* from Rochelle (Rochelle's Group). /l/ present, diphthongal vowel, not glottalised, /k/ absent, preceded by pause, followed by stop

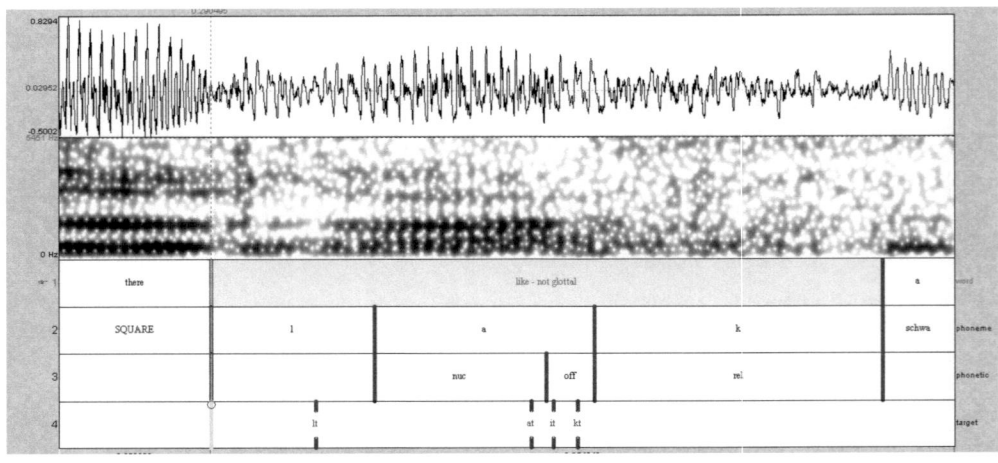

Figure 3.8: Discourse particle *like* from Marama (The Pasifika Group). /l/ present, monophthongal vowel, not glottalised, fricated /k/, preceded by vowel, followed by vowel

distance value of zero, whereas a value of five Bark would be extremely diphthongal. Euclidean distance can therefore be viewed as a gradient measure of how diphthongal a vowel is; the greater the Euclidean distance, the more diphthongal the token.

A token's pitch was extracted automatically at 10ms intervals throughout the vowel using the AMDF method in Emu. The mean pitch for each token was calculated from the extracted values. Pitch measurements at the nucleus and offglide targets were also extracted and they were used to determine whether a token had a steady or moving intonation. Tokens with a transition of 10Hz or more were labelled as 'moving'. Due to limits on time, pitch contours were not corrected by hand in Emu, so results regarding pitch should be viewed with some caution. In order to keep them from biasing results, tokens with a mean pitch that was over two standard deviations away from the mean were assigned the pitch value at the cutoff point.

3.3.2 Results

The raw data is presented in Appendix B, with the numbers of different tokens with each phonetic characteristic listed according to whether the speaker was a CR or a NCR girl. Because each of the factors is best understood within the context of all of the other factors, the results are presented in this chapter within the context of statistical models.

In order to test the relationship between the function of *like* and numerous phonetic factors, three mixed effects models were fit to the production data. Like simple linear and logistic regression models, a mixed effects model allows for numerous predicting factors to be included in a single model. Significance levels and the degree of each effect are calculated whilst keeping the other factors constant. This effectively takes into consideration the influence of the other variables when investigating a particular factor. For example, assume /k/ realisation only patterns systematically with following environment (e.g., it is more likely to be realised when followed by a vowel) and following environment predicts the dependent variable being tested. This could lead to /k/ realisation appearing to be a predicting factor of the dependent variable if following environment is not included in the model.

Another benefit of using mixed effects models is that in addition to allowing the inclusion of fixed effects, such as phonetic and social factors that can systematically predict the form of the dependent variable, random (non-generalisable) effects can be included (Baayen 2008: 263-326). Random effects can be speaker-specific effects or, in experimental work, stimuli-specific effects. For example, in an analysis of reaction time, some participants may be faster than others. If the researcher wants to examine predicting factors above and beyond this participant-specific effect, they could include the participant as a random effect in the model. Including the speaker as a random effect reduces the risk that a single individual will bias results.[19]

The first model presented in this chapter compares realisations of quotative *like* to grammatical functions of *like*. The second compares realisations of quotative *like* to discourse particle *like*, and the third compares realisations of the discourse particle to grammatical functions of *like*. A summary of results of all three models can be found at the end of the section in Table 3.13.

3.3.2.1 Model 1: Grammatical and quotative *like*

Using R, a mixed effects model was fit to the data comparing the quotative with grammatical functions of *like*, modeling the likelihood that the token was the quotative. The speaker was included as a random intercept. Before fitting the model, I assumed an alpha level of 0.05 as the threshold for statistical significance.

A number of factors were tested as potential effects in the model, including vowel duration, preceding and following environment, the different calculations of pitch (mean pitch and steady versus moving pitch), and the speech rate (calculated as syllables per second in both the 5 seconds and 20 seconds of speech surrounding a token).[20] Also tested was whether the speaker was a girl who ate lunch in the CR, whether the /k/ and /l/ were realised, the duration of the closure period of the /k/, and linear as well as non-linear distributions of the Euclidean distance of a token's vowel. In order to determine whether the probability of a speaker using quotative *like* played a role, tested in the model were interactions between phonetic factors and the two calculations of an individual's use of *like*: the number of tokens of quotative *like* per hundred words produced by that speaker and the percentage of all quotatives produced by an individual that were quotative *like*.[21] The number of tokens of the discourse particle observed

---

[19] The random effects included in these models were random intercepts. Random slopes were tested but did not change the reported trends, so the simpler models are included.

[20] Only speech that was produced by the same speaker who produced the tokens was used to calculate speech rate.

[21] Both calculations were tested to determine whether they had any power in predicting the relationship between function and phonetic form, both to inform future work in this area and because they have different theoretical implications. The number of tokens of quotative *like* per hundred words failed to reach significance in the model when in place of the second calculation (p>0.1).

3.3 Phonetic variation of like

Table 3.7: Coefficients of fixed effects for Model 1, comparing the quotative with grammatical functions of *like*

	Estimate	Std. Error	z value	Pr(>|z|)
(Intercept)	0.3366	0.68	0.50	0.6198
DIPH	−0.4367	0.13	−3.46	0.0005
PITCH	0.0072	0.00	3.51	0.0005
LV DURATION	−2.2391	0.59	−3.81	0.0001

for each girl per hundred words produced but was not found to reach significance. Factors reaching significance were included as fixed effects in the model, but some factors that approach significance (p<0.06) are included in the models in order to account for the variation they appear to be predicting (thereby creating a better fit model). The model's fixed effects and their coefficients for the test variables are shown in Table 3.7, and the control variables from the model are shown in Table 3.8.[22] The estimated scale parameter of a model is a measure of how much of the actual variance in the data can be accounted for by the model. Ideally, it is close to 1. The estimated scale parameter for this model is 1.030892, which indicates that it is a good fit.

Fixed effects in the model include the preceding and following environment, the Euclidean distance between F1 and F2 of the nucleus and offglide as a measure of how diphthongal the token's vowel was (DIPH), the mean pitch (PITCH), and the ratio of /l/ to vowel duration (LV DURATION).

The defaults of the model are that the token was preceded by something other than a fricative or a pause and was followed by a consonant (followed by C). For continuous factors, the model assumes a value of zero, even when this value is not present in the data. Therefore, the model assumes as a default that the vowel was completely monophthongal (DIPH = 0) and that the /l/ to vowel duration ratio was zero (LV DURATION = 0), both of which are values that were observed

---

[22] The final model was also fit only to data from girls who had ten or more quotatives (see Table 3.3). All factors reached the same level of significance as in the model reported here. Similarly, the final model was fit first only comparing the quotative with the lexical verb and then comparing it with the adverb. All effects reached significance and were in the same direction as the model presented here with the exception of the value of F2, which did not reach significance in either of the models. This provides additional evidence that the lexical verb and the adverb were similar phonetically.

3 Like: Frequency and phonetic realisations

Table 3.8: Coefficients of control variables for Model 1, comparing the quotative with grammatical functions of *like*

	Estimate	Std. Error	z value	Pr(>|z|)
preceded by pause	−0.8199	0.87	−0.94	0.3482
preceded by fricative	1.7364	0.28	6.21	< 0.0001
followed by pause	0.8526	0.52	1.64	0.1015
followed by V	−0.1981	0.42	−0.47	0.6379
followed by sibilant	−1.8554	0.65	−2.87	0.0041
followed by nasal	−1.0028	0.55	−1.81	0.0697
followed by other voiceless	−1.8175	0.51	−3.53	0.0004
followed by other voiced	−3.1986	0.57	−5.65	< 0.0001

in the data. Tokens with an /l/ to vowel duration ratio of zero were tokens where there was no acoustic evidence of an /l/; the /l/ was dropped. The intercept's estimate given in Table 3.7 is the likelihood in log odds that a token with the default characteristics was quotative *like*. To determine the log odds for tokens that do not match the default criteria, the estimate for binary factors must be added to the default intercept of the model. For example, to determine the likelihood that a token was quotative *like* if it had the default characteristics except that it was followed by a pause, the estimate for tokens followed by pauses (-0.8199) would be added to the estimated intercept (0.3366). For continuous factors, such as Euclidean distance, the product of the factor's coefficient and the token's Euclidean distance is added to the estimated coefficient of the intercept. In calculating log odds of factors for the graphs presented in this chapter, the mean values of continuous factors were used as defaults.

Prior to running the final model, the different preceding environments were run as separate factors in the factor group for the preceding environment.[23]

---

[23] First, the different phonemes which preceded each token were treated as factors. They were then divided depending on voicing and on whether they were continuous. Whether a token was continuous did not significantly predict the function of *like*. Voiceless tokens were less likely to precede the quotative than the grammatical function (p<0.05), but there is no interaction between voicing and whether the preceding environment was a fricative. This makes it unlikely that the shorter /l/ to vowel duration ratio associated with the quotative was due to identifying portions of the /l/ that were voiceless (as a result of coarticulation) as the preceding segment.

They appeared to clump according to whether they were a fricative, a pause, or something else. Therefore, the factor group for the preceding environment that was included in the final model had this three-way distinction. As indicated by the positive coefficient in Table 3.7, tokens that were preceded by a fricative were significantly more likely to be the quotative than a grammatical function when compared to tokens that were preceded by a segment that was non-fricated ($p<0.0001$). Although there was not a significant difference between tokens that were preceded by a pause and by a non-fricated segment, these factors were not collapsed into a single factor in order to maintain consistency across the different production models.

For the factor group of following environment, the model was first tested with each phoneme listed as a separate factor (e.g., /f/, /b/, pause). The following environment was divided into seven discrete factors: followed by an approximant, followed by a pause, a vowel, a sibilant, a nasal, by some other segment that was voiceless, and by some other segment that was voiced. The preceding environment was divided into three discrete factors: preceded by a pause, preceded by a fricative, and preceded by anything else. The model held the fixed effect of following environment constant when testing the other factors, so the predicted effect of other factors was independent from following environment.

A token was significantly less likely to be quotative *like* if it was more diphthongal ($p<0.001$). The higher the Euclidean distance of a vowel, the less likely it was to be the quotative. This was a continuous factor and its relationship with the function of *like* was also continuous; tokens with vowels that were more diphthongal were more likely to be a grammatical function of *like*.

A vowel's mean pitch also significantly predicted whether or not a token was the quotative. The higher the mean pitch, the more likely it was that the token was quotative *like* as opposed to a traditionally grammatical function of *like* ($p<0.001$). This is likely related to the prosodic position in a sentence of the different types of *like*. Though both lexical verb *like* and quotative *like* function as verbs, their syntactic properties differ, affecting their position in a sentence. Impressionistically, lexical verb *like* seemed to be produced in conjunction with a dip in the intonation contour, whereas quotative *like* rarely was and was sometimes part of a rising contour that raised more steeply after the verb.

Tokens with a larger /l/ to vowel ratio have a longer /l/ duration relative to the duration of the vowel. These tokens with a relatively long /l/ were significantly less likely to be quotative *like* than a grammatical function of *like* ($p=0.0001$). Though measures of speech rate failed to reach significance in differentiating between the functions of *like*, using the ratio of /l/ to vowel duration helped to normalise the duration of /l/ across different rates of speech. That the ratio

3 Like: Frequency and phonetic realisations

reached significance in the model suggests that the relationship between /l/ duration and function of *like* was not an artefact of different speech rates across the different functions.

3.3.2.2 Model 2: Quotative and discourse particle *like*

A mixed effects model comparing tokens of the quotative with tokens of the discourse particle was fit to the data, modeling the likelihood that a particular token of *like* was the quotative. As with the first model, speaker was included as a random effect. The same factors as tested in model 1 were tested in model 2. Only those reaching significance were included in the model. These included how diphthongal the token was, the ratio of /l/ to vowel duration, the mean pitch of the token, and the preceding and following environment as described for the previous model. Also reaching significance in the model was an interaction between whether or not the /k/ was dropped and whether the girl was in a group who ate lunch in the CR. Speech rate, frequency of use of quotative and discourse particle *like*, and whether the token had a steady intonation contour failed to reach significance and were not included in the model. The coefficient table for the production model is shown in Table 3.9.

A token was less likely to be a quotative if preceded by a pause than if preceded by a fricative ($p<0.0001$) or any other segment ($p<0.001$). A token was more likely to be a quotative if preceded by a fricative than if preceded by any other segment ($p<0.001$).

A token's Euclidean distance also predicts the function of a token. A token was significantly more likely to be quotative *like* if it was more monophthongal ($p<0.0001$), as indicated by the negative coefficient value. This is also similar to results from model 1.

As with the first model, a token with a higher mean pitch was more likely to be quotative *like* ($p<0.0001$). Again, this is likely related to the words' prosodic position in a sentence. Tokens of quotative *like* were often followed by reported speech in a very high pitch, and the token of quotative *like* itself rarely had the lowest pitch in the phrase. Discourse particle *like*, on the other hand, was produced in conjunction with a dip in the intonation contour. It could have a very low pitch and was often produced with a creaky quality.

As in model 1, a token with a long /l/ duration relative to its vowel duration was less likely to be quotative *like* than to be discourse particle *like* ($p<0.01$). This provides evidence that quotative *like* had a shorter /l/ duration, regardless of speech rate. Similar results were found in model 1, suggesting that quotative *like* was most likely to have a shorter duration ratio, regardless of the non-quotative function with which it was paired.

Table 3.9: Coefficients of fixed effects for Model 2, comparing the quotative with the discourse particle

	Estimate	Std. Error	z value	Pr(>|z|)
(Intercept)	−0.4093	0.56	−0.735	0.4626
DIPH	−0.4671	0.11	−4.212	<0.0001
PITCH	0.0079	0.00	4.501	<0.0001
LV DURATION	−1.4819	0.49	−3.024	0.0025
K-CLOS=N	−0.9035	0.30	−2.987	0.0028
GROUP=NCR	−0.5364	0.34	−1.560	0.1187
K-CLOS=N:GROUP=NCR	1.3050	0.44	2.97	0.0029

Table 3.10: Coefficients of control variables for Model 2, comparing the quotative with the discourse particle

	Estimate	Std. Error	z value	Pr(>|z|)
preceded by pause	−2.8558	0.76	−3.78	0.0002
preceded by fricative	0.8261	0.22	3.78	0.0002
followed by pause	0.0618	0.33	0.19	0.8516
followed by V	0.4689	0.32	1.45	0.1470
followed by sibilant	−0.4713	0.59	−0.80	0.4253
followed by nasal	0.3668	0.48	0.76	0.4475
followed by other voiceless	−0.6591	0.42	−1.56	0.1179
followed by other voiced	−1.7862	0.51	−3.50	0.0005

3 Like: Frequency and phonetic realisations

The model includes a significant interaction between whether the /k/ in a token was realised or not and whether the girl who produced the token was a CR girl or not (p<0.01).[24] A token where the /k/ was dropped was more likely to be quotative *like* if produced by a CR girl, but less likely to be quotative *like* if produced by a NCR girl.[25] This interaction, shown in Figure 3.9, was independent of following environment, as following environment was included as a fixed effect in the model. It seems there were not only differences in pronunciation between the different types of *like* but that different social groups had different realisations for the different functions of *like*.

This interaction was not carried exclusively by quotative *like*; the opposite trend of /k/ realisation was found for the discourse particle. While CR girls were more likely to produce the /k/ in discourse particle *like*, NCR girls were more likely to drop the /k/.

This interaction is not an artefact of the frequency of use of either the quotative or the discourse particle. Though they do not reach significance in the model, if frequency measures are included, the interaction between /k/ realisation and a girl's eating place is still significant. This provides statistical evidence that the interaction is independent of the speaker-specific probability of producing quotative *like*. Interestingly, CR girls were significantly more likely to use the discourse particle than NCR girls (Wilcoxon, p=0.01).[26] But there is no interaction between the frequency of use of the discourse particle and whether the /k/ is realised.[27] Irrespective of how often a girl used quotative and discourse particle *like*, she was more likely to realise the /k/ in quotative *like* than in discourse particle *like* if she was a NCR girl and more likely to drop the /k/ in the quotative than in the discourse particle if she was a CR girl. For example, Juliet (PCs), Barbara (Relaxed Group), and Clementine (Trendy Alternatives) were all CR girls

---

[24] The interaction remains significant if the duration of the /k/ closure is included in the model in place of the discrete measure of whether or not the /k/ was realised. Because the effect appeared to be carried entirely by the tokens where the closure duration was equal to zero as opposed to all other closure durations, the discrete measure was used in the model.

[25] The significance level presented here is for the interaction between CR and /k/ realisation. Separate models fit first to the CR girls' data and then to the NCR girls' data, reveal that while the trend with /k/ realisation is significant for the CR girls (p<0.05), it is not significant for the NCR girls (p>0.7). The arguments presented in this chapter are based on the opposite trends found for the two groups, which is why the interaction's significance level and coefficient are the focus of this discussion.

[26] This is based on the calculation presented in Section 3.2.2.

[27] This was tested with the percentage of all words that were the discourse particle, the percentage of all tokens of *like* that were the discourse particle, and the ratio of quotative to discourse particle tokens produced by a speaker.

3.3 Phonetic variation of like

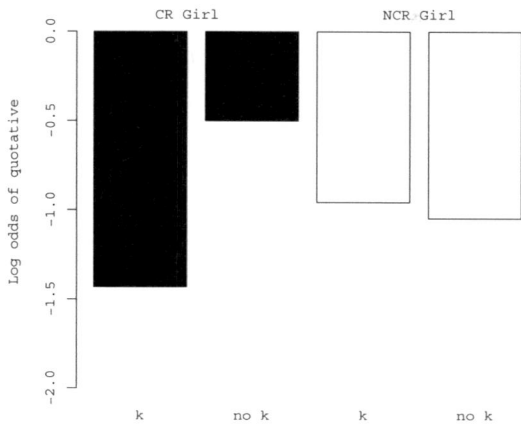

Figure 3.9: Graph of the interaction between whether the /k/ was realised and whether the speaker was in a group who ate lunch in the CR (black) or not (white). The graph is based on the model's predictions. A higher value (i.e. closer to zero) on the y-axis indicates a greater likelihood that the token was quotative *like*.

who were not particularly frequent users of quotative *like* and they produced the /k/ more frequently in quotative *like* than did some of their friends who used quotative *like* more often. However, these girls were more likely to produce the /k/ in the discourse particle than in the quotative, thereby patterning more similarly to their CR friends than with NCR girls who were also infrequent users of quotative *like*.

In regard to monophthongisation, mean pitch, /l/ to vowel duration ratio, and following environment, both discourse particle *like* and grammatical functions of *like* behaved similarly when compared to quotative *like*. However, they involved different interactions: one with /k/ realisation and the speaker-specific probability of a token, and the other with /k/ realisation and the social grouping of the speaker. Whereas the realisation of /k/ was linked to frequency of use for quotative *like*, it did not appear to be linked to frequency of use for the discourse particle. Phonetic differences between grammatical functions of *like* and the discourse particle will be presented in the following section.

3 Like: Frequency and phonetic realisations

3.3.2.3 Model 3: Grammatical and discourse particle *like*

A mixed effects model was fit to the data comparing the discourse particle with grammatical functions of *like*, modelling whether a token was one of the traditionally grammatical functions. Speaker was included as a random effect. Coefficients of the model's fixed effects are shown in Table 3.11 and the model's control variables are shown in Table 3.12.

The preceding and following environment and the F2 value of a token's nucleus target significantly predicted whether a token was a grammatical function. A token that was preceded by a pause or a fricative was less likely to be a grammatical function of *like* than the discourse particle when compared with a token preceded

Table 3.11: Coefficients of fixed effects for Model 3, comparing the discourse particle with grammatical functions of *like*

	Estimate	Std. Error	z value	$Pr(>|z|)$
(Intercept)	4.8433	1.8126	2.67	0.0075
NUC F2	−0.4876	0.1546	−3.15	0.0016
LV DURATION	−0.2231	0.6144	−0.36	0.7165
GROUP=NCR	−0.4758	0.4666	−1.02	0.3079
LV DURATION:GROUP=NCR	1.7159	0.8670	1.98	0.0478

Table 3.12: Coefficients of control variables for Model 3, comparing the discourse particle with grammatical functions of *like*

	Estimate	Std. Error	z value	$Pr(>|z|)$
preceded by pause	−1.7516	0.3915	−4.475	< 0.0001
preceded by fricative	−0.9553	0.2503	−3.82	0.0001
followed by pause	−0.8570	0.4843	−1.77	0.0768
followed by V	0.7412	0.3799	1.95	0.0510
followed by sibilant	1.4890	0.5040	2.95	0.0031
followed by nasal	1.2666	0.5062	2.50	0.0123
followed by other voiceless	0.8749	0.4058	2.16	0.0311
followed by other voiced	1.3631	0.3854	3.54	0.0004

by some other segment (p<0.0001). The difference between tokens preceded by a pause as opposed to a fricative was approaching significance (p=0.06), with tokens preceded by a fricative being more likely to be a grammatical function.

Tokens that were followed by an approximant were significantly less likely to be a grammatical function of *like* than tokens that were followed by a sibilant (p<0.001), a nasal (p<0.05), a voiceless consonant of a different manner of articulation (p<0.05), and a voiced consonant of a different manner of articulation (p<0.001).

Tokens with a higher F2 at the target of the nucleus (i.e. tokens with a nucleus that was less back) were less likely to be a grammatical function of *like* (p<0.01). This suggests that grammatical functions of *like* were more likely to be produced with a backer diphthong nucleus than the discourse particle. Between the two discursive functions, there was no significant difference in F2.

Also reaching significance in the model is an interaction between the /l/ to vowel duration ratio and whether or not the speaker ate lunch in the Common Room (p<0.05); tokens with a long /l/ relative to the vowel were more likely to be the discourse particle if produced by a common room girl and were more likely to be one of the grammatical functions if produced by a non-common room girl. Together with the interaction from model 2, the results suggest that a word's phonetic realisation can depend on a combination of the word's grammatical function and the social characteristics of the speaker who produced it.

A summary of results from all three models is presented in Table 3.13.

3.4 Discussion

The results provide evidence that different functions of *like* have different realisations.[28] The ultimate realisation depends on a combination of a token's grammatical function and the social grouping of the girl who produced it. That the girls' realisations of *like* were systematically different depending on the function of a token suggests that these items are stored in the mind in a way that maintains the distinction. This is discussed in Chapter 5 where I also describe implications of results from the perception experiments presented in Chapter 4. The current section discusses how the results add to previous work on sound change, the discursive status of certain lexical items, and the link between phonetic reduction and a token's probability given the context.

---

[28] It is possible that some of the variation observed between functions is due to effects of prosody and other phonetic cues not investigated here. This is discussed briefly in Section 3.4.4.

Table 3.13: Summary of results from the first three statistical models

type	summary of traits
grammatical	low pitch
	more diphthongal
	long /l/ to vowel duration ratio
	shorter /l/ to vowel duration ratio for CR girls
quotative	high pitch
	less diphthongal
	short /l/ to vowel duration ratio
	more /k/ reduction for CR girls than NCR girls
discourse particle	low pitch
	large F2 value but still diphthongal
	long /l/ to vowel duration ratio
	shorter /l/ to vowel duration ratio for NCR girls
	more /k/ reduction for NCR girls than CR girls

3.4.1 Frequency effects

Previous studies provide evidence that token frequencies correlate with at least some phonetic variables. The majority of previous studies have focused on vowel duration (Bybee 2001; Jurafsky, Bell & Girand 2002; Gahl 2008), but vowel quality and monophthongisation have also been shown to correlate with frequency measures (Munson 2007; Hay, Jannedy & Mendoza-Denton 1999). In these studies, monophthongisation, shorter vowel durations, and a more compact vowel space are associated with tokens that have a higher frequency. In the SGH data, the different measures of relative frequency of use described in Section 3.2.1 did not interact with monophthongisation, vowel duration, or the /l/-vowel duration ratio. Given the amount of previous work that has found a relationship between token frequency and duration, it is surprising that no such effects were observed here. This may be a result of using measurements that reflect the speaker-specific probability of producing a token in a given context (e.g., when speaking, or when producing a quotative) as opposed to an overall approximation of token frequency. Alternatively, it may be related to the fact that, across all speakers, all of the anal-

Table 3.14: Coefficients of fixed effects for Model 4, modeling /k/ reduction for tokens of quotative *like*

	Estimate	Std. Error	z value	Pr(>|z|)
(Intercept)	−8.58498	3.75172	−2.288	0.02212
DIPH	0.92959	0.21775	4.269	<0.0001
LV DURATION	2.26894	0.84877	2.673	0.00751
NUC F2	0.77772	0.28334	2.745	0.00605
GROUP=NCR	1.47449	0.51989	2.836	0.00457
PROB QUOTE	−0.04481	0.02160	−2.075	0.03801

ysed functions of *like* would be classified as highly frequent in previous studies. For example, Bybee (2002) treats words that are observed in corpus data equal to or more than 35 times per million words as high-frequency; all of the analysed functions of *like* were more frequent than this for all speakers in the SGH data.

In the model comparing the quotative with the grammatical functions, there is an interaction between /k/ realisation and the percentage of all quotatives that were quotative *like*. This interaction suggests that the speaker-specific probability of an item in a given context is linked to phonetic reduction in that item. To demonstrate that this effect is independent of the effect of a girl's status as a CR girl or a NCR girl, I have fit a fourth mixed effects model with speaker as a random effect, modeling /k/ realisation and only including tokens of quotative *like*. The model's output is shown for the test items in Table 3.14 and for the control variables in Table 3.15.

The model shows that there is a significant relationship between /k/ realisation and a token's Euclidean distance ($p<0.0001$) and /k/ realisation and the /l/ to vowel duration ratio of a token ($p<0.05$). More diphthongal tokens and tokens with a longer /l/ relative to the vowel were more likely to have the /k/ present. This is not surprising if monophthongisation, /l/ duration reduction, and /k/ dropping are all reductive processes. Tokens that have the /k/ realised were also more likely to have a higher F2 at the nucleus target ($p<0.01$).

The key finding in this model was that for quotative *like* both the speaker's social grouping and how often she used quotative *like* were linked to /k/ realisation. NCR girls were more likely to realise the /k/ than CR girls ($p<0.05$) and the more a girl used quotative *like*, the less likely she was to realise the /k/ in it

3 Like: Frequency and phonetic realisations

Table 3.15: Coefficients of control variables for Model 4, modeling /k/ reduction for tokens of quotative *like*

	Estimate	Std. Error	z value	Pr(>|z|)
preceded by pause	−2.7829	1.78	−1.57	0.1174
preceded by fricative	0.1268	0.38	0.34	0.7360
followed by pause	1.1055	0.56	1.96	0.0495
followed by V	1.1439	0.54	2.12	0.0341
followed by sibilant	2.2012	1.07	2.07	0.0389
followed by nasal	1.1754	0.74	1.59	0.1112
followed by other voiceless	0.4163	0.83	0.50	0.6156
followed by other voiced	17.3702	989.60	0.02	0.9860

($p<0.05$). Both social and frequency effects played a role in predicting whether the /k/ was realised.[29]

Previous work has observed a relationship between the phonetic realisation of a word and its predictability based on contextual information (Jurafsky, Bell & Girand 2002): words that are more predictable given the preceding context undergo more reductive processes. These findings help to interpret the results regarding the relationship between /k/-dropping and the percentage of a speaker's quotatives that were quotative *like*. If the contextual information indicates that a speaker is likely to produce a quotative, the probability of that quotative being *like* (as opposed to some other quotative) is speaker-dependent. Thus, for speakers who have a high percentage of quotatives that are *like*, *like* is more predictable in its local context; for these speakers, /k/ is more likely to be dropped. Conversely, for speakers who have a lower percentage of quotatives that are *like*, *like* is less predictable in its local context and the /k/ is less likely to be dropped.

This supports previous findings that words that are more predictable given the preceding context undergo more reduction. Further, it indicates that predictability needs to be considered at the level of the individual speaker; not all words are equally predictable in all contexts for all speakers.

It is possible that phonetic patterns that derive from speaker-specific, context-dependent probabilities could be exploited as a stylistic resource. Such re-appropriation of phonetic variables could have led to the differences in /k/ realisation

---

[29] Models fit only to the grammatical tokens and to the discourse particle tokens revealed that the social grouping and speaker-specific frequency did not play a significant role in whether or not the /k/ was realised ($p>0.1$ for the effects in both models).

observed between CR and NCR girls. Stylistic resources are constantly recombined in a process of bricolage (Hebdige 1984; Eckert 2005a). While work such as that by Milroy & Milroy (1978) has focused on a community or social group's adoption of (and reassignment of meaning to) variables used by another group, it is also possible that phonetic variability originally driven by speaker-specific probabilities could be manipulated for stylistic means. Due to the multidimensional nature of the stylistic components, the model presented in Chapter 5 predicts that socially-conditioned phonetic variability could arise from probabilistic distributions of the variables based on non-social factors.

3.4.2 Special status of discursive tokens

The only socially-conditioned phonetic variation in the production of *like* was found when observing two discursive functions, quotative *like* and discourse particle *like*: a token was more likely to be quotative *like* if the /k/ was not realised and it was produced by a CR girl or if the /k/ was realised and it was produced by a NCR girl.[30] Why might this be? I argue that their discursive nature and their frequent use make them probable targets of sociophonetic variation.

The frequent occurrence of these discursive items may ensure their status as loci of socially meaningful phonetic variation. Work in sociophonetics has demonstrated that the realisations of frequent items can be socially meaningful and manipulated stylistically (Hay, Jannedy & Mendoza-Denton 1999). The frequent repetition of quotative and discourse particle *like* would provide ample opportunity for these words to become layered with social meaning, but frequency alone can not explain why particular pronunciations become imbued with social meanings. Because patterns of /k/ realisation in quotative and discourse particle *like* were in the opposite direction, this result can not be a matter of ease of processing. I believe that socially meaningful phonetic variation in discursive words is a result of the words themselves carrying socially indexical meanings.

Discursive items, which I define as words used in informal speech situations that are not considered traditionally grammatical but are used across generations of speakers, come to be indexed with social meaning through variation and eventual associations with particular social groups. In her discussion of slang, Bucholtz explains how

> variation in slang use, like music fandom, clothing, and hairstyles, allows teenagers to identify themselves with some of their peers while differen-

---

[30] Of course, frequency of use was related to social characteristics. Here, however, I am focusing on socially-conditioned phonetic variation that was not derivative of frequency.

3 Like: Frequency and phonetic realisations

tiating themselves from others; in short, it enables teenagers to produce distinctive linguistic and cultural styles. (Bucholtz 2006: 251)

Both quotative *like* and discourse particle *like* can be used similarly, a point I will return to shortly.

Lexical items with particularly socially-indexical meanings can serve as vehicles for phonetic variables that in themselves index social meaning. Eckert (1996a) found that words like *all-nighter* and *fight* could be realised by Burnouts with an especially raised /ai/ diphthong. The extreme phonetic realisation, which was associated with the city, emphasised the toughness and rebelliousness that the lexical items themselves also indexed. Chun (2007) found that the pronunciation of the phrase *oh my god* was stylistically manipulated and she argued that words and phrases can index social characteristics, especially when used in conjunction with socially meaningful phonetic variants. That discursive lexical items in particular often index 'youth', 'coolness', and stances associated with a particular social group suggests that their phonetic realisations will be readily manipulated as a means of emphasising social characteristics such as these.

In terms of *like*, there are two levels of association in language ideology: youth culture as distinct from non-youth culture and between the different groups within youth culture. Both quotative and discourse particle *like* are discursive items associated in language ideology with youth culture in the US and the UK (Dailey-O'Cain 2000; Buchstaller 2006), making them prime potential candidates in which to observe phonetic variation that signals 'youth' as well as characteristics associated with youth culture. Though comparable work has yet to be carried out in New Zealand, conversations between girls at the school suggest that speakers of New Zealand English associate *like* with youth culture. After taking part in the perception experiments discussed in Chapter 4, several girls wanted to share their opinions on the discursive functions of *like*, both with me and with each other. In the conversation between Theresa and Esther (Christians) shown in Example 16, Theresa explained how her mother did not understand why she used *like*. Esther's response suggested that the available alternative was undesirable.

(16) Theresa and Esther, Christians. Interview, 24-10.

Theresa: no but they're so bad with like
Mum Mum's like why do you say that
and um

Esther: 'cause otherwise we'd have to use the word said
and that would just be annoying

3.4 Discussion

Though girls in every group at the school used them, discursive functions of *like* were particularly associated with The PCs. In Example 17, Ricky and Marissa talked about how Joanna and Alissa, two PCs, were frequent users of the discursive functions of *like*.

(17) Ricky and Marissa (Goths). Interview, 14-10.

Ricky: in assembly one time when Joanna and Alissa were talking

Marissa: and we sat there
we're like one .
Ricky: duh duh duh duh duh duh duh duh [counting on fingers]
Marissa: duh duh [counting on fingers]
I ran out of fingers within the first five seconds

[laughter]

Marissa: she r- she ran I ran out of fingers
within the first five seconds
Ricky: 'cause she uses it more than I than most people

Interestingly, The PCs whose speech was analysed were not the highest users of quotative *like*. Even Emma, one of the girls explicitly mentioned by others as someone who was a frequent user of *like*, was not one of the most frequent users of either quotative or discourse particle *like* based on the measures presented in Section 3.2. The perception that she was a frequent user likely came from her frequent use of the discourse marker and approximant adverb combined with her highly visible status at the school.

Despite *like* being associated with The PCs, girls in other groups were highly aware that they used it as well. Before the segment shown in (17), Marissa suggested that they try to avoid saying *like* during the morning break. Ricky, knowing how frequently and automatically they used it, stated simply that "it won't work". The widespread use of the lexical items combined with their association with a particular group served to make the discursive functions of *like* a target of socially-meaningful phonetic variation within the school.

Another word with a discursive use that seemed to have a distinct pronunciation at the school from the traditionally grammatical function was the word

111

3 Like: Frequency and phonetic realisations

yes.[31] When girls used *yes* as an exclamation, the vowel was backed and centralised, which strongly contrasted with the fronted, raised variant used in the agreement form of *yes* and most other words containing this vowel. The girls were highly aware of this distinctive pronounciation of exclamation *yes* and in writing they spelled it as 'yuss'. This is another example of how words with discursive meanings can be used in conjunction with distinct pronunciations.

3.4.3 Changes in progress

In NZE, the diphthong /ai/ is involved in two on-going sound changes: the nucleus is shifting back, a phenomenon known as diphthong shift, (Gordon et al. 2004: 149) and the diphthong itself is becoming more monophthongal, which is referred to as glide weakening (Gordon et al. 2004; Chartres 2008). Realisations that are innovative in terms of both glide weakening and diphthong shift can be produced by the same individuals (Chartres 2008). In the current study, the function of *like* was predictable both by how diphthongal and by how backed the vowel was. A backed nucleus was associated with grammatical functions, while a monophthongal vowel was found in the quotative. This suggests that there is a conflict in terms of innovation: quotative *like* was produced with the most innovative realisation in terms of glide weakening and the grammatical functions were produced with the most innovative realisation in terms of diphthong shift. Results described in Chartres (2008) indicate that both glide weakening and diphthong shift are led by males in NZE. Informal discussions with colleagues who are from New Zealand suggest that while a backed nucleus is highly associated with males, a monophthongal realisation is not. Thus, girls at the school may avoid producing variants associated with males and this may be particularly true in contexts such as discursive words that strongly index identity, especially with the discursive functions of *like* that are highly associated with females. Another possibility is that the discursive functions of *like* are more likely to carry primary stress in a sentence. Stressed tokens tend to be more peripheral in a speaker's vowel space than unstressed tokens. However, there was no significant difference observed for vowel duration or whether the pitch was moving or stable, both of which are other acoustic cues for stress. A study on the ideology surrounding the changes in progress in which /ai/ is involved may help to shed light in interpreting the findings presented here.

---

[31] I have also noticed this difference among New Zealanders outside of SGH.

3.4.4 Prosody and phonetic variation

It is well established that prosody can affect articulation. Vowel duration (Edwards, Beckman & Fletcher 1992), formant transitions in diphthongs (Wouters & Macon 2002), glottalistion (Dilley, Shattuck-Hufnagel & Ostendorf 1996), and consonant realisation (Fougeron & Keating 1997) all appear to be linked to prosodic position; greater articulatory effort tends to be observed at the edges of prosodic domains (Fougeron & Keating 1997). While only one of the analysed tokens in the current study occurred at a sentence boundary, this does not ensure that the observed phonetic differences between the different functions of *like* were not in fact due to the token's prosodic position in the sentence. When compared to the discourse particle, quotative *like* was more likely to have a shorter /l/ to vowel duration ratio and a more monophthongal vowel; both of these might be expected if the quotative was more likely to occur in a prosodically less prominent position. However, we might also expect to observe both a shorter vowel duration and a lower rate of /k/ realisation in the quotative. In actuality, there was no significant difference in vowel duration, and /k/ realisation depended on social characteristics of the speaker. While some of the phonetic differences observed between the different functions may be related to frequency, it is unlikely that all of them, /k/ realisation in particular, resulted from prosodic differences. Further work in this area is beyond the scope of this book, but it would certainly be a worthwhile avenue for future work, especially given the fact that the majority of work investigating the effects of prosody on articulation is done in the laboratory.[32]

3.4.5 Identity construction

What is the meaning behind the stylistic variation of /k/ realisation?[33] Speakers actively manipulate linguistic variables and non-linguistic qualities to construct their identities. The variation of /k/ in quotative and discourse particle *like* is no exception. Zwicky (1997) outlines two internal psychosocial mechanisms for the acquisition of identity: identification and avoidance. He argues that an individual can model their behaviour based on characteristics of those who they believe they are similar to or who they would like to be similar to (Identifica-

---

[32] One notable exception to this is Cole et al. (2007), who used speech from a corpus of radio news.
[33] Whether or not the realisation of /k/ is a variable undergoing a sound change in progress is not relevant for this discussion. Either way, it is being used stylistically in the construction of the girls' social identities.

tion). Conversely, individuals can reject behaviour of people who they wish to dissociate themselves from or who they do not believe themselves to be similar to (Avoidance).

At Selwyn Girls' High, norms of dress and behaviour were set by the CR girls. These girls did not adopt 'normal' qualities so much as they determined which linguistic and non-linguistic factors were considered to be 'normal' at the school. In the results presented in this chapter, the CR girls consistently displayed a strong tendency to drop the /k/ in quotative *like* and to produce the /k/ in discourse particle *like*. They conformed to each other in an act of identification. It is also possible that adopting these trends was an act of avoidance of realisations produced by particular individuals from a NCR group.

It is unlikely that NCR girls were conforming to each other's speech. There was no evidence of identification in terms of clothes, values, or lifestyles across the different NCR groups; there was not a common socially-constructed identity that united them. In the production of *like*, NCR girls displayed the opposite trend as CR girls: they were more likely to produce the /k/ in quotative *like* than in discourse particle *like*. The trend was less robust than the trend observed in the speech of the CR girls. It is clear, however, that NCR girls did not adopt the variation observed in the speech of the CR girls. In fact, they showed the opposite trend, providing evidence of avoidance. They rejected the norms of the CR girls and their trends in production were contrary to those of the CR girls from whom they wished to distance themselves.

The PCs were an especially salient group. They were talked about by other groups and were always named first when identifying groups at the school. The discursive functions of *like* were particularly associated with them in the school's language ideology. Taken together, this suggests that it is possible that NCR girls were diverging from The PCs or particular individuals in The PCs rather than from the CR girls as a whole. While CR girls in groups other than The PCs may have been accommodating to The PCs, the evidence does not necessarily support this. The PCs whose speech was analysed for this study did not display the strongest trends in the CR direction. This is true even for those girls who were core members of The PCs, such as Emma and Tracy. It is likely that CR girls as a whole converged on each other's speech rather than accommodated to that of a single group.

That the trends of /k/ realisation result from identification and avoidance finds support in the NCR girls' rejection of non-linguistic norms. There is a close relationship between linguistic features used by a speaker and that speaker's choice in other stylistic components, such as clothing (Bourdieu 1991: 89). Choice of clothing was fairly consistent across the different CR groups, while many NCR girls chose to wear clothes that were dissimilar to those worn by the CR girls. The NCR groups' divergence in choice of clothing took a variety of forms and it is likely that they also deviated from the CR norms in terms of phonetic variables that have not yet been investigated. In terms of /k/ realization for quotative and discourse particle *like*, the different NCR groups seem to have diverged from CR girls in a similar direction. Of course, there was still a great deal of variation across the different NCR groups, even in terms of /k/ realisation. Trends in the speech of individual girls will be discussed in the next section.

The observed differences between CR and NCR girls are a result of identification and avoidance. CR girls' similarities in production of *like* are a result of identification with one another and conforming to each other's speech (and possibly avoiding speech patterns of the NCR girls) and NCR girls' similarities may be due to avoidance and a rejection of the CR girls' norms.

3.4.5.1 Variation at the individual level

In this section, I discuss the patterns of /k/ realisation exhibited by different individuals. I argue that a strong NCR trend in production (i.e. they were more likely to drop the /k/ in discourse particle *like* than in quotative *like*) is associated with individuals who were likely to reject norms, and that a strong CR trend in production (i.e. they were more likely to drop the /k/ in quotative *like* than discourse particle *like*) is associated with a wider range of people: those who actively embraced norms as well as others with alternative motivation. The order of individuals (from speaker with the strongest NCR trend to speaker with the strongest CR trend) is shown in Table 3.16. The coefficients are based on a separate production model fit to the data, modelling the likelihood of producing the /k/. Included in the model was an interaction between whether or not the token was quotative and the random effect of the speaker. The following environment was included as a fixed effect. The estimate for each speaker is the difference between random effect coefficients when the token was the discourse particle and when it was the quotative. The coefficients in the table are a reflection of a speaker's likelihood of producing the /k/ in discourse particle *like* relative to quotative *like*. A larger coefficient means that a speaker was more likely to produce the /k/ in the quotative than in the discourse particle; the more negative the coefficient, the more likely a speaker was to exhibit a strong CR trend in production. These results are also presented in Drager & Hay (2012).

The girl who showed the strongest NCR trend (she was most likely to produce the /k/ in quotative *like* and drop the /k/ in discourse particle *like*) was Santra.

3 Like: Frequency and phonetic realisations

Table 3.16: Likelihood of an individual producing /k/ in discourse particle *like* compared to quotative *like*. Estimates are based on a separate model fit to the production data modelling the likelihood of /k/ realisation, with an interaction between the random effect of a speaker and whether the token was the quotative or the discourse particle. The presented estimate for each speaker is the difference between random coefficients when the token is a discourse particle and when it is a quotative.

Speaker	Sub-group	Group	Estimate
Barbara	Relaxed Group	CR	−1.84791
Clementine	Trendy Alternatives	CR	−1.71651
Rochelle	Rochelle's Group	CR	−1.47306
Rose	Relaxed Group	CR	−1.33595
Holly	Sonia's Group	NCR	−1.26401
Betty	Sporty Group	CR	−1.01303
Meredith	Goths	NCR	−0.85033
Juliet	PCs	CR	−0.74285
Tracy	PCs	CR	−0.72341
Bianca	Geeks	NCR	−0.67159
Emma	PCs	CR	−0.65743
Tania	Goths	NCR	−0.59702
Katrina	Relaxed Group	CR	−0.40379
Sarah	Real Teenagers	NCR	−0.38485
Justine	Trendy Alternatives	CR	−0.38075
Mariah	Geeks	NCR	−0.14698
Theresa	Christians	NCR	−0.09286
Christina	Trendy Alternatives	CR	0.015748
Jane	BBs	CR	0.13346
Marissa	Goths	NCR	0.281689
Kanani	Sporty Group	CR	0.561684
Marama	Pasifika Group	NCR	0.589017
Patricia	Sporty Group	CR	0.746599
Isabelle	Real Teenagers	NCR	0.967743
Vanessa	Goths	NCR	1.024424
Esther	Christians	NCR	1.130588
Joy	Geeks	NCR	1.789199
Santra	Goths	NCR	1.994998

Santra was the central member of The Goths. She was the only goth who wore all black; she was the goth who gave The Goths their name. She questioned everything, loudly and boldly. She had very strong political and social views and she was the only openly bisexual girl in Year 13. If anyone at the school was the most likely to reject norms and rebel against conformity, it was Santra.[34] Perhaps it is unsurprising that out of all of the girls whose speech I analysed, Santra's realisations of quotative and discourse particle *like* were least similar to those of the CR girls.

Other NCR girls also exhibited strong NCR trends. These include Vanessa (The Goths), Joy (The Geeks), Isabelle (The Real Teenagers), Marama (The Pasifika Group), and Esther (The Christians). These were girls who expressed feeling different from other girls at the school and they were proud of these differences.

The girl with the most atypical trend for a CR girl was Patricia from The Sporty Group. Though the majority of her tokens of quotative *like* had the /k/ dropped, she was less likely to produce the /k/ in discourse particle *like* than in quotative *like*. Patricia had some Māori ancestry, though she did not identify strongly as Māori. I mention this because her speech patterns in terms of *like* were similar to those of two other non-Pākehā girls, Marama and Kanani, and because she had some features of Māori English in her speech despite not identifying strongly as Māori. She was also not a central member of her group. Though she liked The Sporty Girls, her closest friends went to schools other than SGH. Most of her social time while away from school was with these other girls. As shown in Example 18, Patricia felt disconnected from the majority of girls at SGH.

(18) Patricia, The Sporty Girls, 24-07

>Patricia: oh yeah
>I just come here and I learn pretty much
>
>[laughter]
>
>Patricia: yeah
>
>KD: that's good
>
>Patricia: yeah I get along with the people but
>I don't really . know

---

[34] Another girl who was highly likely to reject norms was Onya (the Real Teenagers), whose speech was not analysed because she did not take part in the perception experiment. However, it is worth noting that it was upon noticing the NCR trend in Onya's speech that led me to look at the variable in the speech of the other girls.

3 Like: Frequency and phonetic realisations

> you know . that many people really well
> like . say hi to them and stuff but yeah
>
> KD: mm
>
> Patricia: and it was kind of hard
> 'cause I came in at the start of fourth form
> and everyone had made their groups
> . and known each other and stuff
>
> KD: oh yeah
>
> Patricia: and I was just like
> yeah I had to try and fit in then

In fact, Patricia felt so disconnected from The Sporty Girls that she did not refer to them as her group. When using the term 'my group', she was referring to her friends who went to other schools, as shown in Example 19.

(19) Patricia, The Sporty Girls, 24-07

> Patricia: I reckon I'm a lot different at school than I am to the outside school actually
>
> KD: really?
>
> Patricia: yeah
>
> KD: how?
>
> Patricia: um . 'cause I'm more comfortable around you know my own friends and my own group

It is likely that Patricia conformed to the patterns of her friends outside of SGH, with whom she identified more strongly, rather than to those of the SGH group with whom she was friendly.

That girls such as Santra, Marama, and Patricia did not embrace the norms established by the CR girls suggests that their pattern of /k/ realisation for quotative and discourse particle *like* was an active manipulation of a linguistic variable to construct their identity as someone who was distinct from the CR girls.

Like Patricia, Kanani (Sporty Girls) was more likely to produce realisations of *like* associated with NCR girls. Kanani, who was of Pacific Island descent, used to be in The Pasifika Group but changed to The Sporty Girls at the beginning of the year. As a result of the switch, The Pasifika Group was no longer friendly toward her and she wanted nothing to do with them. Though she was extremely friendly and readily accepted by girls in her new group, she resisted becoming a part of the group entirely and would instead seek out my company, sometimes even when I was sitting with another CR group. Outside of school, she spent time with her new group of friends, with friends from other schools, and with her family. Given her previous membership in a NCR group and her continued dismissal of CR norms, it is not surprising that she did not entirely adopt the production patterns of the CR girls. (Though see more on Patricia and Kanani in Chapter 6.)

Two of The Goths, Meredith and Tania, did not exhibit strong NCR trends and were instead more likely to produce /k/ in discourse particle *like* than in quotative *like*. Tania was previously a member of a CR group (Relaxed Group) but had left the group because she felt that the friendship contributed to her eating disorder. Though she was no longer friendly with girls in The Relaxed Group, she interacted occasionally with girls in other CR groups, especially toward the end of the year. She did not reject their expectations as actively as many of her friends in The Goths and her realisations of *like* more closely resembled those of the CR girls.

That Meredith's realisations of *like* patterned more similarly to the CR girls than the NCR girls is surprising; I expected them to pattern with those of her best friend, Vanessa. The motivation behind her adoption of CR trends is rather speculative. It's possible that she adopted variants produced by her other close friend, Tania. It is also possible that she diverged from the speech patterns of Isabelle, with whom she had a falling out earlier in the year. It is also possible that she was less opposed in general to the norms of the CR girls. She wore clothing that could have been worn by members of The Relaxed Group and she had lost a great deal of weight in the previous year, perhaps signalling a willingness to conform to society's expectations of beauty. She was also the Goth who, as discussed in Chapter 2, had first claimed to be "normal". After being met by silence from her friends she changed her stance toward normalcy, claiming that she was weird and stating that normal was boring. Interestingly, both Meredith and Tania were among the girls with the highest rates of discourse particle *like*. This function was used more often by, and associated with, CR girls. Though they were in a NCR group, it seems that Meredith and Tania had patterns of *like* that resembled those of CR girls. That the patterns in their production of *like* were not consistent with those observed for other girls in their group demonstrates how stylistic resources need not have a one-to-one relationship with a social group; there may be alternative motivation behind some variants observed.

3 Like: Frequency and phonetic realisations

Another NCR girl who produced CR-like trends in her production of *like* was Holly (Sonia's Group). Both Holly and Sonia talked about The PCs as though they were friends, though I never saw them interact. Holly did not eat lunch in the CR nor did she sit with The PCs, but from the way she talked about them, it was clear that she looked up to them. She may have adopted similar speech patterns in terms of *like* as a result of identifying with The PCs.

3.4.6 Reflection on influence from researcher

Social characteristics of a researcher can influence the realisation of phonetic variables (Rickford & McNair-Knox 1994). Additionally, varying levels of familiarity with a researcher can influence production (Cukor-Avila & Bailey 2001). How, then, can I be sure that my presence and the constantly shifting interpretation of my identity did not influence the girls' realisations of *like*? The truth is, I can not be sure and in fact, it is unlikely that my presence did not influence their production.

I grew up using both quotative and discourse particle *like* and my native dialect (Southern California English) is a dialect closely associated with discursive functions of *like* in language ideology in the U.S. It is possible that a similar stereotype exists in New Zealand. In fact, different girls at the school informed me that they started using *like* after watching the movie 'Clueless', which was set in Southern California. It is possible that some of the girls accommodated to, or diverged from, my pronunciations of *like*. For this reason, I present a short analysis of *like* from my own speech, both when speaking to CR girls and when speaking to NCR girls.

3.4.6.1 Methodology

Tokens from my speech were selected from recorded interviews with girls whose speech was analysed for the production results presented in this chapter. Because analysis of their speech displayed socially-conditioned variation only for quotative and discourse particle *like*, these were the functions analysed for my speech. Tokens from interviews with CR girls and NCR girls were analysed separately in order to determine whether we had converged on each other's speech. 10 tokens of quotative *like* and 10 tokens of the discourse particle from interviews with girls from CR and NCR groups were analysed, resulting in a total of 40 tokens of *like*. Results based on the girls' speech indicated that the socially-meaningful phonetic variable was the realisation of the /k/. Therefore, this was the only phonetic cue analysed for tokens from my speech.

3.4.6.2 Results

The analysis demonstrates that I overwhelmingly realised the /k/, regardless of the function of *like* and regardless of who I was speaking to. Of all 40 tokens analysed, only three did not have the /k/ present. Two of these were when speaking to NCR girls and included both a quotative and a discourse particle and the other token was a quotative when speaking with girls in a CR group.

3.4.6.3 Discussion

The strong tendency to drop the /k/ in quotative *like* and realise the /k/ in discourse particle *like* that was observed among the CR girls was not found in my speech. In fact, I most often produced tokens of *like* with the /k/ realised, regardless of the discourse pragmatic function or the constellation of stance of the addressee. I did not converge on the speech of either the CR or NCR girls when addressing them; apparently, I am not the skilled accommodator that I thought I was.

3.4.7 Storage of phonetic detail in the mind

The phonetic realisation of *like* at SGH depended on a combination of the function of *like* and the social grouping of the speaker. This poses a challenge for theoretical frameworks with identical, non-probabilistic phonetic representations for homophonous and polysemous words (e.g., Levelt, Roelofs & Meyer 1999), as they would predict a single realisation for all types of *like*. The current findings lend support to production models with a lemma level that is indexed directly to acoustic information, or one in which lemmas with identical phonological forms have separate lexeme levels, each associated with acoustic information. Cognitive models that can account for these results are discussed in Chapter 5. If mental representations are indexed directly to lemma-based representations, it may be possible to observe an effect in perception, where individuals could identify a lemma based solely on phonetic cues in the auditory signal. The following chapter reports on three speech perception experiments conducted at Selwyn Girls' High, with the aim of shedding light on the degree to which listeners are sensitive to the relationship between lemma, social, and phonetic information.

4 Variation in speech perception

This chapter presents results from three perception experiments. First, I provide a short review of the production data and discuss the hypotheses that the experiments set out to test. Then I present the methodology and results from each experiment. Finally, I briefly discuss the theoretical implications of the findings. A more in-depth theoretical discussion can be found in Chapter 5.

As discussed in Chapter 3, acoustic analysis of the girls' speech indicates that different girls produced phonetically different tokens of *like* that varied systematically depending on the token's function and on whether or not the girl was in a group who ate lunch in the common room. Tokens with a higher F2 value at the nucleus target (i.e. a fronter nucleus) were more likely to be a discourse particle than a grammatical function (i.e. either the lexical verb or the adverb). A larger /l/ to vowel duration ratio, a lower mean pitch, and a more diphthongal vowel were more likely to be produced in both the grammatical functions of *like* and the discourse particle than in the quotative. There were also two results that depend on an interaction between social group and the function of *like*. (1) CR girls were more likely to realise the /k/ in the discourse particle than in the quotative, and NCR girls were more likely to realise the /k/ in the quotative than in the discourse particle. (2) CR girls were more likely to produce a long /l/ to vowel duration ratio in the discourse particle compared with the traditionally grammatical functions, and NCR girls were more likely to produce a long /l/ to vowel ratio in the grammatical functions.

These findings provide evidence in favour of acoustically rich or acoustically-informed lemma-level representations and they raise questions about the degree to which the relationship between phonetic, social, and lemma-based information is stored in the mind. If perceivers are sensitive to this relationship during perception, this would provide further evidence that the mental representations are stored in such a way as to allow indexing between the different types of information. Exemplar Theory (see §5.3.2) predicts that both lemma-conditioned and socially-conditioned phonetic variation observed in production should influence an individual's perception of the variants. A series of perception experiments was designed and conducted in order to test this hypothesis.

All Year 13 students were invited to take part in a series of three perception experiments. Forty-two girls chose to take part during the two weeks that the experiment was run. Additional girls offered to take part but, due to time constraints, were not able to participate before the debriefing I gave at the year's last assembly.

The experiments were run using a Praat script and a Gateway laptop computer. Participants listened to the tokens over Sony Dynamic Stereo Headphones (MDR-V300).

As stimuli, all three experiments used clips of speech from informal interviews conducted with girls at the school, so some participants responded to stimuli comprised of their friends' or their own speech. A recording of a male New Zealander reading the question numbers was played prior to an individual question's stimuli.

All auditory stimuli contained the word *like*, where *like* was either the discourse particle, the quotative, or a grammatical function. A token of lexical verb *like* was used as the grammatical function whenever possible, but due to low token numbers for some speakers, the adverb was also sometimes used as it was found to be phonetically similar to lexical verb *like*.[1] I use the term grammatical *like* to refer to the traditionally grammatical functions (as opposed to discourse pragmatic functions) used as stimuli.

Tokens were spliced from the original signal using Praat. They were spliced at the nearest zero-crosspoint to the segment boundaries outlined for the production analysis in Section 3.3.1. All tokens that were labelled as having the /k/ present also had the /k/ released. There were no acoustic modifications made to the waveforms.

After completion of all three perception experiments, participants were recorded reading the context sentences used in the second perception experiment. The list of sentences used as a production task is provided in Appendix C. The production task was conducted with the intention of comparing the production and the perception of *like* for a single speaker. However, during the reading task, girls consistently produced the diphthong and the /k/ for all tokens of *like*, regardless of function or social group.[2] Therefore, acoustic phonetic analysis was

---

[1] Other grammatical functions were not frequent enough in the data to be included in the preliminary phonetic analysis. Compared to all of the discursive functions, lexical verb *like* and adverbial *like* were most phonetically similar in terms of all phonetic factors tested in the production data.

[2] It was my impression that girls were not engaging with the meaning of the words when reading the passage. For example, they often read the first part of a sentence (e.g., *I was like*), paused, and then continued on with the rest of the sentence (e.g., *only two seconds behind*).

not conducted on the reading passage and production trends from spontaneous speech were used instead to compare an individual's production and perception.

A number of girls from a variety of groups were invited to take part in the experiment. Due to lack of interest on their part and time constraints on mine, not all girls who participated in interviews took part in the perception experiment. A total of 42 girls took part, 23 of whom were in groups that ate lunch in the CR.[3] Table 4.1 shows the number of girls from each group who took part in the experiment.

To test the degree to which speaker-specific phonetic trends in production influenced their perception, models were first tested on a subset of the data: responses from the 28 girls whose speech the production results were based on (Chapter 3). As discussed in Section 5.3.2, Exemplar Theory predicts that trends in a speaker's production will influence their perception. However, speaker-specific phonetic information was not found to influence perception significantly, either on its own or as part of an interaction.[4] Therefore, the reported results were based on data from all 42 girls who took part in the experiments.[5]

---

[3] One girl, Kristy (The BBs), was in a group that ate lunch in the CR, but she rarely ate lunch with her friends and would instead do school-sponsored activities during lunchtime. However, she is included as a CR girl in this analysis due to her choice of friends and her acceptance of similar values to the other CR girls.

[4] Although speaker-specific production patterns did not reach significance in the model, the directionality of the patterns' relationship with perception in Experiment 1 suggests that there may be a link between the production and perception of /k/ realisation. Using the difference between the speaker-specific random effects' coefficients of discourse particle *like* and quotative *like* from a production model of /k/ realisation, the speaker-specific likelihood of producing /k/ in the discourse particle relative to the quotative was tested as a predictor in the perception model. Participants who were more likely to realise the /k/ in the discourse particle than the quotative were more likely to identify the first token as the quotative if the second token had the /k/ present, and participants who were less likely to realise the /k/ in the discourse particle than in the quotative were less likely to identify the first token as the quotative if the second token had the /k/ present. In Experiment 1, this trend is approaching significance (p=0.06). It is possible that if acoustic phonetic analysis was conducted on speech for a greater number of speakers, this interaction would reach significance. For questions in Experiment 2 where /k/ presence was mismatched across the two tokens, girls who were more likely to drop the /k/ in discourse particle *like* were more likely to identify the token with the /k/ as the quotative than were girls who were more likely to drop the /k/ in the quotative. This trend is in the expected direction but is not approaching significance (p=0.37).

[5] One participant (a CR girl) did not complete the last two tasks in Experiment 3 because the bell rang and she had to go to class. Her data were not included for Experiment 3.

4 Variation in speech perception

Table 4.1: The number of participants who took part in the perception experiment, by group

CR		NCR	
The PCs	4	Pasifika Group	1
Sporty Girls	2	The Goths	5
Trendy Altern.	4	The Geeks	4
Rochelle's Group	1	Real Teenagers	2
Relaxed Group	4	Sonia's Group	1
The BBs	8	Christians	2
		Sally's Group	3
		A Loner	1
Total	23		19

a) He was like...		b) He was like...	
..."what's that?"		a	b
...wearing this kind of visor thing.		a	b

Figure 4.1: Example question from Experiment 1: Participants matched two auditory tokens that contained *like* (here, *he was like* and *he was like*) to different grammatical contexts provided on the answer-sheet.

4.1 Experiment 1

4.1.1 Methodology

4.1.1.1 The task

In the first experiment, participants were played two clips of speech in a given question, each containing the word *like* spoken by the same girl. The voices of seven girls were included, four of whom were members of CR groups. The stimuli for each question was made up of either the quotative and the discourse particle or a grammatical function of *like* and the discourse particle. For example, in question 2, Isabelle was first heard saying *he was like* where *like* was a discourse particle in the source sentence *and HE WAS LIKE singing along to music* (Interview, 02-05). Isabelle was then heard saying *he was like*, where *like* was the quotative: *do I need to shave my legs and HE WAS LIKE "naw"* (Interview, 02-05). Participants did not hear the disambiguating context. Upon hearing the clips (e.g., *he was like*), they were asked to match each of the auditory stimuli with one of the contexts provided on the answer-sheet, as shown in Figure 4.1.

Participants were told that each of the sound clips was taken from a sentence similar to one of the contexts provided and that there was a one-to-one mapping between a context and an auditory token. In other words, one token was taken from a sentence similar to one of the contexts on the answer-sheet and the other token was taken from a sentence similar to the other context on the answer-sheet. They were asked to circle (a) for the context they felt went with the first sound clip and to circle (b) for the context they felt went with the second sound clip. The majority of girls circled the corresponding letter, but several girls chose instead to draw lines between the text representation of the auditory token on the answer-sheet and the context provided. I treated both response techniques as equivalent during analysis.

4.1.1.2 The stimuli

None of the contexts on the answer-sheet were actual excerpts from the interviews. This allowed for control of the phonological environment that followed *like*. The first sound was matched between contexts of the same question in order to avoid response biases due to coarticulation in the source sentence.

The order of the different functions of *like* was pseudo-randomised. Half of the auditory tokens of grammatical and quotative *like* were played before the discourse particle. Ten of the questions compared grammatical-discourse particle pairs and twenty compared quotative-discourse particle pairs. Grammatical *like* and quotative *like* were not compared in Experiment 1 due to the low number of occurrences where their preceding context was matched.[6] Additionally, because tokens were difficult to find given the low number of recordings I had transcribed at the time of designing the experiment, some tokens were used as stimuli in more than one question. The stimuli are listed in the order they were played in Appendix C.

There was no training session for the experiment and it was hypothesised that participants may fail to respond to the first question. Therefore, the first pair of stimuli was repeated later in the experiment. This resulted in a total of 31 pairs of tokens. After all 31 questions were played, the same 31 questions were repeated in the same order. In the second half of the experiment, the contexts for each question were presented in the same order on the page and the auditory tokens were played in the reverse order; if the discourse particle was played first in the first half, it was played second in the second half. This was done in order to remove a potential effect of token order.

Contexts were presented so that the context containing the discourse particle was first on the page for half of the questions. The context order and the order of auditory stimuli were mismatched, so that half of the time that the discourse particle context was first on the page, the auditory token of discourse particle *like* was played second.

The stimuli for a given question were matched as closely as possible. In some cases, the match was identical at the lexical level (*He was like* and *He was like*). However, in some cases the pair was not identical (*They were like* and *They're like*). This was due to the small number of identical phrases found in spontaneous speech within the recorded interviews for a single girl. Care was taken to match clips that were as similar as possible at the lexical level. In Pākehā (European) New Zealand English, quotative *like* is more likely to occur with the historical present (i.e. present tense morphology with a past temporal reference), as in *he is like*, than with the past tense, as in *he was like*. It is also most likely to occur with the first person singular (e.g., *I was like*) (Buchstaller & D'Arcy 2009). None of the experimental stimuli for a given question differed in both of these respects, but some differed in either tense or person. Questions where the contexts were lexically matched (matched preceding) were labelled separately from those where there was a mismatch. Mismatched questions for which the first token was

---

[6] For example, it would be possible to compare an adverb, as in *oh no it was LIKE the coat tie* (Gina, The PCs, Interview, 16-05), with a quotative, as in *he was dancing naked in my room last night and it was LIKE "dih"* (Isabelle, The Real Teenagers, Interview, 02-05), where both the adverb and the quotative were preceded by *it was*. However, at the time of designing the experiment, too few suitable adverbs were identified.

either in the historical present or in the first person (i.e. questions where the first token had the more frequently observed context for quotative *like* than that of the second token) were labeled as 'likely preceding', and mismatched questions for which the first token was the less frequently observed context compared with the second token were labelled as 'unlikely preceding'.[7]

The auditory stimuli were intentionally designed to represent a wide range of phonetic cues upon which the listeners could potentially rely instead of being representational tokens of the different types of *like* from each group. This was done in order to determine whether participants would use particular phonetic cues to determine what word they had heard and whether their responses were congruent with trends in the girls' production. Phonetic characteristics of the different tokens in the quotative and discourse particle pairs are shown in Table 4.2 and phonetic characteristics of the tokens in the grammatical and discourse particle pairs are shown in Table 4.3. Only phonetic characteristics that significantly predicted the functions in the production models are shown in the corresponding tables. All tokens were played twice.

Table 4.2: Potential phonetic cues in Experiment 1 for quotative-discourse particle stimuli, by type and social group

	CR		NCR	
type	quote	dp	quote	dp
monophthong	2	2	1	0
/k/ present	4	5	6	3
ave. mean pitch	226.3	243.2	217.6	271.3
ave. duration ratio	0.40	0.29	0.31	0.36
matched prec.	5		8	
number of tokens	11	11	10	10

---

[7] There is some evidence that for Māori English speakers, quotative *like* is more likely to be produced in the past tense than in the historical present (D'Arcy 2010). Because the vast majority of the participants in the current study were speakers of Pākehā English, I use the terms 'likely' and 'unlikely' to refer to the organization of the stimuli, although these terms would not be appropriate for an ethnicity-based investigation.

4 Variation in speech perception

Table 4.3: Potential phonetic cues in Experiment 1 for quotative-grammatical stimuli, by type and social group

type	CR		NCR	
	gram	dp	gram	dp
ave. nuc. F2 (Hz)	1574	1535	1381	1451
number of tokens	5	5	5	5

4.1.2 Results

Of the 2604 possible responses, 108 questions were not responded to and are not included in the analysis. Overall, participants performed at chance level when identifying the function of an auditory token of *like* (50.7% correct). A high accuracy rate was not anticipated given the non-representative phonetic features included in the stimuli.

In order to determine whether participants used phonetic cues to identify the word and whether these cues were consistent with trends in production, two mixed effects models were fit to the data from Experiment 1. The first model is based on responses to questions that compared the quotative with the discourse particle and the second model is based on responses to questions that compared the discourse particle to a grammatical function.

4.1.2.1 Experiment 1, Model 1: The quotative and the discourse particle

Model 1 includes responses to 1690 questions comparing the quotative and the discourse particle from all 42 girls who took part in the experiment. It models the likelihood of identifying the first token as the quotative. This was done instead of modelling accuracy in order to test whether participants relied on phonetic cues in the stimulus when identifying a token, independent of the actual function of that token. This was particularly important given the unequal distribution of phonetic cues across the different function types.

The data were fit using R (R Core Development Team 2007) and the lme4 package (Bates & Sarkar 2007). Participant and question number were included as random effects in the model and only factors reaching significance were included as fixed effects. Factors that were tested but not included in the model were degree of monophthongisation, whether the participant was in a CR group, and whether the quotative stimulus had the /k/ realised. Also tested was how far through the experiment the participant was at the time of responding as well as whether the response was during the first or second half of the experiment. Fixed effects that were included in the model, shown in Table 4.4, were whether the first context on the answer-sheet was the quotative (quote second) and the difference between the /l/ to vowel duration ratio of the first and second auditory token (duration ratio diff.). Also included was a three-way distinction between whether the preceding context of the first token was less frequently observed in production with the quotative (preced. unlikely), more frequently observed (preced. likely), or whether the preceding context was matched at the lexical level (preced. match).

An estimated scale parameter is a measure of how the actual variance in the data compares to the variance assumed by the model. For a perfectly fit model, the value would be equal to 1. For this model, the estimated scale parameter is 0.9989158, which indicates that the model is a good fit.

Table 4.4: Experiment 1 coefficients of fixed effects from Model 1, comparing responses to the quotative and the discourse particle

	Estimate	Std. Error	z value	$Pr(>|z|)$
(Intercept)	0.8036	0.1337	6.009	< 0.0001
quote second	−1.0213	0.1056	−9.669	< 0.0001
preced. match	−0.2847	0.1387	−2.053	0.04007
preced. unlikely	−0.4539	0.1706	−2.660	0.00781
duration ratio diff.	−0.7200	0.2519	−2.858	0.00426

The estimates provided for each factor in Table 4.4 are in log odds and can be taken as an indication of how robust the effect of each factor is. The estimate for the intercept is the likelihood of identifying the first token as the quotative given the default factors. The model assumes as defaults that the quotative context is listed first on the answer-sheet and that the first auditory token has a preceding context that is more likely than that of the second auditory token. It also assumes that the difference between the /l/ to vowel duration ratio of the first and second token is zero, which indicates that /l/ to vowel duration ratios of the first and second token were equal to one another. To determine the degree of a categorical factor's effect, that factor's estimate should be added to the intercept's estimate. For gradient factors, such as the difference in duration ratio, the product of the estimate and the value for a given token is added to the intercept's estimate.

Participants were significantly more likely to identify the first auditory token as the quotative if the quotative context was listed first on the answer-sheet ($p<0.0001$). This trend reflects an overall bias for participants to identify the first token heard with the first context on the sheet. This bias is the forced-choice equivalent of an acquiescence response set (the tendency for participants to answer 'yes' for yes/no questions in experimental work), an effect which is commonly found in the psychology literature (cf. Bentler, Jackson & Messick (1971)). The experiment design controlled for this by counterbalancing the auditory stimuli. Therefore, the influence of phonetic cues could be examined above and beyond the response bias. Additionally, including this factor in the model allowed for examination of other potential factors that influenced responses; the model held this constant when testing effects of the other factors.

Participants were less likely to identify the first token as the quotative if the first auditory token of *like* had an 'unlikely preceding' context ($p<0.01$) than if it had a 'likely preceding' context. This was in the expected direction given the trends described in Buchstaller & D'Arcy (2009). Responses to tokens that were matched for preceding context fell between the two mismatched question types. When identifying the function of a token, participants appear to have used their implicit knowledge about the syntactic distribution of contextual information that is associated with quotative *like*. This finding provides evidence that individuals were sensitive to lemma-specific contextual information during perception. In order for perception to be influenced by the preceding context, chunks of speech that carry this syntactic information could be stored and indexed to the stored lemma. Chunks of speech that are larger than a single word could be stored as a cloud of exemplars or an abstract representation.[8] It is also possible that probabilities about context could be updated through experience. These possibilities are discussed further in Chapter 5.

In production, quotative *like* was more likely to have a smaller ratio of /l/ to vowel duration than discourse particle *like*: the /l/ was shorter in quotative *like* than in discourse particle *like*, relative to the duration of the vowel. In perception, participants were less likely to identify the first token as quotative *like* if it had a larger duration ratio than the second token ($p<0.01$). In other words, perceivers'

---

[8] Interestingly, the two Māori English speakers who participated in the experiment responded in the opposite direction from the Pākehā participants with regard to this factor. This is consistent with trends in the production of quotative *like* in Māori and Pākehā Englishes described by D'Arcy (2010). Further work is needed to determine the extent to which perceivers from different social groups use lemma-specific contextual information that is consistent with socially-conditioned trends from production. All girls were included in the analysis presented in this chapter, regardless of ethnicity.

responses were consistent with trends in their production.

These results are discussed in more detail in Chapter 5. First, I present the second model for Experiment 1 and the methodology and results from Experiments 2 and 3.

4.1.2.2 Experiment 1, Model 2: Grammatical functions and the discourse particle

A second model was fit to the data for questions comparing grammatical functions of *like* with the discourse particle, modelling the likelihood of identifying the first token played as the grammatical token. Most of the same potential predictors that were tested in Model 1 were also tested in Model 2 and only those factors that reached significance were included in the model.[9] Model 2 was based on 806 responses from 42 different girls. The estimated scale parameter of the model is 0.9942788.

Table 4.5: Experiment 1 coefficients of fixed effects from Model 2, comparing responses to the discourse particle and grammatical functions of *like*

	Estimate	Std. Error	z value	$Pr(>|z|)$
(Intercept)	0.3933	0.1003	3.923	< 0.0001
gram second	−0.8205	0.1789	−4.586	< 0.0001

As shown in Table 4.5, only one factor was included in the model: whether the grammatical context was listed first on the answer-sheet. The difference between the F2 values of the first and second tokens' nucleus target was not found to significantly predict responses.

Participants were more likely to identify the first token as the grammatical function if the grammatical function was listed first (p<0.0001). This parallels results from Model 1 where participants were more likely to identify the first token as the quotative if the quotative context was listed first. Both of these findings reflect an overall bias with identifying the first auditory token with the first context listed.

There were no questions in Experiment 1 that compared the quotative with a grammatical function of *like* due to the lack of tokens with comparable preceding

---

[9] The likelihood of the preceding context was not tested due to a lack of previous work exploring the distribution of contextual information in production.

4 Variation in speech perception

contexts. In Experiment 2, the preceding context was not included in the auditory stimuli, making a comparison between grammatical functions and the quotative possible.

4.2 Experiment 2

4.2.1 Methodology

4.2.1.1 The task

As in Experiment 1, participants in Experiment 2 were asked to match the word *like*, which had been spliced from spontaneous speech, with the contexts provided. In Experiment 2, however, participants were exposed only to the word *like*. Additionally, the voices of only four girls were used. All were from different groups at the school. The girls were: Tracy (The PCs), Rose (Relaxed Group), Onya (Real Teenagers), and Meredith (The Goths). Two of the girls (Tracy and Rose) were in groups who ate lunch in the CR and two of the girls (Onya and Meredith) were in groups who did not. Voices were selected to cover a range of girls from different groups. Additionally, I used voices of girls for whom a larger amount of speech was transcribed, as this made the tokens more easily identifiable in an automated search.[10]

In contrast to the longer clips in Experiment 1, the shorter clips in Experiment 2 allowed for a three-way comparison between the different functions of *like*. Five of the tokens for each voice were grammatical functions of *like* (either a lexical verb or an adverb), five were quotative *like*, and five were discourse particle *like*. Participants were asked to distinguish between grammatical and quotative *like*, grammatical and discourse particle *like*, and quotative and discourse particle *like*. The two auditory tokens for each question number were produced by the same speaker, and stimuli were blocked for each voice. After responding to 15 questions for each voice, participants were asked if they recognised the voice and were asked to identify the speaker if possible.

The contexts provided on the response sheet differed for each question within a single voice. The same contexts were used across the different voices, but they differed in the order they appeared within a particular question and the order in which the context pairs were listed. For example, the contexts for speaker 1, question 3 were in the following order: *I was like "Only if he asks me himself"* and *I was like only two seconds behind*, whereas they were in the opposite order for

---

[10] To identify tokens to be used as potential stimuli, transcripts were searched using the tool ONZE Miner (Fromont & Hay 2007).

4.2 Experiment 2

speaker 2, question 21. The question and context order are listed in Appendix C. As in Experiment 1, participants were told that the contexts were not the actual contexts from the interview but that they were similar. The manner in which they were similar was not made explicit.

After playing stimuli for all four voices, the first half of the experiment was repeated. The questions were presented in the same order as during the first half, but the order in which the auditory tokens were played within each question was reversed in order to counterbalance potential effects from a response bias based on the tokens' order. The contexts were presented in the same order as found in the first half of the experiment.

4.2.1.2 The stimuli

Potential phonetic cues in the stimuli are shown in Table 4.6 for each of the function types. Each token was played twice, once with each corresponding function type. For example, in the block for Tracy's voice, one discourse particle token (tracy-discp1) was compared with a grammatical token (tracy-like1) and a quotative token (tracy-quote1); and the quotative (tracy-quote1) and the grammatical (tracy-like1) were compared to each other. Only characteristics that were included in the production models are shown in the table. All tokens were played once in the first half of the experiment and then again in the second half.

Table 4.6: Potential phonetic cues in stimuli from Experiment 2, by type and social group

type	CR			NCR		
	quote	lex verb	dp	quote	lex verb	dp
monophthong	4	0	0	2	0	0
/k/ present	6	3	8	6	4	6
ave. dur. ratio	0.269	0.507	0.426	0.286	0.505	0.354
ave. nuc. F2	1619.5	1628.5	1694.26	1598.8	1477.8	1583.5
number of tokens	10	10	10	10	10	10

In Experiment 2, the 42 participants correctly identified the function of *like* 54.1% of the time. As there were only two possible answers in the task, participants' accuracy was roughly at chance. As with Experiment 1, a high rate of accuracy was not anticipated given the mix of phonetic cues included in the stimuli. Three mixed effects models were fit to the data in order to determine

135

4 Variation in speech perception

Table 4.7: Experiment 2 coefficients of fixed effects from Model 1, comparing responses to the quotative and the discourse particle

	Estimate	Std. Error	z value	Pr(>|z|)
(Intercept)	0.16468	0.09152	1.799	0.0720
quote second	−0.29861	0.12929	−2.310	0.0209
duration ratio diff.	−0.55828	0.27063	−2.063	0.0391

the extent to which perceivers relied on phonetic cues in the stimulus to identify the lemma. A number of factors were tested in the models and only those that reached significance were included as fixed effects.

4.2.2 Results

4.2.2.1 Experiment 2, Model 1: The quotative and the discourse particle

For questions that compared the quotative with the discourse particle, a model was fit that modelled the likelihood of identifying the first token as the quotative. It was based on 1650 responses from 42 participants. A number of factors were tested in the model, including the difference between the first and second tokens' Euclidean distance between the F1 and F2 of the vowel's nucleus and offglide. Also tested was whether the participant indicated that they recognised the voice. Only factors that reached significance were included in the model. As shown in Table 4.7, the fixed effects that were included in the model were whether the quotative was listed first on the answer-sheet (quote first) and the difference in the /l/ to vowel duration ratio of the first and second auditory tokens (duration ratio diff.). The estimated scale parameter of the model is 0.994807.

As for results from Experiment 1, participants were less likely to identify the first token as the quotative if the quotative context was listed second on the answer-sheet ($p<0.05$). Again, this reflects an overall bias toward matching the first auditory token with the first context on the sheet.

Also consistent with results from Experiment 1 was the effect of the difference in /l/ to vowel duration ratio between the first and second tokens. Participants were less likely to identify the first token as the quotative if the first token had a longer /l/ duration relative to its vowel than the second token ($p<0.05$). This is consistent with results from Experiment 1 and with results from production.

Table 4.8: Experiment 2 coefficients of fixed effects from Model 2, comparing responses to the quotative and grammatical functions of *like*

	Estimate	Std. Error	z value	Pr(>|z|)
(Intercept)	0.1724920	0.0954958	1.806	0.0709
F2 diff.	0.0011511	0.0005074	2.269	0.0233

4.2.2.2 Experiment 2, Model 2: Grammatical functions and the quotative

A model was fit to the 1652 responses that compared grammatical functions with the quotative, modelling the likelihood that a token was the quotative. The estimated scale parameter for the model is 0.9881647. As shown in Table 4.8, the only fixed effect that reached significance was the difference in F2 between the first and second tokens (F2 diff.).

F2 values were measured at the target of the nucleus in the stimulus tokens. Participants were more likely to identify the first token as the quotative if the first token had a greater F2 value (i.e. a fronter vowel in the nucleus) than the second token ($p<0.05$). Again, the estimated coefficients are in log odds. To determine the robustness of the effect of F2 for a given question, the product of the difference in F2 and the factor's coefficient is added to the estimated coefficient of the intercept. This finding is consistent with production; speakers were more likely to produce a fronter vowel in the nucleus of quotative *like* than in the nucleus of grammatical functions of *like*.

4.2.2.3 Experiment 2, Model 3: Grammatical functions and the discourse particle

A model was also fit to the questions that compared grammatical functions with the discourse particle, modelling the likelihood of identifying the first token as grammatical *like*. There were a total of 1648 responses from 42 different girls. The estimated scale parameter of this model is 0.9883807. As shown in Table 4.9, the only factor included as a fixed effect in the model was the difference in F2 between the first and second tokens.

Participants were less likely to identify the first token as the grammatical function if the F2 of the first token's diphthong nucleus was greater than that of the second token ($p<0.05$). This is consistent with the production results; speakers

Table 4.9: Experiment 2 coefficients of fixed effects from Model 3, comparing responses to the discourse particle and grammatical functions of *like*

	Estimate	Std. Error	z value	Pr(>|z|)
(Intercept)	−0.0416868	0.0756207	−0.5513	0.5815
F2 diff.	−0.0006476	0.0003086	−2.0983	0.0359

were more likely to produce a fronter vowel (with a higher F2) when producing discourse particle *like* than when producing a grammatical function. Though this factor did not reach significance in the model for Experiment 1, the relationship between response and the stimuli's F2 values in Experiment 1 is in the same direction as found in Experiment 2.

The difference in F2 can predict responses in three different models that compared grammatical functions with the discourse particle and the quotative. This is consistent with their behaviour in production. Crucially, the difference in F2 was not found to predict responses to questions that compared the discourse particle with the quotative, and this is also consistent with production.

The results from responses during Experiment 2 are very similar to those from Experiment 1. They provide supporting evidence that perceivers are sensitive to lemma-based phonetic variation. The third experiment investigated the relationship between phonetic, social, and lemma-based information in perception.

4.3 Experiment 3

Though there is growing evidence that perceivers attribute social information to a speaker based on phonetic cues in the stimuli (Giles & Powesland 1975; Bayard 2000; Campbell-Kibler 2007), the extent to which social information can be accessed is less clear in cases when the target social groups are not explicitly discussed by participants. Experiment 3 was designed to test the degree to which perceivers would consistently identify the place where a given girl might eat based on phonetic cues in the stimuli.

4.3 Experiment 3

4.3.1 Methodology

4.3.1.1 The task

In Experiment 3, participants were also asked to respond to isolated auditory tokens of *like*. The tokens were either a quotative or a grammatical function.[11] The speech of ten girls was used and they were equally divided by lunch locale. The CR voices were: Tracy (The PCs), Betty (Sporty Girls), Rachel (Sporty Girls), Anita (Relaxed Group), and Rose (Relaxed Group). The NCR voices were: Vanessa (The Goths), Onya (Real Teenagers), Meredith (The Goths), Isabelle (Real Teenagers), and Sarah (Real Teenagers).

The experiment was divided into three tasks, each with ten questions. Participants were told that the clips were from interviews conducted with Year 13 SGH students. For each question, they were asked to indicate whether they felt that the speaker was probably in a group that sometimes ate lunch in the common room (by circling "Y") or probably in a group that ate lunch outside the common room (by circling "N"). An example question is shown in Figure 4.2. They were also asked if they recognised the voice and to identify the voice if possible. This information was collected in order to determine whether recognition had an effect on responses. The same voices were used in the three tasks and they were played in a different order in the different tasks.

'I like toast.'

Does this person sometimes eat lunch in the Common Room?   Y   N
Do you recognise this voice?   Y   N
If so, who do you think it is?

Figure 4.2: Example question from Experiment 3

For the first task, all tokens were grammatical functions of *like*. Participants were informed that the tokens they would hear were taken from sentences where *like* had the lexical verb meaning, as in the sentence *I like toast*.

---

[11] At the time of designing the experiment, the production analysis had not yet been conducted. In hindsight, it would have been wise to include questions eliciting responses to the discourse particle.

4 Variation in speech perception

For the second task, the tokens were quotative *like*. The girls were informed that the tokens came from sentences similar to *He was like, "Yeah okay."*

For the third task, both the lexical verb and quotative tokens were played for each voice with the appropriate contexts provided. This was done in order to provide participants with a larger amount of lexically-conditioned phonetic information, as it was hypothesised that participant responses would be more accurate when more cues were provided. The token of quotative *like* was played second for each question.

4.3.1.2 The stimuli

Table 4.10 shows the number of tokens in Experiment 3 with phonetic cues that the participants may have used to identify a speaker's eating place. The lexical verb and quotative tokens were played once in the first and second task and these same tokens were repeated in task 3.

Table 4.10: Potential phonetic cues in stimuli from Experiment 3, by type and social group

type	CR		NCR	
	quote	lexical verb	quote	lexical verb
monophthong	2	0	0	0
/k/ present	1	5	3	3
number of tokens	5	5	5	5

4.3.2 Results

Participants in Experiment 3 performed at chance level, correctly identifying the eating place of the girl who produced the stimulus 52.1% of the time across all tasks. Participant responses were most accurate in the first task (with only grammatical functions) and least accurate during the second task (with only the quotative). However, the difference in accuracy between the tasks did not reach significance.

In order to determine whether perceivers used lemma-based phonetic cues when identifying a speaker as someone who ate lunch in the CR or not, a binomial mixed effects model with both question number and participant as random effects was fit to responses from Experiment 3, modelling the likelihood of identifying the speaker as someone who ate lunch in the CR. Of the 1260 possible responses, 36 questions were not responded to and were not included in the analysis.

A number of factors were tested in the model, including whether the stimulus had a vowel that was monophthongal or had a /k/ that was realised. Also tested was the task that the question was in, and whether the participant and stimulus voice were CR girls. Two factors reached significance in the model: (1) whether the participant believed they recognised the voice and (2) whether the question contained a token of quotative *like* with a monophthongal vowel. The coefficients for the model are shown in Table 4.11.

Table 4.11: Experiment 3 coefficients of fixed effects

	Estimate	Std. Error	z value	$Pr(>|z|)$
(Intercept)	0.46790	0.18834	2.484	0.0130
recognise = y	0.97158	0.19703	4.931	< 0.0001
no quotative token	0.04105	0.23599	0.174	0.8619
quote = monophong	0.72789	0.33996	2.141	0.0323

Whether the participant believed they recognised the voice significantly predicted responses, even if they incorrectly identified the speaker. Participants who believed they recognised the voice were more likely to indicate that the speaker was someone who ate lunch in the CR ($p<0.0001$). Participants identified a speaker correctly only 58.7% of the time that they believed they recognised the voice. While this is well above chance, it provides evidence that recognition of a voice does not equate with accurately knowing who the speaker was. In fact, when participants misnamed a speaker, they named someone from the same group as the actual speaker only 18.0% of the time. This suggests that if a voice merely sounded familiar, the speaker was identified as someone who ate lunch in the CR. The tendency to believe that the recognised voices were CR girls is not entirely surprising, as CR girls were more involved in school activities. They were talkative in class, they played sport, and they had leadership roles at the school. With few exceptions, NCR groups interacted with each other rarely and many were actually more likely to interact with CR girls. Therefore, a wider variety of students had exposure to the speech of CR girls. CR girls had less exposure to NCR girls (and their speech) than to other CR girls, and NCR girls had more exposure to CR girls (and their speech) than to girls from other NCR groups.

Also included in the model is whether the question contained a token of quotative *like* that had a monophthongal vowel. Participants were significantly more likely to identify the voice as someone who ate lunch in the CR if the question contained a token of quotative *like* with a monophthongal vowel than if it contained a token of quotative *like* with a diphthongal vowel (p<0.05). In production, NCR girls were more likely to produce variants of quotative *like* with a more diphthongal vowel (Wilcoxon, p<0.01).[12] The fact that participants were significantly more likely to identify tokens with monophthongal vowels as having been produced by a CR girl suggests that they used their knowledge of sociophonetic trends in production to identify the eating place of the speaker; monophthongal vowels were more likely to be observed in the speech of CR girls and, in perception, tokens with this phonetic characteristic were more likely to be identified as having been produced by a CR girl.

4.4 Discussion

In Experiments 1 and 2, participants were sensitive to the /l/ to vowel duration ratio in the stimuli when distinguishing between quotative *like* and the discourse particle. This duration trend in perception was consistent with the duration trend in production. Likewise, when responding to questions that included a grammatical token of *like*, participants in Experiment 2 responded to how fronted the diphthong's nucleus was in a way that was consistent with production. Taken together, these results suggest that perceivers can use their knowledge of lemma-conditioned phonetic variation from production to identify lemmas in perception.[13]

In Experiment 1, participants also relied on syntactic information to identify whether or not a given token was quotative *like*. Their responses were consistent

---

[12] This did not reach significance in the production model because it did not interact with function type; NCR girls were more likely to produce more diphthongal tokens, regardless of function type.

[13] If indeed the production trend regarding /l/ to vowel duration ratio is a result of prosodic position, individuals' sensitivity to the /l/ to vowel duration ratio in perception may reflect an ability to use this phonetic cue to extrapolate the likelihood of prosodic trends, which are then used during the experiment to determine the likelihood of the token being a particular function of *like*. Cutler & Clifton (1984) found little evidence to suggest that speakers use lexical stress to identify grammatical categories. This apparent conflict between their results and the results presented in this book may be due to differences between the methodologies, different types of stress, or other factors not discussed here.

with lemma-conditioned syntactic variation in production. This suggests that participants were not only sensitive to lemma-conditioned phonetic variation but also lemma-conditioned contextual variation.

Participants in Experiment 3 were more likely to identify voices as NCR girls if the participant did not believe they recognised the voice and if the stimulus contained a token of quotative *like* that had a monophthongal vowel. Here again, perception is consistent with production: CR girls were more likely to produce monophthongal vowels in the different functions of *like*. This provides some evidence that perceivers were sensitive to sociophonetic trends from production when identifying the eating place of each girl.

4.4.1 Lack of social effects in function identification tasks

In the production model, there is a significant interaction between whether the speaker was a CR girl and whether the /k/ was realised. In Chapter 3, I argued that the observed interaction was a result of the girls' identification with, and avoidance of, norms established by the CR girls. But why was there no evidence of perceivers' sensitivity to this socially-conditioned variation?

In the clips of speech that were used as stimuli, the recording ended directly after the token of *like*. In Experiment 3, all of the tokens of *like* where the /k/ was realised were also released (and were, therefore, easily identifiable as having the /k/ present). However, the participants had no way of knowing that if a /k/ was present, it would be released. Tokens with a velar closure but without a release are difficult to identify as having the /k/ present unless they are followed by another segment, particularly a vocalic segment. Without the following environment included in the stimuli, participants may not have been able to distinguish between tokens where the /k/ was realised and tokens where it was dropped, leading them to rely on phonetic information other than the presence or absence of /k/.[14]

Another possibility is that observing sociophonetic effects in perception relies on the degree to which the perceivers are aware of the linguistic variable and possibly also its tendency to pattern with certain social characteristics. Results from

---

[14] This may also be responsible for the lack of a significant correlation between a participant's production and their perception. Realisation of /k/ was the phonetic variable that varied most across different speakers; there was little variation for the other phonetic factors across the different discursive pragmatic functions. For example, with little deviation from the widespread trend of producing a monophthong in quotative *like* and a diphthong in other functions, it was statistically unlikely to observe an effect of production on perception in regards to the diphthong.

4 Variation in speech perception

Hay, Nolan & Drager (2006) provide some evidence that sociophonetic trends in perception are stronger for variables for which the variation is above the level of consciousness in the community; vowels with realisations that are more stigmatised and commented on are affected more than other vowels and the effect is strongest for lexical items that are strongly associated with these highly salient realisations. At SGH, the girls were not aware of the variation in /k/ realisation across the different functions of *like*; it was not commented on and they expressed surprise when I described some preliminary results regarding the differences in /k/ realisation across the different functions for the different groups. Awareness of a sociolinguistic variable does not appear to be necessary in order for that variable to covary with social group, stance, and style during speech production. In contrast, some level of awareness may be necessary to observe sensitivity to such trends in speech perception or else a larger number of tokens per experiment and a larger number of subjects may be required to observe the more subtle trends that we might expect when examining the perception of patterns that are below the level of consciousness.

A third possibility is that the lack of an effect is due to experiment design. I intentially chose tokens that were not representative of the two groups, thinking that it would help tease apart whether listeners were using the variables I identified during analysis or some other cues in the signal. However, the stimuli are not balanced for the different phonetic variants and the variants present in the stimuli may be "at odds" with other cues in the signal, making it less likely that listeners would/could use social information when completing the task.

4.4.2 Theoretical implications

These results provide evidence that perceivers are sensitive to the relationship between phonetic, social, and lemma-based information during perception. In production, phonetic variation depends on the social group of the individual and the function of the token. In perception, individuals are sensitive to the relationship between phonetic and lemma-based information. They also extract community-specific social information about the speaker, depending on whether they recognise the speaker's voice and whether a token has a monophthongal vowel. This suggests that social, phonetic, and lemma-based (syntactically/semantically-defined) information is stored in, or indexed to, the lexicon and can be accessed during the perception of speech.

The results also provide evidence that individuals store and use information about the surrounding context. Quotative *like* is most frequently found in the first person and in the historical present, and individuals appear to have used this information to identify the lemma. This suggests that not only are probabilities of contextual information beyond the word level stored in the mind but moreover that they are used during speech processing.

These findings are consistent with an exemplar-based model of speech perception and production in which utterances are stored in the mind complete with fine-grained phonetic detail and indexed with other social and contextual information observed at the time of the utterance (Johnson 1997; Pierrehumbert 2001; 2002). The results presented here indicate that such information must include the grammatical function of a token. Possibilities for how this information may be stored will be discussed in the following chapter.

5 Toward a cognitive model of stylistic variation in identity construction

In this chapter I discuss the results presented in this book within the context of two probabilistic linguistic models of language use: one that uses Bayesian statistics to calculate the probability of the different interpretations of an ambiguous sentence (Jurafsky 1996; Narayanan & Jurafsky 2002) and one where utterances are stored as separate exemplars complete with phonetic detail (Johnson 1997; Pierrehumbert 2001). I then present a usage-based model of speech production and perception that has multidimensional representations of stylistic features abstracted over detailed episodic memories. First, I briefly summarise the results presented in this book.

5.1 Summary of results

5.1.1 Maintaining and rejecting norms

At SGH, there were a number of norms that were established and maintained by the girls. Based on whether a group ate lunch in the common room (CR) or not (NCR), I have used the terms CR and NCR to differentiate between the girls who created and conformed to the school's norms, thereby perpetuating the norms themselves (CR), and the girls who rejected the norms and did not conform to them (NCR). The CR and NCR groups form constellations of stance: the CR girls viewed themselves as "normal" whereas the NCR girls viewed themselves as "weird" or "different". These stances were reflected in the girls' styles: there were commonalities in the linguistic and non-linguistic stylistic components observed among the girls in different CR groups, and while NCR girls varied across groups in terms of the stylistic features they adopted, they shared a common trend in that their identities were constructed in opposition to the styles of the CR girls.

5 Toward a cognitive model of stylistic variation in identity construction

5.1.2 Patterns in production

As presented in Chapter 3, there was phonetic variation across the different functions of the word *like* and some of this variation depended on whether the speaker ate lunch in the CR or not. Tokens of quotative *like* were more likely to be monophthongal, have a higher mean pitch, and have a shorter /l/ to vowel duration ratio than tokens of discourse particle *like* and traditionally grammatical functions. Tokens of grammatical functions were more likely to have a lower F2 value in the nucleus than the discourse particle. There were also two interactions involving the realisation of /k/:

(1) When comparing the two discursive functions, there was an interaction between /k/ realisation and where the speaker ate lunch: CR girls were more likely to realise the /k/ in the discourse particle than in the quotative, whereas NCR girls were less likely to realise the /k/ in the discourse particle than in the quotative.

(2) In the model comparing the discourse particle with the traditionally grammatical functions, there was an interaction between the /l/ to vowel duration ratio and the speaker's social group: CR girls were more likely to produce the discourse particle with a long /l/ whereas NCR girls were more likely to produce the grammatical functions of *like* with a long /l/.

Section 3.4.5 discussed how the individual girls' use of phonetic variants in the word *like* was related to the degree to which they accepted or rejected norms. Because a girl's eating place reflected her stance as "normal" or "different", this finding provides evidence that linguistic variables are correlated with a speaker's stance and that speakers actively adopt and reject linguistic variants as part of the construction of their identity.

5.1.3 Patterns in perception

As discussed in Chapter 4, the girls were sensitive during perception to some of these lemma-based phonetic differences from production. For questions comparing the quotative with the discourse particle, participants were more likely to identify a token as the quotative if it had the shorter /l/ to vowel duration ratio, a tendency that was consistent with trends observed in production. For questions in Experiment 2 that compared a traditionally grammatical function with either of the discursive functions, participants were more likely to identify tokens as the grammatical function if they had a lower F2 target in the nucleus. This trend was

5.1 Summary of results

also consistent with production. Although not all trends from production were observed in perception, all phonetic-based trends manifested in the perception data reflected the trends in the production data. A summary of these results is shown in Table 5.1.

Table 5.1: Summary of perception results from Experiments 1 and 2

factor	gram/quote	quote/dp	gram/dp
nucF2	X		X
EucD			
pitch			
duration ratio		X	
glott			
k present			

In addition to the perception results outlined above, there was an effect of syntactic information on lemma identification. In Experiment 1 there was contextual information preceding the token of *like* and it was not matched at the lexical level for all questions (e.g., *He was like* vs. *He is like*). Participants were more likely to identify the token as the quotative when preceded by the contexts that Buchstaller & D'Arcy (2009) found to be the most frequent for the quotative in New Zealand English. This provides evidence that individuals can use probabilisitic contextual information during speech processing.

In Experiment 3, participants were more likely to identify a voice as belonging to someone who ate lunch in the CR if they indicated that they recognised the voice. Due to CR girls' high visibility at the school, girls from all groups had extensive exposure to the speech of CR girls, and when a perceiver indicated recognition of a voice (even if they incorrectly identified that voice), they were more likely to indicate that the voice belonged to a CR girl. Perceivers were also more likely to identify the speaker as a CR girl if the stimulus contained a token of quotative *like* that had a monophthongal vowel. Because CR girls were more likely to produce monophthongal vowels in all of the functions of *like* analysed, this provides evidence that perceivers were sensitive to sociophonetic trends from production when identifying the eating place of the speaker during perception.

In the following sections, I discuss the theoretical implications of the quantitative results from production and perception, and I present an experience-based

5 Toward a cognitive model of stylistic variation in identity construction

model in which both linguistic and non-linguistic stylistic components are indexed to a speaker's style.

5.2 Social theory

5.2.1 Phonetic information and identity construction

In constructing their personae, individuals sometimes make conscious decisions about what symbols to adopt based on the meanings indexed to the symbols. For example, Eckert (2005a) describes how particular girls at Palo Alto High School adopted components of other groups' styles that indexed only those characteristics with which they identified (Eckert 2005a: 457). These components were then recombined as part of a process of *bricolage*, a term coined by Lévi-Strauss (1974) that refers to the disassembly of an existing whole into parts that can be recombined in the creation of a new whole. However, the meanings indexed to the stylistic components can be different for different individuals. For example, Supré is a chain of stores in Australia and New Zealand that sells clothing, much of which is revealing and inexpensive. They give free canvas bags of different colours to people who purchase clothes from their shop. At SGH, the use of Supré bags carried a particular social meaning that was usually described as "skanky". While some girls felt that all Supré bags indexed "skanky", others felt that only the hot pink ones carried this meaning and that bags in other colours, like black, were an indication that the user liked a bargain. This example helps to portray how individuals segment styles into meaningful elements but the meanings are not necessarily the same for all individuals in a community.

As with clothing, linguistic variables can be manipulated depending on their indexation to socially-constructed meanings. Zwicky (1997) explains how speakers can adopt variants associated with individuals with whom they identify (identification). Alternatively, they can avoid using variants that are associated with individuals who they do not want to be similar to or do not believe themselves to be similar to (avoidance). A speaker can also identify with (or avoid) a particular style shared across numerous individuals, as opposed to associated with a single individual.

As discussed in §3.4.2, both quotative and discourse particle *like* are highly frequent words that are themselves imbued with social meaning. I argue that this makes them likely loci of socially-meaningful phonetic variation. At SGH, girls in the different constellations of stance adopted and rejected linguistic variables to construct their social personae. I argue that CR girls conformed to each other in terms of their realisation of /k/ in quotative and discourse particle *like*, whereas NCR girls did not conform to one another; the similar trends in terms of /k/ realisation resulted from a common divergence from the speech of the CR girls. This similarity among girls in NCR groups may be due to chance or, as discussed in §3.4, it may be due to the exploitation of trends already present in the distribution of /k/ realisation that arose as a function of how likely a speaker was to use quotative *like*.

In the following section, I discuss how stylistic variation as part of identity construction can be incorporated into a hybrid model that uses both episodic and abstracted representations: it is possible that both acoustically-rich exemplars and abstract representations of multi-dimensional social information are stored and accessed during the production and perception of speech.

5.3 Probabilistic linguistics

The results provide evidence that mental representations of phonetic information are acoustically-detailed and that their distributions are stochastic: patterns involving gradient phonetic information such as duration and diphthongisation can be observed in both production and perception. There are several ways that this probabilistic and acoustically-detailed information could be represented. It is possible that the probabilities are abstracted from the signal such that exposure to new utterances updates the previously stored probabilities (Norris & McQueen 2008). Another possibility is that the utterances themselves are stored and frequency distributions arise as a function of this storage (Pierrehumbert 2001). There is also the possibility that stored representations are made up of some combination of episodic memories, abstracted categories, and distributional probabilities. For example, exemplars of utterances could be stored complete with acoustic detail and used while accessing phonetic information, and probabilities and categories could be abstracted and stored (rather than computed online) for processing of higher-level (e.g., syntactic) information. Different levels of the grammar may rely on different levels of representations but, as evidenced by the link between phonetic, contextual, social and lemma-based information observed in the SGH data, these stored representations must be indexed to one another.

5.3.1 Bayesian model of syntactic parsing

In a Bayesian model of speech processing, probability distributions over a set of encountered variables are stored. They are then used during speech process-

5 Toward a cognitive model of stylistic variation in identity construction

ing to determine the most likely candidate given the specific context (Norris & McQueen 2008) and social information associated with a linguistic form can influence what is identified as the most likely candidate (Casasanto 2009). Norris & McQueen (2008) implemented a Bayesian model of speech processing based on phonemes (called Shortlist B) and they state that the model could just as easily be implemented using other units at a prelexical level of processing, including bundles of features and position-specific allophones (Norris & McQueen 2008: 362). They assume that "word recognition necessarily involves a comparison of the evidence in the current acoustic input with stored knowledge about the phonological form of words" (Norris & McQueen 2008: 379). It is unclear from their description whether this "knowledge about the phonological form" could include detailed phonetic information such as the probability of a segment being observed with a particular duration. In their Bayesian model of phonetic imitation, Nielsen & Wilson (2008) use feature representations (+spread glottis) to encode phonetic detail (VOT), and something similar could be implemented in Shortlist B. Results from the perception experiments presented in Chapter 4 indicate that fine phonetic detail such as the duration of the /l/ relative to the vowel duration affects a perceiver's identification of a word and therefore such information needs to be stored in a form that maintains the multidimensional and gradient nature of the phonetic signal.

Although Bayesian models have yet to be applied to the production and comprehension of patterns involving fine phonetic detail, they are successful at predicting trends in human parsing of syntactic structure during reading tasks. Narayanan & Jurafsky (1998; 2002) implemented a Bayesian-based model in which probabilities of preceding contextual information, such as tense, contribute to the overall probability of different interpretations of thematically ambiguous structures; the model prunes parses that have a low probability. As described by Narayanan & Jurafsky (2002: 59), *the cop arrested* is ambiguous: *the cop* could be the agent, as in *the cop arrested the crook*, or the theme, as in *the cop arrested by the detective was guilty of taking bribes*. Because *cop* is most likely to be the agent when followed by *arrested*, reading times are slower when it is the theme. Their model predicts this because it incorporates probability distributions specifying the most likely tense and argument structure for every verb.

The perception results presented in Chapter 4 provide evidence that perceivers were influenced by the preceding context of a lemma and that the effect of the preceding context was consistent with previously observed trends from production. In ambiguous contexts such as *I was like*, where *like* could be either the quotative or the discourse particle, participants were more likely to identify tokens as the quotative if they were preceded by the first person pronoun. Buchstaller & D'Arcy (2009) found that in New Zealand English, quotative *like* is more frequently found with the first person pronoun than with the third person pronoun. Therefore, an interpretation where a token of *like* is the quotative has a higher probability when the preceding context is in the first person than the third person. In the task, perceivers were simply asked to identify which of the two tokens of *like* was the quotative and which was the discourse particle; the task did not require a comparison of probabilities across all words in that context. In Narayanan and Jurafsky's model, each interpretation of an utterance receives a probability based on previous experience. The tense and person most often encountered with quotative *like* would contribute to the overall probability of an interpretation of the utterance where *like* is the quotative. This would bias responses toward identifying a token as quotative *like* when the preceding contextual information is that which is most frequently observed.

If context-dependent probabilities of lemmas are stored, they may also be accessed during speech production. Jurafsky, Bell & Girand (2002) found that the probability of a word given its context was linked to the duration of that word; the more predictable the word, the more likely it was to have a shorter duration. The interaction between /k/ realisation and relative frequency of use that was observed in the SGH data supports Jurafsky, Bell & Girand's (2002) finding and provides evidence that the effect is speaker-specific; if, when producing a quotative, a speaker's probability of producing quotative *like* is high, a token of quotative *like* that is produced is less likely to have the /k/ present.

Another model that could account for the observed bias in lemma identification is one that computes the probabilities online during speech processing. This online computation could occur in a model where each lemma from the context is stored as a cloud of exemplars, and lemma-level exemplars from a given utterance are either indexed to each other or stored as an utterance-complete exemplar. An exemplar model of speech production and perception is discussed in the next section.

5.3.2 Exemplar Theory

A model of speech production and perception that relies on the storage and retrieval of acoustically-rich detail is based in Exemplar Theory. In an exemplar model of speech production and perception, utterances are stored in the mind as episodic memories (exemplars) (Pisoni 1997) complete with acoustically detailed information (Goldinger 1997; Pierrehumbert 2001; 2002). For example, if a listener hears a speaker produce an utterance such as *look at the cat*, the theory assumes that the listener stores the word *cat* with all of the acoustic detail inherent in the signal. This includes the quality of the /a/, speaker-specific qualities such as nasality and, if the /t/ was released, the exact quality of the release. The stored exemplar for *cat* is indexed to exemplars from the rest of the utterance. Phrases that are encountered at a very high frequency can be stored as a single representation (Bybee 2006). Attention paid to speech influences the activation of the exemplars through attention weights on the exemplars (Nosofsky 1986). Greater attention results in greater weight, which in turn results in greater activation.

Phonetic information in the signal is indexed to a separate cloud of phoneme-level exemplars. For the utterance *look at the cat*, the attributes of [k] in *cat* are indexed to a label /k/. This phoneme-level exemplar is in the same cloud, or is even the same label, as the phoneme-level exemplar /k/ that is indexed to the attributes of [k] from *look*. Pierrehumbert (2006) refers to this type of model that combines acoustically-rich exemplars with abstract labels as a hybrid model. She argues that it can account for results which provide evidence that speaker-specific information is stored (e.g., Goldinger 1997) as well as results that suggest abstractions are required, such as the opposite effects on word recognition of two highly correlated factors: likely phonotactics and neighborhood density (Vitevitch & Luce 1999).

In addition to linguistic contextual information, exemplars are indexed to a myriad of other factors that are stored at the time of the utterance. These include the formality of the situation and the social characteristics of the person who produced the utterance (Johnson 1997; Foulkes & Docherty 2006). Again, salience plays a role. Non-linguistic information is only stored if it was available at the time of the utterance and if it may be important to the perceiver (Johnson 1997: 147). A sketch of this indexation is shown in Figure 5.1 for an exemplar cloud of the word *fishing* within the context of Trudgill's (1972) finding that females were more likely to realise word final /ŋ/ as the velar nasal [ŋ] whereas males were more likely to realise it as the alveolar nasal [n]. Exemplars representing encountered utterances produced by males and females are indexed both to the phoneme level (e.g., /ŋ/) and to characteristics of the speaker who produced the utterance (e.g., male).

During production, the final realisation is a result of averaging over an entire region of an exemplar cloud. There is not a one-to-one mapping of activated exemplar to the token that is ultimately perceived or produced (Pierrehumbert 2001). This is in contrast to some presentations of exemplar models where a one-to-one mapping is assumed (Griffiths et al. 2007). Exemplars which have

5.3 Probabilistic linguistics

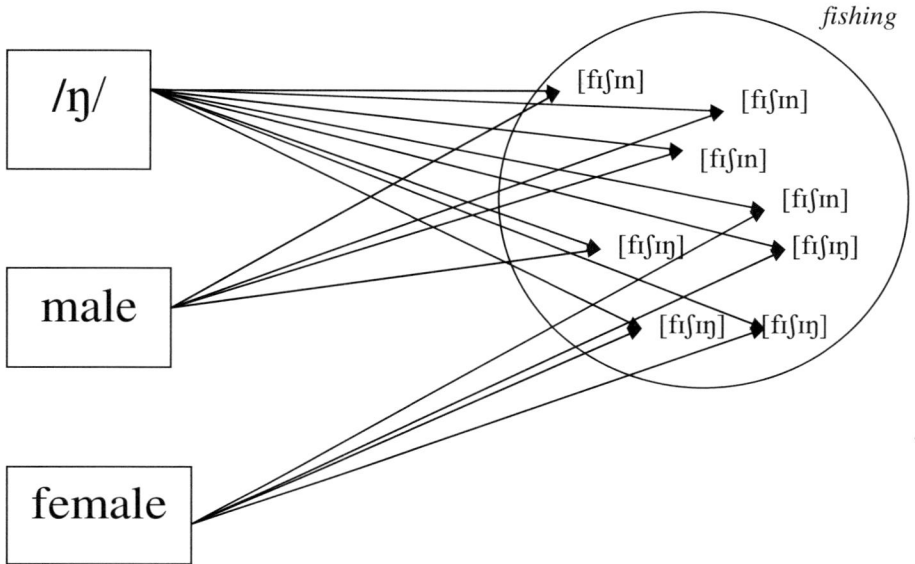

Figure 5.1: Sketch of exemplar model based on results from Trudgill (1972) with distributions of remembered exemplars of the word *fishing*. Each exemplar is indexed to a label for phonemic category (/ŋ/) and speaker sex (male and female).

been activated recently and those which are activated frequently carry the highest weight values, resulting in a bias in production toward variants resembling these exemplars. As with perception, non-linguistic information indexed to the exemplars can bias which variants are produced. After storage, exemplars immediately begin to decay and frequent activation slows decay. This activation can occur through encountering an acoustically similar utterance.

The region of an exemplar cloud that is activated during production may be selected as a result of its indexation to social factors with which the speaker identifies. Additionally, social characteristics of an addressee activate social exemplars, thereby biasing production toward the speech of that addressee in ways that depend on the speaker's attitudes toward the interlocutor (Drager, Hay & Walker 2010; Babel 2012). This prediction is consistent with the well-known effects of audience design and speech accommodation (Bell 1984; Giles, Coupland & Coupland 1991; Hay, Jannedy & Mendoza-Denton 1999).

During perception, exemplars are activated to varying levels depending on their similarity to the incoming utterance. If incoming social information closely matches a previously stored social exemplar, the linguistic exemplar indexed to the social information will receive partial activation. These partially-activated exemplars reach full activation faster than acoustically similar exemplars that are not indexed to a relevant social exemplar, resulting in a bias in perception depending on the perceived social characteristics of the speaker (Strand & Johnson 1996; Niedzielski 1999; Hay, Warren & Drager 2006).

Thus, exemplar-based models such as these predict a bias in both production and perception toward socially relevant exemplars. Additionally, because different words with the same wordform are indexed to different lemma-specific phonetic information, exemplar models predict that (1) there can be lemma-conditioned phonetic variation in production that patterns according to exposure (a speaker's realisations will resemble those of other speakers with whom they regularly interact) and (2) individuals can use phonetic information based on trends in production to identify a lemma during speech perception. And because exemplars are stored complete with acoustically-detailed information, it predicts that trends in production can be phonetically gradient and that individuals will be sensitive to acoustically-detailed information during the perception of speech.

It is important to keep in mind that the mental representations reflect what was perceived, not what was produced or, even, what could potentially have been perceived. This means that a number of factors, including attention, influence the form of the representation (Foulkes & Hay 2015).

In many cases, exemplar-based models and Bayesian-based models behave similarly. Pierrehumbert (2002) states that an exemplar model of speech production and perception should be viewed as

> a logical schema rather than taking it as a literal picture of activity in the brain. Any model which stores implicit and incrementally updatable frequency distributions over a cognitive map will show similar behaviour; it is not important that all percepts are individuated as separate memories in the long term. (Pierrehumbert 2002: 113)

Even if episodic traces of acoustically-rich utterances are not stored, each utterance could update the system in such a way that probabilities (with their base in frequency distributions) could be stored. However, as evidenced by the work in the previous two chapters, this needs to include probabilities of very detailed, acoustically-rich information as well as very rich social information.

In conceptualising this logical schema, it may help to view different modes of representation for different levels of the grammar. Rich phonetic detail of specific episodes may be stored and may influence both production and perception, and probabilities may also be abstracted and stored, influencing the production and perception of higher-level processes such as those involving syntactic information. For example, a Bayesian-based model could account for the effect of surrounding contextual information on lemma identification in Experiment 1 and an exemplar-based model could account for the lemma-conditioned phonetically gradient trends observed in production and the sensitivity to these trends observed in perception.

5.4 Indexation of social information

In current exemplar-based models, such as those described by Johnson (1997) and Hay, Warren & Drager (2010), the representation of social information that is indexed to acoustically-rich exemplars is consistent with variationist work from the First and Second Waves of variation studies, where phonetic variables are treated as indexed directly to social categories. These categories can be broad, as in the sketch in Figure 5.1, or can be locally constructed.

However, the representation of social information is much richer than this indexation would suggest. In this section, I step through how, in the construction of social personae, the adoption and rejection of linguistic and non-linguistic features might be understood within an exemplar-based hybrid model.

Work in the Third Wave treats linguistic variables as directly indexed to style. Style is complex; it is comprised of socially-meaningful components that can shift in meaning depending on other components indexed to the style. From situation to situation, the style of a single speaker can shift, sometimes subtly, sometimes dramatically.

A speaker's stance can serve to create that speaker's style. For example, if a speaker views themselves as "different" from the norm, they create their individual style through the expression of this stance. At SGH, goths and geeks created different styles from one another but because their stance was in opposition to a third group (e.g., The PCs or the CR girls as a whole), some of their styles could have components that resembled each other (e.g., patterns of /k/ realisation in quotative and discourse particle *like*).

Mendoza-Denton, Hay & Jannedy (2003) state that a usage-based probabilistic model is

> entirely compatible with a view of the social world that relies on gradually built up social categories that emerge from experiences that surround individuals as social actors. (Mendoza-Denton, Hay & Jannedy 2003: 136)

5 Toward a cognitive model of stylistic variation in identity construction

Yet, no one has spelled out how stylistic variation occurs within the context of a probabilistic linguistic model. One challenge that arises when trying to do so is that potential stylistic components not only come to be imbued with social meaning based on the presence of an item, activity, or characteristic but also from the absence of wearing certain items or from not taking part in certain activities. For example, Santra (The Goths, NCR) wore black clothes and the colour of the clothes was meaningful in that it helped to construct her social persona. But also meaningful was that Santra did not wear mini skirts or bright colours. One day when she wore a green shirt, someone commented that they had never seen her wear a bright colour before. Santra confessed that she didn't feel like herself and was looking forward to going home so that she could change clothes. Refraining from participating in certain activities (e.g., wearing bright colours), both linguistic and non-linguistic, can itself be socially meaningful and helps to contribute to a speaker's style. But if exemplar clouds are based on previously encountered occurrences, how does the lack of a characteristic or item of clothing become a stylistic component? The model presented here addresses this through the indexation of a speaker's style to different parts of multidimensional stylistic features: the part of the distribution to which a speaker's style is indexed indicates the degree to which that component is adopted in the construction of her style. Both identification and avoidance can occur through comparing how different styles index different parts of multidimensional representations of stylistic components.

In Figure 5.2, I present a sketch of Santra's (The Goths, NCR) style and Betty's (The Sporty Girls', CR) style within the context of an exemplar model of speech production and perception. Of course, a speaker's style is multidimensional and shifts depending on the situation. A speaker's shifting style may not be the overt abstraction implied by the sketch in Figure 5.2. Instead, components may be indexed to a representation of the speaker and that speaker's style could arise with particular patterns of activation over the components. This could account for how styles shift in ways that are sometimes subtle and sometimes dramatic. For simplicity, the styles modelled here represent the general styles that were consistently observed for the girls within the context of the school. Each of the components is based on their own cloud of exemplars, where the stored exemplars are representations of previous encounters with each of the girls.

In order for the lack of an item to become socially meaningful, comparisons must be made between potential stylistic components observed in a social arena. Different individuals will vary probabilistically in how they are indexed to these components and the components themselves become more socially meaningful

5.4 Indexation of social information

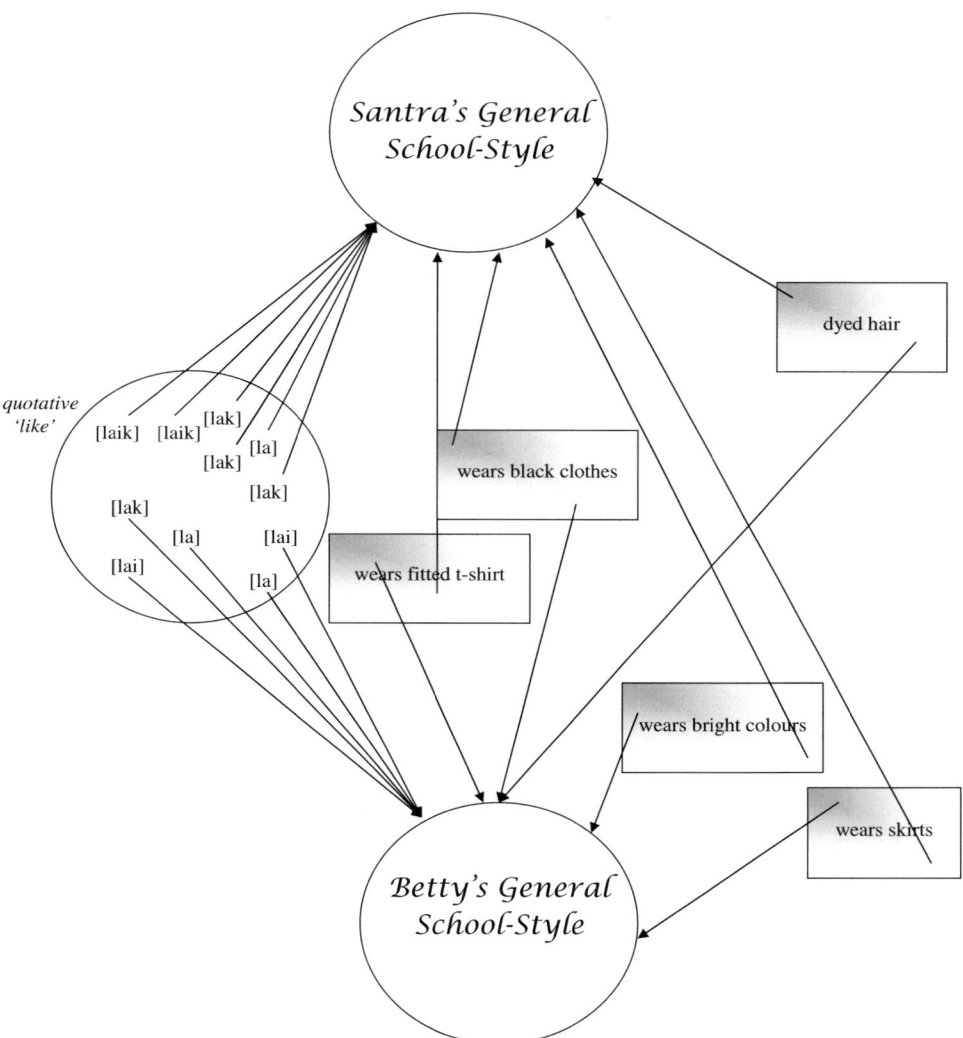

Figure 5.2: Sketch of two speakers' styles and their linguistic and non-linguistic components. The portion of the shaded box that is indexed reflects the degree to which an individual adopts or rejects that characteristic when constructing a given style.

5 Toward a cognitive model of stylistic variation in identity construction

the further apart the sections are that the different styles index. In Figure 5.2, this is displayed through indexing different regions of multidimensional components; different parts of the multidimensional representations are indexed depending on the likelihood of a girl possessing that item or characteristic. Here, I have treated the horizontal plane within each shaded box as frequency across time (e.g., some girls were more likely to wear a skirt than others) and the vertical plane as another dimension at a given point in time, such as the number of items worn in that colour or the length of a skirt when worn. For example, 'wears black' is labelled as a stylistic component and the styles of different girls are indexed to different parts of this abstract representation depending both on how often they wear black and, when wearing black, how much of their clothing is black. The style represented for Betty is indexed to the whiter region of the box, indicating that she wears black less than half of the time and, when even wearing black, does not wear many items that are black. This indexation reflects the probability that a single speaker will adopt one of these stylistic components, thereby constructing their personal style. Indexation can occur not only through the storage of exemplars based on experience with an individual, but through the comparison of that individual with others.

Not all items or characteristics that could potentially be components of an individual's style become imbued with social meaning. For example, both Santra and Betty wore tight-fitting t-shirts. Donning this type of shirt was not particularly meaningful in differentiating their different styles; this is reflected in their indexation to a similar space within this potential component. However, the colour of the top was potentially meaningful: Betty's might be blue or black depending on the day whereas Santra's was almost certainly black.

That indexation of stylistic components relies on comparisons also ensures that the lack of an item or characteristic is meaningful only within the context of a given social arena. This is desirable because traits that are completely absent from the reality of the social arena do not meaningfully affect an individual's style. For example, that Santra did not wear a tiara was not socially meaningful because none of the girls wore tiaras to school.

Linguistic variation, like the variation found among other stylistic components, can be converged upon or diverged from depending on both the speaker's attitudes toward an individual and how similar they believe they are to the individual. As with other stylistic components, indexation may occur not only between a speaker's style and a phonetically-rich exemplar representing an utterance produced by that speaker, but also through the absence of producing a particular variant. A sketch of this relationship is shown in Figure 5.3. While the sketch shows only two dimensions, the model is not limited in this way. Furthermore, it is important to note that speakers can shift their indexations between different parts of the mutlidimensional space and that this shift can occur throughout an interaction.

As with non-linguistic elements, linguistic components of style are multidimensional, with different styles indexed to different parts of the distribution. The dimensions represented in Figure 5.3 are frequency of use (along the horizontal plane) and the likelihood of realising the /k/ in any given token (along the vertical plane). For example, Marama's General School-Style is indexed to the portion of the distribution of quotative *like* where there is a relatively low likelihood of dropping the /k/ in addition to a lower frequency of use of the quotative when compared with many of her peers. In contrast, her School-Style is indexed to the portion of the distribution of discourse particle *like* where there is a high likelihood of dropping the /k/ and a low frequency of using the discourse particle relative to other girls at the school. Of course, other dimensions would include other information, such as the duration of a segment and the frequency bands of the formants. Such indexation to multidimensional representations of linguistic variables predicts that identity construction will result in convergence among speakers constructing similar styles to one another. Because distributions of these indices can be compared across different speakers, it also predicts divergence by individuals wishing to differentiate themselves from a particular style; indexation to the multidimensional space can be manipulated through comparison of stored indices of other speakers' styles to the space. A speaker can index a space that is void of exemplars and can do so in relation to the observed behaviour of the other speakers.

These patterns of activation over the multitude of components that comprise a style can explain how vowel shifts can occur within an exemplar-based hybrid model. In Pierrehumbert's (2001) model, vowel shifts could only be driven by a speaker producing variants outside the realm of previously stored exemplars as a result of random noise; there is no socially-driven motivation for vowel shifts built in to the model. However, it is highly unlikely that vowel shifts result entirely from random noise: individuals who lead vowel shifts are the same individuals who lead other stylistic changes (Labov 2001). For example, elementary school girls who produce the most extreme phonetic variants are the same individuals who begin wearing nail polish or lacy underwear (Eckert 1996b); they are the individuals who first adopt the most extreme components of styles from the heterosexual marketplace in the construction of their identity within an emerging peer social order. The model presented here, which combines

5 Toward a cognitive model of stylistic variation in identity construction

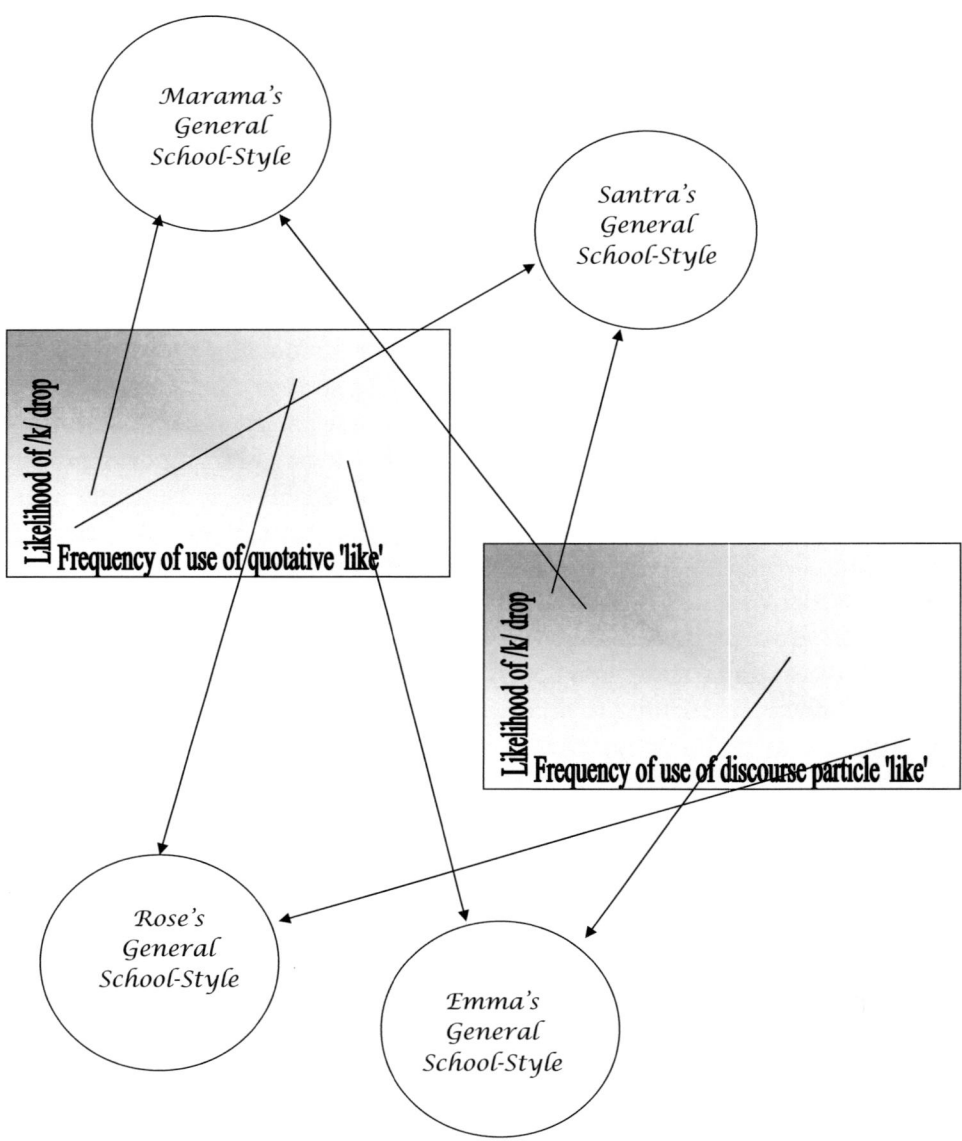

Figure 5.3: Sketch of indexation between multidimensional linguistic components and speakers' styles. For simplicity, only two dimensions are shown: frequency of using quoative *like* is shown on the x-axis and the likelihood of dropping the /k/ is on the y-axis.

acoustically-detailed episodic memories with multi-dimensional abstractions of the acoustic space, allows speakers to index these spaces that are potentially void of acoustically-rich exemplars. This indexation can have a direct effect on the variants produced; speakers constructing personae that are extreme within the context of a social arena can produce variants that are extreme in comparison to other speakers in that arena. Linguistic variation is a stylistic resource and the manner in which it is stored must allow for the construction of a speaker's identity.

5.5 Conclusion

In this chapter, I discussed two probabilistic models of language use and I described how they can account for the results presented in the preceding two chapters. The most comprehensive model may be some combination of these, incorporating both stored exemplars of utterances complete with acoustic detail and abstracted probabilities of phrase structures. In a model where clouds of phonetically-rich exemplars contribute to abstractions of multidimensional stylistic components, it is possible to account for phonetic variation that patterns according to stylistic choices made by the speaker.

6 Looking forward

> They may change their roles, their styles of acting, even the dramas in which they play; but – as Shakespeare himself of course remarked – they are always performing.
>
> (Geertz 1973: 35–36)

Individuals manipulate linguistic variables in the construction of their identities, displaying their communicative competence within the context of the social world in which they participate. Probabilistic models provide a means of uniting social and linguistic theory and this unification has been a driving force behind the methods and analyses used for this book.

In Chapters 2 and 3, the analysis concerned both the individual girls' styles constructed within the school and the components that make up this style, with a particular emphasis on stylistic phonetic variation of different words. The results presented in Chapter 4 display how individuals can use phonetic information when identifying a word, even when the words are identical at the phonological level, and that listeners can identify the function of a word and, to some extent, attribute social characteristics to the speakers based on phonetic information in the stimulus. In Chapter 5, I presented a probabilistic model of speech production, perception and identity construction in which multidimensional stylistic components are indexed to a speaker's style. My hope is that this model will serve as a stepping stone from which to explore the integration of social and linguistic theory in future work.

In the remainder of this chapter, I present one possible avenue of inquiry that I believe will aid our understanding of the way in which mental representations of sociolinguistic variables are accessed during the production and perception of speech, ultimately leading to a better understanding of human cognition.

6 Looking forward

6.1 Speakers as style-creators

Variationist sociolinguists who examine style are increasingly turning their attention to the individual (Eckert 1996a; 2011; Podesva 2011). This is important because individuals create stance and style during interaction and, therefore, stance and style need to be examined as processes that emerge in context (see e.g., Coupland (2007); Kiesling (2009); Rampton (2013). For example, Bucholtz (2010: 110–115) demonstrates how quotative variants used by high school students were influenced by a combination of the speaker's stance and their social group: preppy students were more likely to use *be all* when taking a neutral stance, whereas non-preppy students were more likely to use *be all* when taking a non-neutral stance. In her study on phonetic realisations of bilingual children, Kattab (2013) shows how the children sometimes adopt phonetic features from their parents' non-native English accents to do social work, shifting between native-like and non-native-like realisations in socially-meaningful ways. This work demonstrates how a single linguistic variant can be used to achieve multiple (and, in some cases, quite different) social goals. Work by Schilling-Estes demonstrates how speakers' sociolinguistic variants shift as a function of both their stances and the variants produced by their interlocutors (Schilling-Estes 2004). Finally, Kirtley (2015) demonstrates how individual speakers use different phonetic variants for social purposes, many of which can be perceived both as being consistent with a particular trait (e.g., masculinity) and as highlighting different aspects of that trait (e.g., the many different ways of being masculine and of doing masculinity).

When examining stance-taking and style-making by individuals, it is important to keep in mind the social groups to which these speakers orient. It is believed that linguistic forms are directly indexed to stances and that the linguistic forms become indirectly indexed with social groups who regularly take or are believed to take those stances (Bucholtz 2009; Du Bois 2007). Alternatively, it seems plausible that speakers wishing to construct a certain style or take a particular stance may do so by drawing on pre-existing indexations between (or ideologies around) linguistic forms and social groups. The reality is likely a combination of these, where a variable that is ideologically linked with a group is adopted to take stances that are habitually taken or are associated with that group, and that those variables can then become indexed with new social categories via the stances they enact.

In this book, I have examined stance and style across social groups and, though I recognise that stances and styles are not stagnant, I have largely treated them this way in my analysis. I have done this due to time restrictions and because I believe that variation in interaction has the most explanatory power when situated within a larger context for that variation. During stancetaking, speakers do not select linguistic variants out of the blue: the variants are indexed to social meanings (social meanings that can be multiple and complex) through ideologies around what kinds of people produce what variants. Therefore, understanding the ideologies and the ways in which variables pattern across social groups is important for understanding how the variables are manipulated in the construction of stance and style in interaction.

With this in mind, in Drager (2016a) I revisited the SGH data to gain insight into how the girls manipulated realisations of quotative and discourse particle *like* when taking various stances in interaction. The phonetic analysis was restricted to the tokens analysed for Chapter 3 of this book and focused on tokens from narratives that included references to other groups or individuals. The speakers' stances toward the referents were identified (removing those that were ambiguous or unknown) and the tokens were compared within the speech of a single individual.

Three trends emerged from this analysis that are especially noteworthy. The first is that, for some speakers, their interactional stances appear to be related to the frequency with which they produce discourse particle *like*. For example, The Goths (a non-Common Room group) frequently produced discourse particle *like*, but they did not produce any tokens when making claims about how they were different from other "normal" girls at SGH. Because the discursive functions of *like* are highly associated with Common Room groups (and The PCs in particular), the absence of discourse particle *like* in these segments helps to highlight that The Goths are different from the Common Room groups. The second trend that emerged is that some speakers' realisations of discourse *like* contained little phonetic variation.[1] The only speaker to produce both the quotative and discourse particle as [laik] for all of the analysed tokens was Mariah (The Geeks), who not only consistently realised the /k/ but produced it with a long release. Mariah generally produced clear speech, including the release of other stops, such as /t/. Articulation of stop releases is ideologically associated with intelligence, a trait that was valued by members of The Geeks, and strong releases have also been found to be used by geek girls in the United States (Bucholtz 1998: 125). Thus, Mariah's realisations of *like* help to construct her personal style.

---

[1] I noticed this during the analysis presented in Chapter 3 but, at the time, failed to comment on the importance of it for the construction of social meaning.

6 Looking forward

A third trend that emerged concerns the realisations of quotative *like* in which the speakers' evaluations of the referents differ, resulting in a change in footing (Goffman 1981). The speech of two girls, Patricia and Kanani (both from The Sporty Group, a CR group), is especially revealing. Patricia and Kanani were the two CR girls whose patterns of realisations of *like* were most similar to the NCR girls (see Section 3.4.5.1). In Chapter 3, I attributed this to their particular social histories and backgrounds: Kanani was formerly a member of a NCR group (so may still have had some NCR group speech characteristics) and Patricia's closest friends went to other schools (and her friends' patterns of realisations of *like* are unknown). However, after examining how *like* was used in interaction, I now believe Patricia and Kanani were doing something much more complicated and socially-meaningful: they seem to have been manipulating their realisations of quotative *like* as a part of their stancetaking toward the person whose speech they were reporting. An example from Kanani's speech is shown in Example 20.

(20) 1 Kanani: I remember this chick rung up (.) for my brother
      2   and um (.)
      3   hh she's like$_1$ "hi is Kimo there please"
      4   I'm like$_2$ "oh he's in the toilet at the moment" (.)
      5   she's like$_3$ (.) "thanks"
      6   <laughter>
      7 Rose: I would've been like "oh actually he's just
                    [really constipated"]
      8 KD: ["he's doing poos"]
      9 Rose: yeah
      10   <laughter:>
      11 Kanani: and then my brother came and got the phone
      12   and he's like$_4$ <raises eyebrows>
      13   he went off the phone he's like$_5$ "what a dick"

In this example, Kanani is telling a story about her popular and attractive brother, Kimo, receiving a phone call from a woman, a "chick" (line 1) who she had never met. Kanani was very close with her brother - she was very family-oriented in general - and didn't necessarily approve of the woman who called. Within the context of the conversation, Kanani positions herself as family-oriented and

6.1 Speakers as style-creators

down-to-earth, and the woman who rings up as coquettish and silly. These positionings align with the realisations of quotative *like*: when preceding her own or her brother's speech, the quotative is realised with a less diphthongal vowel and no /k/ (the "CR realisation"), whereas when introducing the speech of the woman on the phone, the vowel is diphthongal and the /k/ is present (the "NCR realisation"). These trends do not appear to result from phonological environment or speech rate: $like_5$ (line 13) is followed by /w/, an environment which promotes the realisation of /k/ in quotative *like*, but the /k/ is not realised. Likewise, given the relatively quick speech rate in $like_1$ (line 3), we might expect a monophthongal vowel but, in fact, the vowel is diphthongal.

Table 6.1: Phonetic realisations of tokens of *like* found in Example (20), adapted from Table 5 in Drager (2016b). The Euclidean distance (EucD) is shown in Bark and speech rate is syllables per second in the IP surrounding the token but does not include the token itself.

token	referent	EucD	/k/ present	syllables/sec
$like_1$	woman	2.24	y	4.88
$like_2$	Kanani	1.36	n	6.47
$like_3$	woman	2.53	y	2.78
$like_4$	brother	0.31	n	5.26
$like_5$	brother	1.53	n	4.08

In other words, when reporting the speech of someone who she aligned with, Kanani produces quotative *like* with a monophthongal vowel and non-realised /k/ (the CR realisation), whereas she produces it with a diphthongal vowel and [k] when reporting the speech of someone who she does not know or respect. This suggests that Kanani does not have imperfect acquisition of the variable as a result of changing from a non-Common Room to a Common Room group; instead, she demonstrates a sophisticated knowledge of both systems and appears to use it as a narrative device. In fact, it is possible that her social history provided her with greater (unconscious) control of the variable as a result of having greater exposure.

Some other girls (e.g., Meredith, Isabelle, and Patricia) demonstrate analogous trends, with appropriate realisations for their group (CR or NCR). For other speakers, a trend is less clear (or is non-existent as in the case of Mariah) and the analysis is complicated by ambiguous or unknown stances. Additionally, other

6 Looking forward

factors such as speech rate and pitch that are linked with the phonetic variables of interest are not controlled for in this type of analysis, which limits the data one can reliably use to examine variation of this type.[2]

In my estimation, the finding that phonetic realisations of quotative *like* are conditioned by interactional stance is more suggestive than conclusive due to the relatively small number of speakers and data points that demonstrate the trend. But, given the fact that other researchers have demonstrated that the form of the quotative (e.g., *be like* vs. *be all*) varies by stance, we might actually expect that the realisations of these highly salient words would vary, particularly when - like in these data - *be like* so strongly dominates the quotative system of all of the speakers. It is worth noting that the variation in the realisation of discourse *like* does not negate the quantitative findings presented in this book. Because only some individuals seem to vary their realisations of quotative *like* in this way and because the girls so frequently voice their own or their friend's speech, the trends reported in Chapter 3 do seem to be the most frequent realisations. In fact, the distinction between CR and NCR realisations is needed to interpret the stance-based variation reported by Drager (2016a). Taken together, the work suggests that speakers can use probabilistic patterns of sociolinguistic variables (including those tied with locally-constructed social categories) to help take stances during the course of an interaction, but much more work along these lines is needed.

6.2 Concluding remarks

The findings presented in this book demonstrate the benefits of combining qualitative and quantitative analysis and of examining variation in both production and perception. While I do not advocate abandoning traditional variationist description by any means, I do believe that inroads will be made by variationists who choose to explore multiple avenues of inquiry. In continuing the progression of social theory through the investigation of linguistic variation, sociolinguistics will benefit from increased focus on variation in speech perception in addition to production, using computational models to explore sociolinguistic assumptions and predictions, examining the behaviour of individuals within a single interaction, and using insights from other areas of empirical linguistics such as laboratory phonology. Additionally, laboratory phonology will benefit from incorporating more socially-informed data and analyses, not only by examining speakers' and listeners' social characteristics but moving toward a more

---

[2] Variation in speech rate and pitch can, of course, be socially meaningful. When they are, variation in related phonetic variables may in fact be an epiphenomenon.

nuanced treatment of socially-conditioned variation that includes a focus on the individual and the individual's goals in interaction. As sociolinguists have long argued, the division of language into the social and the non-social is artificial; the time is ripe for social theory and linguistic theory to be examined together within the context of unified models of language use.

Appendix

A Measures of familiarity

This appendix provides the names of girls in each group. Also provided is a number indicating how well I felt I knew each girl, where 5 is highly familiar and 1 is knew by name and sight only.

Girls who took part in the perception experiment and whose speech was analysed for the production study are marked with two crosses (++). Girls who only took part in the perception experiment are marked with a single cross (+).

A.1 CR Groups

A.1.1 The Sporty Girls

Table A.1: The Sporty Girls, by how central to group and how well I felt I knew them.

NAME	CENTRALITY TO GROUP	HOW CLOSE WITH ME
Naomi	main	3
Stella	main	3
Rachael	main	3
Elise	core	2
Candice	core	2
Patricia ++	fringe	3
Ruby	core	2
Betty ++	fringe	4
Kanani (previously of The Pasifika Group) ++	fringe	5

A *Measures of familiarity*

A.1.2 The PCs

Table A.2: The PCs, by how central to group and how well I felt I knew them.

NAME	CENTRALITY TO GROUP	HOW CLOSE WITH ME
Joanna	main	2
June	core/main	1
Tracy ++	core	4
Juliet ++	core	4
Emma ++	core	4
Kim	core	3
Pixie	core	3
Kendra	core	3
Daphne	core	3
Darby	core	2
Marilyn	core	2
Aurora	core	1
Zindri	core	1
Gabrielle	core	1
Minnie	core	1
Gina	fringe	2
Noelle	fringe	1
Amber	fringe	1
Cleo	fringe	1
Katya	fringe	1

A.1.3 Trendy Alternatives

Table A.3: The Trendy Alternatives, by how central to group and how well I felt I knew them.

NAME	CENTRALITY TO GROUP	HOW CLOSE WITH ME
Justine ++	main	3
Kelly	core	4
Clementine ++	core	3
Jewel	core	3
Carla	core	3
Christina ++	core	3
Felicity	core	2
Lily	fringe	5
Pascal +	fringe	4

A.1.4 Rochelle's Group

Table A.4: Rochelle's Group, by how central to group and how well I felt I knew them.

NAME	CENTRALITY TO GROUP	HOW CLOSE WITH ME
Rochelle ++	main	5
Camden	main/core	5
Chantelle	core	2
Mindy	core	2
Lorna (also friends with The Relaxed Group)	fringe	2

A Measures of familiarity

A.1.5 The BBs

The original BBs included Star, Madison, Jaclyn, Zara, Gwen, and Priscilla. The other half of the merged group (originally referred to as Pam's group) included Pam, Odette, Glenda, Jane, Shannon, Annie, Brooke, Andrea, Natasha, Ursula, Denise, Laura, and Maya. In Table A.5, names followed by an asterisk denote members of the subgroup usually referred to as the BBs. The other girls were a part of what was originally referred to as Pam's Group.

Table A.5: The BBs, by how central to group and how well I felt I knew them.

NAME	CENTRALITY TO GROUP	HOW CLOSE WITH ME
Star *	main	2
Madison *	main	3
Pam	main	3
Jaclyn *	core	3
Zara *	core	1
Priscilla *	core	1
Gwen *	fringe	3
Glenda +	core	4
Jane ++	core	3
Andrea +	core	5
Maya + (previously of The PCs)	core	4
Annie	core	3
Natasha	core	3
Ursula (previously of The PCs)	core	3
Brooke +	core	2
Becky	core	2
Shannon	core	1
Kristy +	core	1
Laura +	fringe	3
Odette	fringe	2
Tori +	fringe	1
Denise	fringe	1
Alexis (also friends with Cecily's Group)	fringe	1
Karen (also friends with Cecily's Group)	fringe	1

A.1.6 The Relaxed Group

Table A.6: The Relaxed Group, by how central to group and how well I felt I knew them.

NAME	CENTRALITY TO GROUP	HOW CLOSE WITH ME
Rose ++	main	5
Megan	main	4
Barbara ++	core	4
Anita +	core	4
Katrina ++	core/fringe	4
Lorna (also friends with Rochelle's Group)	fringe	2

A Measures of familiarity

A.2 NCR Groups

A.2.1 The Pasifika Group

Table A.7: The Pasifika Group, by how central to group and how well I felt I knew them.

NAME	CENTRALITY TO GROUP	HOW CLOSE WITH ME
Masina	main	3
Marama ++	core	4
Ariana	core	3
Angel	core	2
Ripeka	core	1

A.2.2 The Goths

Table A.8: The Goths, by how central to group and how well I felt I knew them.

NAME	CENTRALITY TO GROUP	HOW CLOSE WITH ME
Santra ++	main	4
Vanessa ++	core	5
Meredith ++	core	4
Marissa ++	core	4
Tania (previously of The Relaxed Group) ++	core	3
Stevie	core	1
Melinda	core	1
Judith	core	1
Bianca (previously of The Geeks) ++	fringe	5

A.2.3 The Real Teenagers

Table A.9: The Real Teenagers, by how central to group and how well I felt I knew them.

NAME	CENTRALITY TO GROUP	HOW CLOSE WITH ME
Onya	main	5
Claudia	main	3
Renee	main	3
Isabelle ++	core	5
Sarah ++	core	4
Alex (also friends with Cecily's Group)	fringe	5
Sally	fringe	4
Camelia	fringe	1

A.2.4 The Christians

Table A.10: The Christians, by how central to group and how well I felt I knew them.

NAME	CENTRALITY TO GROUP	HOW CLOSE WITH ME
Esther ++	main	5
Theresa ++	main	4

A *Measures of familiarity*

A.2.5 Sonia's Group

Table A.11: Sonia's Group, by how central to group and how well I felt I knew them. There were other girls in this group who I did not come to know.

NAME	CENTRALITY TO GROUP	HOW CLOSE WITH ME
Sonia	core	1
Holly ++	core	1

A.2.6 The Geeks

Table A.12: The Geeks, by how central to group and how well I felt I knew them.

NAME	CENTRALITY TO GROUP	HOW CLOSE WITH ME
Mariah ++	main	5
Joy ++	main	4
Kristen +	core	3
Nisha	core	3
Jamie	core	2
Aluna	core	2
Valentina	core	2
Aerial (previously of The Relaxed Group)	core	2
Bianca (also friends with The Goths)	fringe	4

A.2.7 Cecily's Group

Table A.13: Cecily's Group, by how central to group and how well I felt I knew them.

NAME	CENTRALITY TO GROUP	HOW CLOSE WITH ME
Cecily +	main	3
Sally	core	4
Alex (also friends with The Real Teenagers)	core	5
Pania +	core	2
Keira +	core	2
Lindsey	core	1
Erin	core	1
Alexis (also friends with The BBs)	fringe	1
Karen (also friends with The BBs)	fringe	1

A.2.8 Loners

Table A.14: Loners, by how well I felt I knew them. They were not friends and did not form a group; they are only shown together in the table for convenience.

NAME	HOW CLOSE WITH ME
Charlie +	2
Polly	1

B Production data

In this Appendix, the number of tokens with the different phonetic characteristics are listed separately for CR and NCR girls. The minimum pitch and the maximum pitch are identical for several tokens because tokens with a pitch more than two standard deviations from the mean were reassigned the pitch at the cutoff point (i.e. 76.44Hz for tokens with especially low pitches and 353.90Hz for tokens with especially high pitches). This was done in order to keep these tokens from biasing results. The maximum values for the F2 target at the nucleus may appear higher than would be expected for tokens of /a/. This is at least partly due to the fact that monophthongisation did not only occur through the lowering of F2 (and raising of F1) in the offglide but also a shift in F2 in the nucleus.

B Production data

Table B.1: Counts of tokens with particular phonetic features, by type.

feature	CR grammatical	quotative	discourse particle	NCR grammatical	quotative	discourse particle
total tokens	97	119	160	107	120	132
preceded by fricative	15	73	49	25	82	52
preceded by pause	4	0	28	6	2	24
preceded by other	78	46	83	76	36	56
followed by C	68	43	85	78	43	73
followed by pause	3	30	33	8	33	30
followed by V	26	46	42	21	44	29
min EucD (Bark)	0.0112	0.0000	0.0383	0.0736	0.0130	0.1272
mean EucD (Bark)	1.8000	1.2770	1.7620	2.0840	1.7190	2.0000
max EucD (Bark)	5.9370	4.3120	4.9170	4.8390	5.7690	5.0000
min nuc F2 (Bark)	7.907	9.136	10.08	8.777	8.764	9.826
mean nuc F2 (Bark)	11.320	11.410	11.620	11.110	11.460	11.340
max nuc F2 (Bark)	12.630	12.840	12.730	12.870	12.830	13.080
full glott	24	37	43	21	13	29
mid glott	10	15	22	12	16	23
no glott	63	67	95	74	91	80
min pitch (Hz)	76.44	76.44	76.44	82.4	76.44	76.44
mean pitch (Hz)	212.40	225.10	201.90	202.4	238.50	204.30
max pitch (Hz)	353.90	353.90	353.90	353.90	353.90	353.90
min duration ratio	0.0000	0.0000	0.0000	0.0000	0.0000	0.0000
mean duration ratio	0.4610	0.3591	0.4676	0.4850	0.3032	0.3814
max duration ratio	1.5060	1.5540	1.7630	1.5670	0.9441	1.2600
/k/ not realised	32	70	54	31	35	43
/k/ realised	65	49	106	76	85	89
a	5	29	6	5	12	5
ai	27	41	48	26	23	38
ak	4	7	0	1	1	3
aik	61	42	106	75	84	86

C Stimuli for perception experiments

This appendix provides additional information on the perception experiments described in Chapter 4. First, example answersheets for each experiment and the production task are provided. For the production task, participants read the sentences only once through. There were no instructions provided.

Next, the auditory tokens for each question are listed for each experiment, and they are labelled by type. Due to the difficulty of finding stimuli for Experiment 1 that were matched at the lexical level, some tokens were used for more than one question. It is possible that participants' exposure to the token the first time influenced their response to that token the second time. However, the results do not seem to be dependent on such an effect as they were replicated in Experiment 2 where there were no re-plays of tokens across different questions that compared the same functions.

C Stimuli for perception experiments

#_____

For this portion of the experiment, you will be asked to match recorded speech to the contexts provided. Although the provided context sentences are similar to what was actually said during the interview, these are not the actual sentences. All speech is taken from previously recorded interviews at the school. The speech you will hear is always two different utterances containing the word 'like'. For each question, the utterances are spoken by the same girl.

For each question, please read the two sentences. Then, match each example of 'like' that you hear to the sentence you feel it is MOST LIKELY to have come from. Circle (a) if the sentence goes with the first 'like' you heard, and circle (b) if the sentence goes with the second 'like' you heard. Please do not circle both (a) and (b) for any given question. Please answer all questions.

Work quickly and don't worry too much about your answer. There are no right or wrong answers here- I am simply interested in your intuitions regarding these words.

		1st sound	2nd sound
1. a.) I was like… b.) I was like…			
…gonna go til I heard that.		a	b
… "Go and grab it."		a	b
2. a.) He was like… b.) He was like…			
…"What's that?"		a	b
… wearing this kind of visor thing.		a	b
3. a.) It's like… b.) It was like…			
…something I've heard before but different.		a	b
… some guy she met at a party.		a	b
4. a.) He's like… b.) You're like…			
…hoping for the impossible.		a	b
…"Huh?"		a	b

Figure C.1: Answersheet for Experiment 1

5. a.) She was just like…   b.) She's like…

   …not all that.   a   b

   …"No way!"   a   b

6. a.) You like…   b.) I like…

   …sleeping in.   a   b

   …sat down with them   a   b

7. a.) It was like…   b.) It's like…

   …"Hmmm…"   a   b

   …hotter than the Sahara.   a   b

8. a.) It's like…   b.) It's like…

   …not has hard as you'd expect.   a   b

   …nothing I've ever seen before.   a   b

9. a.) She's like…   b.) She's like…

   …one of my closest friends.   a   b

   …"Well, maybe tomorrow."   a   b

10. a.) She was like…   b.) She was like…

   …"Oh cool."   a   b

   …only a little bit ahead.   a   b

11. a.) I like…   b.) They like…

   …go in to town after school.   a   b

   …going to town.   a   b

C Stimuli for perception experiments

12. a.) And they were like…   b.) And they're like…

    …"Instead of what?"   a   b

    …in front of the classroom or something.   a   b

13. a.) They're like…   b.) They're like…

    …"Um… okay…"   a   b

    …underneath the car for some reason.   a   b

14. a.) …he like…   b.) …he like…

    Does _____ snowboard?   a   b

    Does _____ snowboarding?   a   b

15. a.) I like…   b.) You like…

    …dancing more than he does.   a   b

    …do this funny dance.   a   b

16. a.) I was like…   b.) They were like…

    …"Really?"   a   b

    …really happy about it.   a   b

17. a.) He was like…   b.) He was like…

    …looking right at me when he said it.   a   b

    …"Look up."   a   b

18. a.) It's like…   b.) It was like…

    …having an effect.   a   b

    …"Who?"   a   b

19. a.) I was like…   b.) I was like…

   …an overly curious cat.   a   b

   …already going to go.   a   b

20. a.) It's just kind of like…   b.) It's like…

   …I wanted to but I didn't.   a   b

   …"I guess."   a   b

21. a.) She was like…   b.) She was like…

   …"No, I don't think so."   a   b

   …not able to just walk away.   a   b

22. a.) I like…   b.) You like…

   …him too much.   a   b

   …have so much luck it's crazy.   a   b

23. a.) It was like…   b.) It's like…

   …just down the road.   a   b

   …"Just kidding!"   a   b

24. a.) They're like…   b.) The girls are like…

   …"Can't you tell the difference?"   a   b

   …complaining to the teacher.   a   b

25. a.) I was like…   b.) I was like…

   …"Where do you think you're going?"   a   b

   …wishing he could go as well.   a   b

C Stimuli for perception experiments

26. a.) We were like…   b.) We were like…

   …opening the windows.   a   b

   …"Oh- are you sure?"   a   b

27. a.) …you like…   b.) …you like…

   I know that ____ when I ask questions.   a   b

   I know that ____ wish it were different.   a   b

28. a.) They're like…   b.) They were like…

   …"So, hun. What's your sign?"   a   b

   …so hot.   a   b

29. a.) Your Mum's like…   b.) She's like…

   …the only person I know who'd say that.   a   b

   …"That's exactly what I was thinking!"   a   b

30. a.) I was like…   b.) I was like…

   …gonna go til I heard that.   a   b

   … "Go and grab it."   a   b

31. a.) I like…   b.) You like…

   …swim almost every day.   a   b

   …swimming after school.   a   b

32. a.) I was like…   b.) I was like…

   …gonna go til I heard that.   a   b

   … "Go and grab it."   a   b

33. a.) He was like…   b.) He was like…

   …"What's that?"   a   b

   … wearing this kind of visor thing.   a   b

34. a.) It was like…   b.) It's like…

   …something I've heard before but different.   a   b

   … some guy she met at a party.   a   b

35. a.) You're like…   b.) He's like…

   …hoping for the impossible.   a   b

   …"Huh?"   a   b

36. a.) She's like…   b.) She was just like…

   …not all that.   a   b

   …"No way!"   a   b

37. a.) I like…   b.) You like…

   …sleeping in.   a   b

   …sat down with them   a   b

38. a.) It's like…   b.) It was like…

   …"Hmmm…"   a   b

   …hotter than the Sahara.   a   b

39. a.) It's like…   b.) It's like…

   …not has hard as you'd expect.   a   b

   …nothing I've ever seen before.   a   b

C Stimuli for perception experiments

40. a.) She's like…   b.) She's like…

   …one of my closest friends.   a   b

   …"Well, maybe tomorrow."   a   b

41. a.) She was like…   b.) She was like…

   …"Oh cool."   a   b

   …only a little bit ahead.   a   b

42. a.) They like…   b.) I like…

   …go in to town after school.   a   b

   …going to town.   a   b

43. a.) And they're like…   b.) And they were like…

   …"Instead of what?"   a   b

   …in front of the classroom or something.   a   b

44. a.) They're like…   b.) They're like…

   …"Um… okay…"   a   b

   …underneath the car for some reason.   a   b

45. a.) …he like…   b.) …he like…

   Does _____ snowboard?   a   b

   Does _____ snowboarding?   a   b

46. a.) You like…   b.) I like…

   …dancing more than he does.   a   b

   …do this funny dance.   a   b

47. a.) They were like…   b.) I was like…

   …"Really?"   a   b

   …really happy about it.   a   b

48. a.) He was like…   b.) He was like…

   …looking right at me when he said it.   a   b

   …"Look up."   a   b

49. a.) It was like…   b.) It's like…

   …having an effect.   a   b

   …"Who?"   a   b

50. a.) I was like…   b.) I was like…

   …an overly curious cat.   a   b

   …already going to go.   a   b

51. a.) It's like…   b.) It's just kind of like…

   …I wanted to but I didn't.   a   b

   …"I guess."   a   b

52. a.) She was like…   b.) She was like…

   …"No, I don't think so."   a   b

   …not able to just walk away.   a   b

53. a.) You like…   b.) I like…

   …him too much.   a   b

   …have so much luck it's crazy.   a   b

C Stimuli for perception experiments

54. a.) It's like…   b.) It was like…

   …just down the road.   a   b

   …"Just kidding!"   a   b

55. a.) The girls are like…   b.) They're like…

   …"Can't you tell the difference?"   a   b

   …complaining to the teacher.   a   b

56. a.) I was like…   b.) I was like…

   …"Where do you think you're going?"   a   b

   …wishing he could go as well.   a   b

57. a.) We were like…   b.) We were like…

   …opening the windows.   a   b

   …"Oh- are you sure?"   a   b

58. a.) …you like…   b.) …you like…

   I know that ____ when I ask questions.   a   b

   I know that ____ wish it were different.   a   b

59. a.) They were like…   b.) They're like…

   …"So, hun. What's your sign?"   a   b

   …so hot.   a   b

60. a.) She's like…   b.) Your Mum's like…

   …the only person I know who'd say that.   a   b

   …"That's exactly what I was thinking!"   a   b

61. a.) I was like…   b.) I was like…

    …gonna go til I heard that.   a   b

    … "Go and grab it."   a   b

62. a.) You like…   b.) I like…

    …swim almost every day.   a   b

    …swimming after school.   a   b

C Stimuli for perception experiments

#_____

For this portion of the experiment, you will be asked to match recorded speech to the contexts provided. Although the provided context sentences are similar to what was actually said during the interview, these are not the actual sentences. All speech is taken from previously recorded interviews at the school. The speech you will hear is always two different instances of the word 'like' spoken by the same girl.

For each question, please read the two sentences. Then, match each example of 'like' that you hear to the sentence you feel it is MOST LIKELY to have come from. Circle 1 if the sentence goes with the first 'like' you heard, and circle 2 if the sentence goes with the second 'like' you heard. Please do not circle both 1 and 2 for any given question. Please answer all questions.

Work quickly and don't worry too much about your answer. There are no right or wrong answers here- I am simply interested in your intuitions regarding these words.

Speaker #1

1. He doesn't even like her.   1   2

   He doesn't even like help unless he's asked to.   1   2

2. We're like "No, can't be bothered."   1   2

   Does Fleur like Nathan?   1   2

3. I was like "Only if he asks me himself."   1   2

   I was like only two seconds behind.   1   2

4. She really shouldn't say like anything.   1   2

   She said they like anything and everything.   1   2

5. Would Sam like to join us?   1   2

   I'm like "Too bad."   1   2

6. He's like the best boyfriend I've ever had.   1   2

   He's like "That's the funniest thing I've ever seen!"   1   2

Figure C.2: Answersheet for Experiment 2

7.	I like knowing the truth.	1	2
	I like know that something must've happened.	1	2
8.	Does Pam like rugby?	1	2
	I'm like "Ring me."	1	2
9.	I was just like "Two or three weeks."	1	2
	I was just like too tired to do anything.	1	2
10.	They like don't have any idea what's next.	1	2
	They like doing nothing on Sundays.	1	2
11.	She's like "The other one."	1	2
	Will Liz like the flowers?	1	2
12.	She's like "No. Not interested."	1	2
	She's like not really that pretty on the inside.	1	2
13.	We like when they say stupid stuff like that.	1	2
	We like went up the street a bit.	1	2
14.	They're like "That sucks."	1	2
	Does Claire like that class?	1	2
15.	You were like yelling at randoms on the street.	1	2
	You were like "Yeah, thanks."	1	2

Do you recognise this voice?   Y   N

If so, who do you think it is?_____

C Stimuli for perception experiments

Speaker #2

16.	He doesn't even like help unless he's asked to.	1	2
	He doesn't even like her.	1	2
17.	Would Sam like to join us?	1	2
	I'm like "Too bad."	1	2
18.	You were like yelling at randoms on the street.	1	2
	You were like "Yeah, thanks."	1	2
19.	I like know that something must've happened.	1	2
	I like knowing the truth.	1	2
20.	Does Pam like rugby?	1	2
	I'm like "Ring me."	1	2
21.	I was like only two seconds behind.	1	2
	I was like "Only if he asks me himself."	1	2
22.	She said they like anything and everything.	1	2
	She really shouldn't say like anything.	1	2
23.	Will Liz like the flowers?	1	2
	She's like "The other one."	1	2
24.	She's like "No. Not interested."	1	2
	She's like not really that pretty on the inside.	1	2
25.	We like went up the street a bit.	1	2
	We like when they say stupid stuff like that.	1	2

26.	We're like "No, can't be bothered."		1	2
	Does Fleur like Nathan?		1	2
27.	He's like the best boyfriend I've ever had.		1	2
	He's like "That's the funniest thing I've ever seen!"		1	2
28.	They like doing nothing on Sundays.		1	2
	They like don't have any idea what's next.		1	2
29.	They're like "That sucks."		1	2
	Does Claire like that class?		1	2
30.	I was just like "Two or three weeks."		1	2
	I was just like too tired to do anything.		1	2

Do you recognise this voice?   Y   N

If so, who do you think it is?_____

Speaker #3

31.	We like when they say stupid stuff like that.		1	2
	We like went up the street a bit.		1	2
32.	Will Liz like the flowers?		1	2
	She's like "The other one."		1	2
33.	You were like yelling at randoms on the street.		1	2
	You were like "Yeah, thanks."		1	2

C Stimuli for perception experiments

34.	I like know that something must've happened.	1	2
	I like knowing the truth.	1	2
35.	We're like "No, can't be bothered."	1	2
	Does Fleur like Nathan?	1	2
36.	I was just like "Two or three weeks."	1	2
	I was just like too tired to do anything.	1	2
37.	He doesn't even like help unless he's asked to.	1	2
	He doesn't even like her.	1	2
38.	Does Claire like that class?	1	2
	They're like "That sucks."	1	2
39.	I was like "Only if he asks me himself."	1	2
	I was like only two seconds behind.	1	2
40.	She said they like anything and everything.	1	2
	She really shouldn't say like anything.	1	2
41.	I'm like "Ring me."	1	2
	Does Pam like rugby?	1	2
42.	He's like the best boyfriend I've ever had.	1	2
	He's like "That's the funniest thing I've ever seen!"	1	2
43.	They like doing nothing on Sundays.	1	2
	They like don't have any idea what's next.	1	2

44.	I'm like "Too bad."	1	2
	Would Sam like to join us?	1	2
45.	She's like "No. Not interested."	1	2
	She's like not really that pretty on the inside.	1	2

Do you recognise this voice?   Y   N

If so, who do you think it is?_____

Speaker #4

46.	He doesn't even like her.	1	2
	He doesn't even like help unless he's asked to.	1	2
47.	Does Pam like rugby?	1	2
	I'm like "Ring me."	1	2
48.	He's like the best boyfriend I've ever had.	1	2
	He's like "That's the funniest thing I've ever seen!"	1	2
49.	She really shouldn't say like anything.	1	2
	She said they like anything and everything.	1	2
50.	Does Fleur like Nathan?	1	2
	We're like "No, can't be bothered."	1	2
51.	I was like "Only if he asks me himself."	1	2
	I was like only two seconds behind.	1	2

C Stimuli for perception experiments

52.	I like know that something must've happened.	1	2
	I like knowing the truth.	1	2
53.	I'm like "Too bad."	1	2
	Would Sam like to join us?	1	2
54.	I was just like "Two or three weeks."	1	2
	I was just like too tired to do anything.	1	2
55.	They like don't have any idea what's next.	1	2
	They like doing nothing on Sundays.	1	2
56.	She's like "The other one."	1	2
	Will Liz like the flowers?	1	2
57.	She's like not really that pretty on the inside.	1	2
	She's like "No. Not interested."	1	2
58.	We like when they say stupid stuff like that.	1	2
	We like went up the street a bit.	1	2
59.	Does Claire like that class?	1	2
	They're like "That sucks."	1	2
60.	You were like yelling at randoms on the street.	1	2
	You were like "Yeah, thanks."	1	2

Do you recognise this voice?   Y   N

If so, who do you think it is?_____

\#_____

For this portion of the experiment, you will hear words and (given the context in which they come from) you will be asked to indicate whether you think the speaker is someone who hangs out in the Common Room or not. For each question, you should first read the sentence. You will hear the word 'like' that is taken from a sentence similar to the one for that question. Circle Y if you think that the speaker is probably someone who eats lunch in the Common Room, and circle N if you think that the speaker is probably someone who eats lunch outside the Common Room.

All of the people you will hear in this experiment are Year 13 students here at the school.
Remember to work quickly and try to go with your first intuition.

The following words you will hear are the word 'like', as in the sentence:

'I like toast.'

1. Does this person sometimes eat lunch in the Common Room?   Y   N

    Do you recognise this voice?   Y   N

    If so, who do you think it is? _____

2. Does this person sometimes eat lunch in the Common Room?   Y   N

    Do you recognise this voice?   Y   N

    If so, who do you think it is? _____

3. Does this person sometimes eat lunch in the Common Room?   Y   N

    Do you recognise this voice?   Y   N

    If so, who do you think it is? _____

4. Does this person sometimes eat lunch in the Common Room?   Y   N

    Do you recognise this voice?   Y   N

    If so, who do you think it is? _____

Figure C.3: Answersheet for Experiment 3

C Stimuli for perception experiments

5. Does this person sometimes eat lunch in the Common Room?   Y   N

   Do you recognise this voice?   Y   N

   If so, who do you think it is? _____

6. Does this person sometimes eat lunch in the Common Room?   Y   N

   Do you recognise this voice?   Y   N

   If so, who do you think it is? _____

7. Does this person sometimes eat lunch in the Common Room?   Y   N

   Do you recognise this voice?   Y   N

   If so, who do you think it is? _____

8. Does this person sometimes eat lunch in the Common Room?   Y   N

   Do you recognise this voice?   Y   N

   If so, who do you think it is? _____

9. Does this person sometimes eat lunch in the Common Room?   Y   N

   Do you recognise this voice?   Y   N

   If so, who do you think it is? _____

10. Does this person sometimes eat lunch in the Common Room?   Y   N

    Do you recognise this voice?   Y   N

    If so, who do you think it is? _____

The following words you will hear are the word 'like', as in the sentence:

'He was like, 'Yeah okay.''

11. Does this person sometimes eat lunch in the Common Room? Y   N

Do you recognise this voice?   Y   N

If so, who do you think it is? _____

12. Does this person sometimes eat lunch in the Common Room? Y   N

Do you recognise this voice?   Y   N

If so, who do you think it is? _____

13. Does this person sometimes eat lunch in the Common Room? Y   N

Do you recognise this voice?   Y   N

If so, who do you think it is? _____

14. Does this person sometimes eat lunch in the Common Room? Y   N

Do you recognise this voice?   Y   N

If so, who do you think it is? _____

15. Does this person sometimes eat lunch in the Common Room? Y   N

Do you recognise this voice?   Y   N

If so, who do you think it is? _____

16. Does this person sometimes eat lunch in the Common Room? Y   N

Do you recognise this voice?   Y   N

If so, who do you think it is? _____

C Stimuli for perception experiments

17. Does this person sometimes eat lunch in the Common Room?   Y   N

Do you recognise this voice?   Y   N

If so, who do you think it is? _____

18. Does this person sometimes eat lunch in the Common Room?   Y   N

Do you recognise this voice?   Y   N

If so, who do you think it is? _____

19. Does this person sometimes eat lunch in the Common Room?   Y   N

Do you recognise this voice?   Y   N

If so, who do you think it is? _____

20. Does this person sometimes eat lunch in the Common Room?   Y   N

Do you recognise this voice?   Y   N

If so, who do you think it is? _____

~Please turn to the next page and read the instructions for the next portion of the experiment.

For this portion of the experiment, you will hear two different instances of the word 'like' spoken by the same person. One has the meaning as in the sentence 'I like toast', and the other has the meaning as in the sentence 'He was like, 'Yeah okay.'' All of the people you will hear in this experiment are Year 13 students here at the school.

Your job is to listen carefully to each person say the words and to determine whether they are someone who sometimes eats lunch in the Common Room or not. You will also be asked to indicate whether or not you recognise the voice and who you think the speaker is.

Remember to work quickly and try to go with your first intuition.

Speaker #1

    21. I like toast.
    22. He was like, "Yeah okay."

Does this person sometimes eat lunch in the Common Room?   Y   N

Do you recognise this voice?   Y   N

If so, who do you think it is?_____

Speaker #2

    23. I like toast.
    24. He was like, "Yeah okay."

Does this person sometimes eat lunch in the Common Room?   Y   N

Do you recognise this voice?   Y   N

If so, who do you think it is?_____

Speaker #3

    25. I like toast.
    26. He was like, "Yeah okay."

Does this person sometimes eat lunch in the Common Room?   Y   N

Do you recognise this voice?   Y   N

If so, who do you think it is?_____

C Stimuli for perception experiments

Speaker #4

27. I like toast.
28. He was like, "Yeah okay."

Does this person sometimes eat lunch in the Common Room?   Y   N

Do you recognise this voice?   Y   N

If so, who do you think it is?_____

Speaker #5

29. I like toast.
30. He was like, "Yeah okay."

Does this person sometimes eat lunch in the Common Room?   Y   N

Do you recognise this voice?   Y   N

If so, who do you think it is?_____

Speaker #6

31. I like toast.
32. He was like, "Yeah okay."

Does this person sometimes eat lunch in the Common Room?   Y   N

Do you recognise this voice?   Y   N

If so, who do you think it is?_____

Speaker #7

33. I like toast.
34. He was like, "Yeah okay."

Does this person sometimes eat lunch in the Common Room?   Y   N

Do you recognise this voice?   Y   N

If so, who do you think it is?_____

Speaker #8

    35. I like toast.
    36. He was like, "Yeah okay."

Does this person sometimes eat lunch in the Common Room?   Y   N

Do you recognise this voice?   Y   N

If so, who do you think it is?_____

Speaker #9

    37. I like toast.
    38. He was like, "Yeah okay."

Does this person sometimes eat lunch in the Common Room?   Y   N

Do you recognise this voice?   Y   N

If so, who do you think it is?_____

Speaker #10

    39. I like toast.
    40. He was like, "Yeah okay."

Does this person sometimes eat lunch in the Common Room?   Y   N

Do you recognise this voice?   Y   N

If so, who do you think it is?_____

C Stimuli for perception experiments

1. He doesn't even like her.
2. He doesn't even like help unless he's asked to.
3. We're like "No, can't be bothered."
4. Does Fleur like Nathan?
5. I was like "Only if he asks me himself."
6. I was like only two seconds behind.
7. She really shouldn't say like anything.
8. She said they like anything and everything.
9. Would Sam like to join us?
10. I'm like "Too bad."
11. He's like the best boyfriend I've ever had.
12. He's like "That's the funniest thing I've ever seen!"
13. I like knowing the truth.
14. I like know that something must've happened.
15. Does Pam like rugby?
16. I'm like "Ring me."
17. I was just like "Two or three weeks."
18. I was just like too tired to do anything.
19. They like don't have any idea what's next.
20. They like doing nothing on Sundays.
21. She's like "The other one."
22. Will Liz like the flowers?
23. She's like "No. Not interested."
24. She's like not really that pretty on the inside.
25. We like when they say stupid stuff like that.
26. We like went up the street a bit.
27. They're like "That sucks."
28. Does Claire like that class?
29. You were like yelling at randoms on the street.
30. You were like "Yeah, thanks."

Figure C.4: Production Task

Table C.1: The auditory stimuli played for each question in Experiment 1, listed by order played.

num.	(N)CR	voice	type1	type2	person	tense	preced.	token1	token2
1	CR	Rose	d	q	match	match	match	rose-Iwaslike1discp	rose-Iwaslike1quote
2	NCR	Isabelle	d	q	match	match	match	isabelle-hewaslike1discp	isabelle-hewaslike2quote
3	CR	Rose	g	d	match	mismatch	no info	rose-it'slike1prep	rose-itwaslike1discp
4	CR	Tracy	d	q	mismatch	match	likely	tracy-he'slike1discp	tracy-you'relike1quote
5	NCR	Isabelle	q	d	match	mismatch	unlikely	isabelle-shewasjustlike1quote	isabelle-she'slike1discp
6	NCR	Onya	g	d	mismatch	match	no info	onya-youlike1main	onya-Ilike2discp
7	CR	Rose	d	q	match	mismatch	unlikely	rose-itwaslike1discp	rose-it'slike3quote
8	CR	Rachael	d	g	match	match	match	rachael-it'slike1discp	rachael-it'slike2prep
9	NCR	Onya	d	q	match	match	match	onya-she'slike1	onya-she'slike1quote
10	NCR	Isabelle	d	q	match	match	match	isabelle-shewaslike1discp	isabelle-shewaslike1quote
11	CR	Rose	g	d	mismatch	match	no info	rose-Ilike1main	rose-theylike1discp
12	CR	Tracy	d	q	match	mismatch	unlikely	tracy-andtheywerelike2discp	tracy-andthey'relike1quote
13	NCR	Onya	q	d	match	match	match	onya-they'relike1quote	onya2may-they'relike1
14	NCR	Isabelle	g	d	match	match	match	isabelle-helike1main	isabelle-helike1discp
15	CR	Tracy	g	d	mismatch	match	no info	tracy-Ilike1main	tracy-youlike1discp
16	CR	Daphne	q	d	mismatch	match	likely	daphne-Iwaslike1quote	daphne-theywerelike1discp
17	NCR	Isabelle	q	d	match	match	match	isabelle-hewaslike1quote	isabelle-hewaslike1discp
18	NCR	Sarah	d	q	match	mismatch	likely	sarah-it'slike4discp	sarah-itwaslike1quote
19	CR	Rose	d	g	match	match	match	rose-Iwaslike1discp	rose-Iwaslike1prep
20	CR	Rachael	q	d	match	match	match	rachael-it'sjustkindoflike1	rachael-it'slike1discp
21	NCR	Isabelle	q	d	match	match	match	isabelle-shewaslike2quote	isabelle-shewaslike1discp
22	NCR	Onya	d	g	mismatch	match	no info	onya-Ilike1discp	onya-youlike1main
23	CR	Rose	d	q	match	mismatch	unlikely	rose-itwaslike1discp	rose-it'slike2quote
24	NCR	Onya	d	q	match	match	match	onya2may-they'relike2	onya-thegirlsarelike1quote
25	CR	Rose	q	d	match	match	match	rose-they'relike1quote	rose-Iwaslike1discp
26	NCR	Onya	q	d	match	match	match	onya-wewerelike2	onya-wewerelike3
27	NCR	Isabelle	d	g	match	match	match	isabelle-youlike1discp	isabelle-yalike1main
28	CR	Rose	q	d	match	mismatch	likely	rose-they'relike1quote	rose-theywerelike
29	CR	Tracy	q	d	match	match	match	tracy-yourmum'slike1quote	tracy-she'slike1discp
30	CR	Rose	d	q	match	match	match	rose-Iwaslike1discp	rose-Iwaslike1quote
31	NCR	Onya	d	g	mismatch	mismatch	no info	onya-Ilike3discp	onya-youlike1main

C Stimuli for perception experiments

Table C.2: The auditory stimuli played for each question in Experiment 2, listed by order played (1-30).

num.	(N)CR	voice	type1	type2	token1	token2	context1	context2
1	CR	Rose	g	d	rose-like3	rose-discp1	g	d
2	CR	Rose	q	g	rose-quote2	rose-like4	q	g
3	CR	Rose	d	q	rose-discp1	rose-quote1	q	d
4	CR	Rose	d	g	rose-discp5	rose-like9	d	g
5	CR	Rose	q	g	rose-quote4	rose-like9	g	q
6	CR	Rose	q	d	rose-quote2	rose-discp2	d	q
7	CR	Rose	g	d	rose-like10	rose-discp6	g	d
8	CR	Rose	g	q	rose-like3	rose-quote1	g	q
9	CR	Rose	q	d	rose-quote4	rose-discp5	q	d
10	CR	Rose	g	d	rose-like8	rose-discp3	d	g
11	CR	Rose	g	q	rose-like8	rose-quote3	q	g
12	CR	Rose	d	q	rose-discp6	rose-quote5	q	d
13	CR	Rose	d	g	rose-discp2	rose-like4	g	d
14	CR	Rose	g	q	rose-like10	rose-quote5	q	g
15	CR	Rose	d	q	rose-discp3	rose-quote3	d	q
16	NCR	Meredith	g	d	meredith-like1main	meredith-like1discp	d	g
17	NCR	Meredith	g	q	meredith-like5main	meredith-like5quote	g	q
18	NCR	Meredith	q	d	meredith-like2quote	meredith-like2discp	d	q
19	NCR	Meredith	d	g	meredith-like4discp	meredith-like4main	d	g
20	NCR	Meredith	g	q	meredith-like1main	meredith-like1quote	g	q
21	NCR	Meredith	d	q	meredith-like1discp	meredith-like1quote	d	q
22	NCR	Meredith	g	d	meredith-like5main	meredith-like5discp	g	d
23	NCR	Meredith	q	g	meredith-like2quote	meredith-like2main	g	q
24	NCR	Meredith	q	d	meredith-like4quote	meredith-like4discp	q	d
25	NCR	Meredith	g	d	meredith-like3main	meredith-like3discp	d	g
26	NCR	Meredith	g	q	meredith-like3main	meredith-like3quote	g	g
27	NCR	Meredith	d	q	meredith-like3discp	meredith-like3quote	d	q
28	NCR	Meredith	d	g	meredith-like2discp	meredith-like2main	g	d
29	NCR	Meredith	q	g	meredith-like4quote	meredith-like4main	q	g
30	NCR	Meredith	d	q	meredith-like5discp	meredith-like5quote	q	d

Table C.3: The auditory stimuli played for each question in Experiment 2, listed by order played. (31-60)

num.	(N)CR	voice	type1	type2	token1	token2	context1	context2
31	CR	Tracy	d	g	tracy-discp1	tracy-like1	g	d
32	CR	Tracy	q	g	tracy-quote1	tracy-like1	g	q
33	CR	Tracy	d	q	tracy-discp2	tracy-quote2	d	q
34	CR	Tracy	g	d	tracy-like4	tracy-discp4	d	g
35	CR	Tracy	q	g	tracy-quote3	tracy-like3	q	g
36	CR	Tracy	q	d	tracy-quote1	tracy-discp1	q	d
37	CR	Tracy	d	g	tracy-discp3	tracy-like3	d	g
38	CR	Tracy	g	q	tracy-like4	tracy-quote4	g	q
39	CR	Tracy	q	d	tracy-quote5	tracy-discp5	q	d
40	CR	Tracy	d	g	tracy-discp5	tracy-like5	g	d
41	CR	Tracy	g	q	tracy-like2	tracy-quote2	q	g
42	CR	Tracy	q	d	tracy-quote3	tracy-discp3	d	q
43	CR	Tracy	g	d	tracy-like2	tracy-discp2	g	d
44	CR	Tracy	q	g	tracy-quote5	tracy-like5	q	g
45	CR	Tracy	d	q	tracy-discp4	tracy-quote4	q	d
46	NCR	Onya	d	g	onya-discp1	onya-like6	g	d
47	NCR	Onya	q	g	onya-quote1	onya-like6	g	q
48	NCR	Onya	d	q	onya-discp2	onya-quote2	d	q
49	NCR	Onya	g	d	onya-like9	onya-discp4	d	g
50	NCR	Onya	g	q	onya-like7	onya-quote2	g	q
51	NCR	Onya	q	d	onya-quote1	onya-discp1	q	d
52	NCR	Onya	d	g	onya-discp5	onya-like10	d	g
53	NCR	Onya	g	q	onya-like9	onya-quote4	q	g
54	NCR	Onya	d	q	onya-discp4	onya-quote4	q	d
55	NCR	Onya	d	g	onya-discp3	onya-like8	d	g
56	NCR	Onya	q	g	onya-quote3	onya-like8	q	g
57	NCR	Onya	q	d	onya-quote5	onya-discp5	d	q
58	NCR	Onya	g	d	onya-like7	onya-discp2	g	d
59	NCR	Onya	q	g	onya-quote5	onya-like10	g	q
60	NCR	Onya	q	d	onya-quote3	onya-discp3	d	q

C Stimuli for perception experiments

Table C.4: The auditory stimuli played for each question in Experiment 3, listed by order played.

task	num.	(N)CR	voice	type1	type2	token1	token2
1	1	CR	Anita	g	na	anita-like1	na
1	2	NCR	Vanessa	g	na	vanessa-like1	na
1	3	NCR	Onya	g	na	onya-like6	na
1	4	CR	Rose	g	na	rose-like9	na
1	5	NCR	Meredith	g	na	meredith-like1	na
1	6	CR	Rachel	g	na	rachel-like1	na
1	7	CR	Tracy	g	na	tracy-like2	na
1	8	NCR	Isabelle	g	na	isabelle-like2	na
1	9	CR	Betty	g	na	betty-like1	na
1	10	NCR	Sarah	g	na	sarah-like1	na
2	11	NCR	Isabelle	q	na	isabelle-quote5	na
2	12	NCR	Onya	q	na	onya-quote4	na
2	13	CR	Rose	q	na	rose-quote2	na
2	14	NCR	Sarah	q	na	sarah-quote1	na
2	15	CR	Rachel	q	na	rachael-quote1	na
2	16	CR	Betty	q	na	betty-quote1	na
2	17	NCR	Vanessa	q	na	vanessa-quote1	na
2	18	CR	Anita	q	na	anita-quote2	na
2	19	NCR	Meredith	q	na	meredith-quote6	na
2	20	CR	Tracy	q	na	tracy-quote1	na
3	21–22	CR	Betty	g	q	betty-like1	betty-quote1
3	23–24	NCR	Isabelle	g	q	isabelle-like2	isabelle-quote5
3	25–26	CR	Rose	g	q	rose-like9	rose-quote2
3	27–28	NCR	Onya	g	q	onya-like6	onya-quote4
3	29–30	CR	Rachel	g	q	rachel-like1	rachel-quote1
3	31–32	NCR	Sarah	g	q	sarah-like1	sarah-quote1
3	33–34	CR	Tracy	g	q	tracy-like2	tracy-quote1
3	35–36	NCR	Vanessa	g	q	vanessa-like1	vanessa-quote1
3	37–38	CR	Anita	g	q	anita-like1	anita-quote2
3	39–40	NCR	Meredith	g	q	meredith-like1	meredith-quote6

D Perception experiment data

Participants' responses are displayed in Tables D.1 and D.2 for Experiment 1, Tables D.3-D.5 for Experiment 2, and Tables D.6-D.8 for Experiment 3.

Table D.1: Characteristics of quote−dp questions in Experiment 1 where the first token was identified as the quotative, by whether the participant was in a CR or a NCR group.

feature questions comparing	CR girl quote−dp	NCR girl quote−dp	CR and NCR quote−dp
total number subjects	23	19	42
total questions answered	916	774	1690
total 1st token labeled as quote	465	383	848
quote first on sheet	278	231	509
1st token's context more likely	110	73	183
1st and 2nd tokens' context matched	271	242	513
1st token's context less likely	84	68	152
1st token mean EucD	1.5930	1.5400	1.5690
2nd token mean EucD	1.6180	1.6720	1.6430
mean EucD diff. (Bark)	−0.02538	−0.13280	−0.07388
1st token mean nuc F2 (Bark)	11.25	11.19	11.23
2nd token mean nuc F2 (Bark)	11.49	11.45	11.47
mean nuc F2 diff. (Bark)	−0.2379	−0.2554	−0.2458
1st token mean duration ratio	0.33900	0.32670	0.33350
2nd token mean duration ratio	0.35020	0.34520	0.34790
mean duration ratio diff.	−0.01120	−0.01844	−0.01447
1st token [k] present, 2nd token [k] absent	93	84	177
1st token [k] absent, 2nd token [k] present	74	65	139
[k] present for both tokens	118	83	201
[k] absent for both tokens	180	151	331

D Perception experiment data

Table D.2: Characteristics of gram−dp questions in Experiment 1 where the first token was identified a grammatical function, by whether the participant was in a CR or a NCR group.

feature questions comparing	CR gram−dp	NCR gram−dp	CR and NCR gram−dp
total number subjects	23	19	42
total questions answered	435	371	806
total 1st token labeled as gram	235	197	432
gram first on sheet	179	158	337
1st token mean EucD	1.1450	1.1750	1.1580
2nd token mean EucD	2.1720	2.3090	2.2350
mean EucD diff. (Bark)	−1.0270	−1.1350	−1.0760
1st token mean nuc F2 (Bark)	11.610	11.680	11.640
2nd token mean nuc F2 (Bark)	11.180	11.150	11.170
mean nuc F2 diff. (Bark)	0.4210	0.5324	0.4718
1st token mean duration ratio	0.6032	0.5812	0.5918
2nd token mean duration ratio	0.5878	0.6098	0.5992
mean duration ratio diff.	0.0017	−0.004056	−0.0009248
1st token [k] present, 2nd token [k] absent	35	35	70
1st token [k] absent, 2nd token [k] present	29	28	57
[k] present for both tokens	90	69	159
[k] absent for both tokens	81	65	146

Table D.3: Characteristics of quote–dp questions in Experiment 2 where the first token was identified as the quotative, by whether the participant was in a CR or a NCR group.

feature questions comparing	CR girl quote–dp	NCR girl quote–dp	CR and NCR quote–dp
total number subjects	23	19	42
total questions answered	906	744	1650
total 1st token labeled as quote	456	375	831
quote first on sheet	250	195	445
1st token mean EucD	1.5330	1.5250	1.5290
2nd token mean EucD	1.5150	1.5820	1.5450
mean EucD diff. (Bark)	0.01807	−0.05693	−0.01577
1st token mean nuc F2 (Bark)	11.59	11.60	11.59
2nd token mean nuc F2 (Bark)	11.57	11.65	11.61
mean nuc F2 diff. (Bark)	0.01299	−0.04582	−0.01355
1st token mean duration ratio	0.3178	0.3198	0.3187
2nd token mean duration ratio	0.3406	0.3281	0.3350
mean duration ratio diff.	−0.022830	−0.008376	−0.016310
1st token [k] present, 2nd token [k] absent	58	49	107
1st token [k] absent, 2nd token [k] present	69	46	115
[k] present for both tokens	236	205	441
[k] absent for both tokens	93	75	168

D Perception experiment data

Table D.4: Characteristics of quote−gram questions in Experiment 2 where the first token was identified as the quotative, by whether the participant was in a CR or a NCR group.

feature questions comparing	CR girl quote−gram	NCR girl quote−gram	CR and NCR quote−gram
total number subjects	23	19	42
total questions answered	905	747	1652
total 1st token labeled as quote	494	398	892
quote first on sheet	234	183	462
1st token mean EucD	1.4480	1.4700	1.4580
2nd token mean EucD	1.4800	1.4550	1.4690
mean EucD diff. (Bark)	−0.03204	0.01479	−0.01114
1st token mean nuc F2 (Bark)	11.45	11.44	11.44
2nd token mean nuc F2 (Bark)	11.37	11.38	11.37
mean nuc F2 diff. (Bark)	0.08333	0.05636	0.07130
1st token mean duration ratio	0.3845	0.3853	0.3849
2nd token mean duration ratio	0.4194	0.4097	0.4151
mean duration ratio diff.	−0.03488	−0.02442	−0.03021
1st token [k] present, 2nd token [k] absent	131	102	233
1st token [k] absent, 2nd token [k] present	208	162	370
[k] present for both tokens	131	115	246
[k] absent for both tokens	24	19	43

Table D.5: Characteristics of gram–dp questions in Experiment 2 where the first token was identified as the grammatical function, by whether the participant was in a CR or a NCR group.

feature questions comparing	CR girl gram–dp	NCR girl gram–dp	CR and NCR gram–dp
total number subjects	23	19	42
total questions answered	910	738	1648
total 1st token labeled as quote	441	366	807
quote first on sheet	248	202	450
1st token mean EucD	1.9500	1.9290	1.9400
2nd token mean EucD	1.9180	1.9580	1.9360
mean EucD diff. (Bark)	0.0316	−0.02898	0.004128
1st token mean nuc F2 (Bark)	11.45	11.47	11.46
2nd token mean nuc F2 (Bark)	11.54	11.48	11.51
mean nuc F2 diff. (Bark)	−0.08344	−0.01363	−0.05178
1st token mean duration ratio	0.4406	0.4398	0.4402
2nd token mean duration ratio	0.4321	0.4389	0.4352
mean duration ratio diff.	0.008490	0.0008953	0.005046
1st token [k] present, 2nd token [k] absent	88	66	154
1st token [k] absent, 2nd token [k] present	87	76	163
[k] present for both tokens	238	197	435
[k] absent for both tokens	28	27	55

D Perception experiment data

Table D.6: Characteristics of the grammatical functions in Experiment 3, Task 1 for questions where the voices were identified as someone who ate lunch in the CR. The total possible based only on questions answered is shown in parentheses.

feature	CR	NCR	CR and NCR
total questions identified as CR	151 (228)	111 (182)	262 (410)
actual voice = CR	87 (114)	56 (90)	143 (204)
recognise voice	41 (46)	25 (37)	66 (83)
voice = extroverted	92 (136)	76 (110)	168 (246)
min EucD (Bark)	0.08728 (0.08728)	0.08728 (0.08728)	0.08728 (0.08728)
mean EucD (Bark)	1.63000 (1.62400)	1.69600 (1.62200)	1.65800 (1.62300)
max EucD (Bark)	2.85800 (2.85800)	2.85800 (2.85800)	2.85800 (2.85800)
min duration ratio	0.1751 (0.1751)	0.1751 (0.1751)	0.1751 (0.1751)
mean duration ratio	0.3772 (0.3770)	0.3725 (0.3760)	0.3752 (0.3766)
max duration ratio	0.5245 (0.5245)	0.5245 (0.5245)	0.5245 (0.5245)
[k] realised	125 (183)	88 (145)	213 (328)

Table D.7: Characteristics of the quotatives in Experiment 3, Task 2 for questions where the voices were identified as someone who ate lunch in the CR. The total possible based only on questions answered is shown in parentheses.

feature	CR	NCR	CR and NCR
total questions identified as CR	159 (211)	116 (188)	275 (399)
actual voice = CR	78 (106)	58 (94)	136 (200)
recognise voice	18 (24)	30 (40)	48 (64)
voice = extroverted	102 (127)	67 (112)	
min EucD (Bark)	0.0832 (0.0832)	0.0832 (0.0832)	0.0832 (0.0832)
mean EucD (Bark)	1.2800 (1.2720)	1.2250 (1.2620)	1.2570 (1.2680)
max EucD (Bark)	3.6340 (3.6340)	3.6340 (3.6340)	3.6340 (3.6340)
min duration ratio	0.1576 (0.1576)	0.1576 (0.1576)	0.1576 (0.1576)
mean duration ratio	0.3478 (0.3490)	0.3199 (0.3459)	0.3361 (0.3475)
max duration ratio	0.7271 (0.7271)	0.7271 (0.7271)	0.7271 (0.7271)
[k] realised	70 (84)	52 (75)	122 (159)

Table D.8: Differences between the grammatical function and the quotative in Experiment 3, Task 3 for questions where the voices were identified as someone who ate lunch in the CR. The total possible based only on questions answered is shown in parentheses.

feature	CR	NCR	CR and NCR
total questions identified as CR	135 (214)	118 (184)	253 (398)
actual voice = CR	72 (108)	57 (92)	129 (200)
recognise voice	35 (42)	35 (47)	70 (89)
voice = extroverted	83 (128)	73 (111)	156 (239)
min EucD diff. (Bark)	-1.0780 (-1.0780)	-1.0780 (-1.0780)	-1.0780 (-1.0780)
mean EucD diff. (Bark)	1.3440 (1.2280)	1.2240 (1.2930)	1.2880 (1.2580)
max EucD diff. (Bark)	6.3530 (6.3530)	6.3530 (6.3530)	6.3530 (6.3530)
min duration ratio diff.	-0.12140 (-0.12140)	-0.12140 (-0.12140)	-0.12140 (-0.12140)
mean duration ratio diff.	0.31020 (0.32450)	0.28800 (0.31860)	0.29990 (0.32170)
max duration ratio diff.	1.06800 (1.06800)	1.06800 (1.06800)	1.06800 (1.06800)
gram. [k] realised, quote [k] not realised	78 (130)	63 (110)	141 (240)
gram. [k] not realised, quote [k] realised	27 (42)	26 (37)	53 (79)
both [k] realised	30 (42)	29 (37)	59 (79)

References

Agar, Michael H. 1980. *The professional stranger: An informal introduction to ethnography*. New York: Academic Press.

Anderson, Gisle. 2001. *Pragmatic markers and sociolinguistic variation: A relevance-theoretic approach to the language of adolescents*. Amsterdam: Benjamins.

Aylett, Matthew & Alice Turk. 2004. The Smooth Signal Redundancy Hypothesis: A functional explanation for relationships between redundancy, prosodic prominence, and duration in spontaneous speech. *Language and Speech* 47(1). 31–56.

Aylett, Matthew & Alice Turk. 2006. Language redundancy predicts syllabic duration and the spectral characteristics of vocalic syllable nuclei. *Journal of the Acoustical Society of America* 119(5). 3048–3058.

Baayen, R. Harald. 2008. *Analyzing linguistic data. A practical introduction to statistics*. Cambridge: Cambridge University Press.

Babel, Molly. 2012. Evidence for phonetic and social selectivity in spontaneous phonetic imitation. *Journal of Phonetics* 40(1). 177–189.

Baker, Rachel E. & Ann R. Bradlow. 2009. Variability in word duration as a function of probability, speech style, and prosody. *Language and Speech* 52(4). 391–413.

Barras, Claude, Edouard Geoffrois, Zhibiao Wu & Mark Liberman. 2001. Transcriber: Development and use of a tool for assisting speech corpora production. *Speech Communication* 33(1–2). 5–22.

Bates, Douglas & Deepayan Sarkar. 2007. Lme4: Linear mixed-effects models using s4 classes. http://r-forge.r-project.org/projects/lme4, Accessed on 2008-08-08.

Bayard, Donn. 2000. The cultural cringe revisited: Changes through time in Kiwi attitudes toward accents. In Allan Bell & Koenraad Kuiper (eds.), *New Zealand English*, 297–324. Wellington: Victoria University Press.

Bell, Allan. 1984. Language style as audience design. *Language in Society* 13. 145–204.

References

Bell, Allan, Jason M. Brenier, Michelle Gregory, Cynthia Girand & Dan Jurafsky. 2009. Predictability effects on durations of context and function words in conversational English. *Journal of Memory and Language* 60. 92–111.

Bentler, Peter M., Douglas N. Jackson & Samuel Messick. 1971. Identification of content and style: A two-dimensional interpretation of acquiescence. *Psychological Bulletin* 76(3). 186–204.

Biber, Douglas, Susan Conrad & Rani Reppen. 1998. *Corpus linguistics: Investigating language structure and use*. Cambridge: Cambridge University Press.

Bock, Kathryn. 1995. Sentence production: From mind to mouth. In Joanne L. Miller & Peter D. Eimas (eds.), *Handbook of perception and cognition, vol. 11: Speech, language, and communication*, 181–216. Orlando, FL: Academic Press.

Bod, Rens, Jennifer Hay & Stefanie Jannedy (eds.). 2003. *Probabilistic linguistics*. Cambridge, MA: MIT Press.

Boersma, Paul. 1997. How we learn variation, optimality, and probability. In R. J. J. H. van Son (ed.), *Proceedings of the Institute of Phonetic Sciences 21*, 43–58. Amsterdam: University of Amsterdam.

Boersma, Paul & David Weenink. 2005. *Praat: Doing phonetics by computer (Version 4.3.24)*. http://www.praat.org/, Accessed on 2005-27-09.

Bourdieu, Pierre. 1991. *Language and symbolic power*. Cambridge, MA: Harvard University Press.

Breiman, Leo, Jerome H. Friedman, Richard A. Olshen & Charles J. Stone. 1984. *Classification and regression trees*. Belmont, CA: Wadsworth.

Bucholtz, Mary. 1998. Geek the girl: Language, femininity and female nerds. In Natasha Warner, Jocelyn Ahlers, Leela Bilmes, Monica Oliver, Suzanne Wertheim & Melinda Chen (eds.), *Gender and belief systems*, 119–131. Berkeley, CA: Berkeley Women & Language Group.

Bucholtz, Mary. 2006. Word up: Social meanings of slang in California youth culture. In Leila Monaghan & Jane E. Goodman (eds.), *A cultural approach to interpersonal communications*, 243–267. Oxford: Blackwell.

Bucholtz, Mary. 2009. From stance to style: Gender, interaction and indexicality in Mexican immigrant youth slang. In Alexandra Jaffe (ed.), *Sociolinguistic perspectives on stance*, 146–170. Oxford: Oxford University Press.

Bucholtz, Mary. 2010. *White kids: Language, race and styles of youth identity*. Cambridge: Cambridge University Press.

Buchstaller, Isabelle. 2006. Social stereotypes, personality traits and regional perception displaced: Attitudes towards the 'new' quotatives in the U. K. *Journal of Sociolinguistics* 10(3). 362–381.

Buchstaller, Isabelle & Alexandra D'Arcy. 2009. Localized globalization: A multi-local, multivariate investigation of quotative 'be like'. *Journal of Sociolinguistics* 13(3). 291–313.

Bybee, Joan. 2001. *Phonology and language use*. Cambridge: Cambridge University Press.

Bybee, Joan. 2002. Word frequency and context of use in the lexical diffusion of phonetically conditioned sound change. *Language Variation and Change* 14. 261–290.

Bybee, Joan. 2006. From usage to grammar: The mind's response to repetition. *Language* 82(4). 711–744.

Campbell-Kibler, Kathryn. 2007. Accent, (ING), and the social logic of listener perceptions. *American Speech* 82. 32–64.

Campbell-Kibler, Kathryn, Penelope Eckert, Norma Mendoza-Denton & Emma Moore. 2006. *The elements of style*. Columbus, November 2006.

Casasanto, Laura Staum. 2009. How do listeners represent sociolinguistic knowledge? *Proceedings from Cognitive Science 2009*. 2341–2346.

Casasanto, Laura Staum. 2010. What do listeners know about sociolinguistic variation? *University of Pennsylvania Working Papers in Linguistics* 15(2). 40–49.

Cassidy, Steve. 2007. *The Emu Speech Database System, version 1.9*. http://emu.sourceforge.net/, Accessed 2007-30-08.

Charon, Joel M. 1995. *Symbolic interactionism. An introduction, an interpretation, an integration*. Englewood Cliffs, NJ: Prentice-Hall.

Chartres, Laura. 2008. Changing values: An analysis of the PRICE phoneme for eight speakers of New Zealand English. *New Zealand English Journal* 22. 9–23.

Chomsky, Noam. 1965. *Aspects of the theory of syntax*. Cambridge, MA: MIT Press.

Chomsky, Noam. 1986. *Knowledge of language: Its nature, origin, and use*. New York: Praeger.

Chun, Elaine. 2007. *"Oh my god!": Stereotypical words at the intersection of sound, practice, and social meaning*. Philadelphia, October 2007.

Clopper, Cynthia G. & David B. Pisoni. 2004. Homebodies and army brats: Some effects of early linguistic experience and residential history on dialect categorization. *Language Variation and Change* 16(1). 31–48.

Cole, Jennifer, Heejin Kim, Hansook Choi & Mark Hasegawa-Johnson. 2007. Prosodic effects on acoustic cues to stop voicing and place of articulation: Evidence from Radio News speech. *Journal of Phonetics* 35(2). 180–209.

Coupland, Nikolas. 2007. *Style: Language variation and identity*. Cambridge: Cambridge University Press.

References

Cukor-Avila, Patricia & Guy Bailey. 2001. The effects of the race of the interviewer on sociolinguistic fieldwork. *Journal of Sociolinguistics* 5(2). 252–270.

Cutler, Anne & Charles Clifton Jr. 1984. The use of prosodic information in word recognition. In Herman Bouma & Don G. Bouwhuis (eds.), *Attention and performance X*, 183–196. Hillsdale, NJ: Erlbaum.

Dailey-O'Cain, Jennifer. 2000. The sociolinguistic distribution of and attitudes toward focuser *like* and quotative *like*. *Journal of Sociolingistics* 4(1). 60–80.

Daly, Nicola & Paul Warren. 2001. Pitching it differently in New Zealand English: Speaker sex and intonation patterns. *Journal of Sociolinguistics* 5(1). 85–96.

D'Arcy, Alexandra. 2005. *Like: Syntax and development.* University of Toronto PhD thesis.

D'Arcy, Alexandra. 2007. *Like* and language ideology: Disentangling fact from fiction. *American Speech* 82(4). 386–419.

D'Arcy, Alexandra. 2010. Quoting ethnicity: Constructing dialogue in Aotearoa/ New Zealand. *Journal of Sociolinguistics* 14(1). 60–88.

de Saussure, Ferdinand. 1983 [1916]. *Course in general linguistics.* LaSalle, IL: Open Court.

Dilley, Laura, Stefanie Shattuck-Hufnagel & Mari Ostendorf. 1996. Glottalisation of word-initial vowels as a function of prosodic structure. *Journal of Phonetics* 24. 423–444.

Docherty, Gerard & Paul Foulkes. 1999. Newcastle upon Tyne and Derby: Instrumental phonetics and variationist studies. In Paul Foulkes & Gerard Docherty (eds.), *Urban voices: Accent studies in the British Isles*, 47–71. London: Arnold.

Drager, Katie. 2006. Social categories, grammatical categories, and the likelihood of "like" monophthongisation. In Paul Warren & Catherine I. Watson (eds.), *Digital proceedings of the 11th Australasian International Conference on Speech Science and Technology*, 384–87. Auckland: University of Auckland.

Drager, Katie. 2008. *Ethnographic Acoustics: Socially-conditioned phonetic variation of quotative like.* Chicago, January 2008.

Drager, Katie. 2009b. *A sociophonetic ethnography of Selwyn Girls' High.* University of Canterbury: Doctoral dissertation.

Drager, Katie. 2010. Sensitivity to grammatical and sociophonetic variability in perception. *Laboratory Phonology* 1(1). 93–120.

Drager, Katie. 2011a. Sociophonetic variation and the lemma. *Journal of Phonetics* 39(4). 694–707.

Drager, Katie. 2011b. Speaker age and vowel perception. *Language and Speech* 54(1). 99–121.

Drager, Katie. 2016a. Constructing style: Phonetic variation in discursive functions of *like*. In Heike Pichler (ed.), *Discourse-pragmatic variation and change in English: New methods and insights*. Cambridge: Cambridge University Press.

Drager, Katie. 2016b. Constructing style: Phonetic variation in quotative and discourse particle 'like'. In Heike Pichler (ed.), *New directions in discourse-pragmatic variation change: Views from englishes across the world*. Cambridge: Cambridge University Press.

Drager, Katie & Jennifer Hay. 2012. Exploiting random intercepts: Two case studies in sociophonetics. *Language Variation and Change* 24(1). 59–78.

Drager, Katie, Jennifer Hay & Abby Walker. 2010. Pronounced rivalries: Attitudes and speech production. *Te Reo* 53. 27–53.

Du Bois, John W. 2007. The stance triangle. In Robert Englebretson (ed.), *Stancetaking in discourse: Subjectivity, evaluation, interaction*, 139–182. Amsterdam: John Benjamins.

Eckert, Penelope. 1989. *Jocks and burnouts: Social categories and identity in the high school*. New York: Teachers College Press.

Eckert, Penelope. 1996a. (ay) goes to the city: Exploring the expressive use of variation. In Gregory R. Guy, Crawford Feagin, Deborah Schiffrin & John Baugh (eds.), *Towards a social science of language: Papers in honor of William Labov*, vol. 1, 47–68. Philadelphia: John Benjamins.

Eckert, Penelope. 1996b. Vowels and nail polish: The emergence of linguistic style in the preadolescent heterosexual marketplace. In Natasha Warner, Jocelyn Ahlers, Leela Bilmes, Monica Oliver, Suzanne Wertheim & Mel Chen (eds.), *Proceedings of the 1996 Berkeley Women and Language Conference*, 183–190. Berkeley: Berkeley Women & Language Group.

Eckert, Penelope. 2000. *Linguistic variation as social practice*. Oxford: Blackwell.

Eckert, Penelope. 2005a. Phonetic reduction and categorisation in exemplar-based representation: Observations on a Dutch discourse marker. *Journal of Sociolinguistics* 12(4). 287–311.

Eckert, Penelope. 2005b. *Variation, convention, and social meaning*. Oakland, January 2005.

Eckert, Penelope. 2011. Language and power in the preadolescent heterosecual market. *American Speech* 86(1). 85–97.

Eckert, Penelope & Sally McConnell-Ginet. 1999. New generalizations and explanations in language and gender research. *Language in Society* 28. 185–201.

Edwards, Jan, Mary E. Beckman & Janet Fletcher. 1992. The articulatory kinematics of final lenthening. *Journal of the Acoustical Society of America* 89(1). 369–382.

References

Fougeron, Cécile & Patricia A. Keating. 1997. Articulatory strengthening at edges of prosodic domains. *Journal of the Acoustical Society of America* 101(6). 3728–3740.

Foulkes, Paul & Gerard Docherty. 2006. The social life of phonetics and phonology. *Journal of Phonetics* 34(4). 409–438.

Foulkes, Paul, Gerard J. Docherty & Dominic J. Watt. 2005. Phonological variation in child directed speech. *Language* 81(1). 177–206.

Foulkes, Paul & Jennifer Hay. 2015. The emergence of sociophonetic structure. In Brian MacWinney & William O'Grady (eds.), *The handbook of language emergence*, 292–313. Malden, MA: Wiley Blackwell.

Fromont, Robert & Jennifer Hay. 2007. *ONZE Miner*. http://onzeminer.sourceforge.net/, Accessed 2007-04-05. Christchurch, New Zealand: ONZE Project, University of Canterbury.

Gahl, Susanne. 2008. 'Time' and 'thyme' are not homophones: The effect of lemma frequency on word durations in a corpus of spontaneous speech. *Language* 84(3). 474–496.

Geertz, Clifford. 1973. *The interpretation of cultures*. New York: Basic Books.

Giles, Howard, Nikolas Coupland & Justine Coupland. 1991. Accommodation theory: Communication, context, and consequence. In Howard Giles, Justine Coupland & Nikolas Coupland (eds.), *Contexts of accommodation: Studies in emotion and social interaction*, 1–68. Cambridge: Cambridge University Press.

Giles, Howard & Peter F. Powesland. 1975. *Speech style and social evaluation*. London: Academic Press.

Goffman, Erving. 1981. *Forms of talk*. Philadelphia, PA: University of Pennsylvania Press.

Goldinger, Stephen D. 1997. Words and voices: Perception and production in an episodic lexicon. In Keith Johnson & John W. Mullennix (eds.), *Talker variability in speech processing*, 33–66. San Diego: Academic Press.

Gordon, Elizabeth, Lyle Campbell, Jennifer Hay, Margaret Maclagan, Andrea Sudbury & Peter Trudgill. 2004. *New Zealand English: Its origins and evolution*. Cambridge: Cambridge University Press.

Gray, Alison. 1988. *Teenangels: Being a New Zealand teenager*. Wellington: Allen & Unwin.

Griffiths, Thomas L., Kevin R. Canini, Adam N. Sanborn & Daniel J. Navarro. 2007. Unifying rational models of categorization via the hierarchical dirichlet process. In Danielle S. MacNamara & J. Gregory Trafton (eds.), *Proceedings of the twenty-ninth annual conference of the Cognitive Science Society*, 317–322. Austin, TX: Cognitive Science Society.

Hall-Lew, Lauren & Sonya Fix. 2012. Perceptual coding reliability of (l)-vocalization in casual speech data. *Lingua* 122(7). 794–809.

Harrington, Jonathan & Steve Cassidy. 1999. *Techniques in speech acoustics*. Dordrecht: Kluwer Academic Publishers.

Hay, Jennifer & Joan Bresnan. 2006. Spoken syntax: The phonetics of giving a hand in New Zealand English. *The Linguistic Review* 23(3). 321–349.

Hay, Jennifer, Stefanie Jannedy & Norma Mendoza-Denton. 1999. Oprah and /ay/: Lexical frequency, referee design and style. In John J. Ohala, Yoko Hasegawa, Manjari Ohala, Daniel Granville & Ashlee C. Bailey (eds.), *Proceedings of the 14th international congress of phonetic sciences*, 1389–1392. San Francisco: University of California.

Hay, Jennifer & Margaret A. Maclagan. 2010. Social and phonetic conditioners on the frequency and distribution and degree of 'intrusive /r/' in New Zealand English. In Dennis Preston & Nancy Niedzielski (eds.), *A reader in sociophonetics*, 41–70. New York: Mouton de Gruyter.

Hay, Jennifer, Aaron Nolan & Katie Drager. 2006. From fush to feesh: Exemplar priming in speech perception. *The Linguistic Review* 23(3). 351–79.

Hay, Jennifer, Paul Warren & Katie Drager. 2006. Factors influencing speech perception in the context of a merger-in-progress. *Journal of Phonetics* 34(4). 458–484.

Hay, Jennifer, Paul Warren & Katie Drager. 2010. Short-term exposure to one dialect affects processing of another. *Language and Speech* 53(4). 447–471.

Hebdige, Dick. 1984. *Subculture: The meaning of style*. New York: Methuen.

Holmquist, Jonathan C. 1985. Social correlates of a linguistic variable: A study in a Spanish village. *Language in Society* 14. 192–203.

Hymes, Del. 1972. On communicative competence. In John Bernard Pride & Janet Holmes (eds.), *Sociolinguistics: selected readings*, 269–293. Harmondsworth: Penguin.

Johnson, Keith. 1997. Speech perception without speaker normalization. In Keith Johnson & John Mullennix (eds.), *Talker variability in speech processing*, 146–165. San Diego: Academic Press.

Jurafsky, Dan. 2003. Probabilistic modeling in psycholinguistics: Linguistic comprehension and production. In Rens Bod, Jennifer Hay & Stefanie Jannedy (eds.), *Probabilistic linguistics*, 39–96. Cambridge, MA: MIT Press.

Jurafsky, Daniel. 1996. A probabilistic model of lexical and syntactic access and disambiguation. *Cognitive Science* 20(2). 137–194.

References

Jurafsky, Daniel, Allan Bell & Cynthia Girand. 2002. The role of lemma in form variation. In Carlos Gussenhoven & Natasha Warner (eds.), *Laboratory phonology 7* (Phonology and Phonetics 4(1)), 3–34. New York: Mouton de Gruyter.

Kattab, Ghada. 2013. Phonetic convergence and divergence strategies in English-Arabic bilingual children. *Linguistics* 52(2). 439–472.

Kiesling, Scott F. 2009. Style as stance: Stance as the explanation for patterns of sociolinguistic variation. In Alexandra Jaffe (ed.), *Sociolinguistic perspectives on stance*, 171–194. Oxford: Oxford University Press.

Kirtley, M. Joelle. 2015. *Language, identity, and non-binary gender in Hawai'i*. to appear December 2015. University of Hawai'i at Mānoa: Doctoral dissertation.

Kondo, Dorinne K. 1986. Dissolution and reconstitution of self: Implications for anthropological epistemology. *Cultural Anthropology* 1(1). 74–88.

Labov, William. 1963. The social motivation of a sound change. *Word* 19. 273–309.

Labov, William. 1966. *The social stratification of English in New York City*. Washington D.C.: Center for Applied linguistics.

Labov, William. 1972a. *Sociolinguistic patterns*. Pennsylvania: University of Pennsylvania Press.

Labov, William. 1972b. Some principles of linguistic methodology. *Language in Society* 1. 97–120.

Labov, William. 2001. *Principles of linguistic change: Social factors*. Oxford: Blackwell.

Labov, William. 2007. Transmission and diffusion. *Language* 83(2). 344–387.

Labov, William, Malcah Yaeger & Richard Steiner. 1972. *A quantitative study of sound change in progress*. Philadelphia: US Regional Survey.

Ladefoged, Peter. 2003. *Phonetic data analysis: An introduction to fieldwork and instrumental techniques*. Oxford: Blackwell.

Lave, Jean & Etienne Wenger. 1991. *Situated learning: Legitimate peripheral participation*. Cambridge: Cambridge University Press.

Lavoie, Lisa M. 2002. Subphonemic and suballophonic consonant variation: The role of the phoneme inventory. In Tracy A. Hall (ed.), *ZAS papers in linguistics 28*, 39–54.

Levelt, Willem J. M., Ardi Roelofs & Antje S. Meyer. 1999. A theory of lexical access in speech production. *Behavioral and Brain Sciences* 22. 1–38.

Lévi-Strauss, Claude. 1974. *The savage mind*. London: Weidenfeld & Nicolson.

Lewis, Stacy. 2009. Making meaning through mocking: A case of the FAKE people. In Julia de Bres, Janet Holmes & Meredith Marra (eds.), *Proceedings of the 5th biennial international gender and language association conference IGALA 5*, 1–16. Wellington: Victoria University of Wellington.

Maclagan, Margaret A., Elizabeth Gordon & Gillian Lewis. 1999. Women and sound change: Conservative and innovative behaviour by the same speakers. *Language Variation and Change* 11(1). 19–41.

Mani, Lata. 1990. Multiple mediations: Feminist scholarship in the age of mulitnational reception. *Feminist Review* 35. 25–41.

Mendoza-Denton, Norma. 2008. *Homegirls: Language and cultural practice among Latina youth gangs.* Oxford: Blackwell.

Mendoza-Denton, Norma, Jennifer Hay & Stefanie Jannedy. 2003. Probabilistic sociolinguistics: Beyond variable rules. In Rens Bod, Jennifer Hay & Stefanie Jannedy (eds.), *Probabilistic linguistics*, 97–138. Cambridge, MA: MIT Press.

Milroy, James. 1992. *Linguistic variation and change.* Oxford: Blackwell.

Milroy, James & Lesley Milroy. 1978. Belfast: Change and variation in an urban vernacular. In Peter Trudgill (ed.), *Sociolinguistic patterns in British English*, 19–36. London: Edward Arnold.

Milroy, Lesley. 1987. *Observing and analysing natural language.* Oxford: Blackwell.

Milroy, Lesley & Matthew Gordon. 2003. *Sociolinguistics: Method and interpretation.* Oxford: Blackwell.

Munson, Benjamin. 2007. Lexical access, lexical representation, and vowel articulation. In Jennifer Cole & José I. Hualde (eds.), *Laboratory phonology 9* (Phonology and Phonetics 4(3)), 241–264. New York: Mouton de Gruyter.

Munson, Benjamin & Nancy Pearl Solomon. 2004. The effect of phonological neighborhood density on vowel articulation. *Journal of Speech, Language, and Hearing Research* 47(5). 1048–1058.

Narayan, Kirin. 1993. How native is a "native" anthropologist? *American Anthropologist* 95(3). 671–686.

Narayanan, Srini & Daniel Jurafsky. 1998. Bayesian models of human sentence processing. In *Proceedings of 20 th annual conference of the Cognitive Science Society (cogsci)*, 752–757. Erlbaum.

Narayanan, Srini & Daniel Jurafsky. 2002. A Bayesian model predicts human parse preference and reading time in sentence processing. In Thomas Glen Dietterich, Suzanna Becker & Zoubin Ghahramani (eds.), *Advances in neural information processing systems 14*, 59–65. Cambridge, MA: MIT Press.

Niedzielski, Nancy. 1999. The effect of social information on the perception of sociolinguistic variables. *Journal of Language and Social Psychology* 18(1). 62–85.

Nielsen, Kuniko & Colin Wilson. 2008. A hierarchical bayesian model of multilevel phonetic imitation. In Natasha Abner & Jason Bishop (eds.), *Proceedings* of the 27th West Coast Conference on Formal Linguistics, 335–343. Somerville: Cascadilla.

Norris, Dennis & James M. McQueen. 2008. Shortlist B: A Bayesian model of continuous speech recognition. *Psychological Review* 115(2). 257–395.

Nosofsky, Robert M. 1986. Attention, similarity, and identification-categorization relationship. *Journal of Experimental Psychology* 115(1). 39–57.

Ochs, Elinor. 1990. Cultural universals in the acquisition of language. *Papers and Reports on Child Language Development* 29. 1–19.

Peterson, Gordon E. & Harold L. Barney. 1952. Control methods used in a study of the vowels. *The Journal of the Acoustical Society of America* 24(2). 175–184.

Pierrehumbert, Janet. 2001. Exemplar dynamics: Word frequency, lenition and contrast. In Joan Bybee & Paul J. Hopper (eds.), *Frequency effects and emergent grammar*, 137–158. Amsterdam: John Benjamins.

Pierrehumbert, Janet. 2002. Word-specific phonetics. In Carlos Gussenhoven & Natasha Warner (eds.), *Laboratory phonology 7* (Phonology and Phonetics 4(1)), 101–139. New York: Mouton de Gruyter.

Pierrehumbert, Janet. 2006. The next toolkit. *Journal of Phonetics* 34(6). 516–530.

Pisoni, David B. 1997. Some thoughts on "normalization" in speech perception. In Keith Johnson & John W. Mullennix (eds.), *Talker variability in speech processing*, 9–32. San Diego: Academic Press.

Podesva, Robert J. 2011. Salience and the social meaning of declarative contours: Three case studies of gay professionals. *Journal of English Linguistics* 39(3). 233–264.

Pomerantz, Shauna. 2008. *Girls, style, and school identities: Dressing the part*. New York: Palgrave Macmillan.

R Development Core Team. 2007. *R: A Language and Environment for Statistical Computing*. http://www.R-project.org, Accessed 2007-07-07. Vienna, Austria: R Foundation for Statistical Computing.

Rabinow, Paul. 1977. *Reflections on fieldwork in Morocco*. Berkeley: University of California Press.

Rampton, Ben. 2013. Styling in a language learned later in life. *The Modern Language Journal* 97(2). 360–382.

Rickford, John & Faye McNair-Knox. 1994. Addressee- and topic- influenced style shift: A quantitative sociolinguistic study. In Douglas Biber & Edward Finegan (eds.), *Sociolinguistic perspectives on register*, 235–276. Oxford: Oxford University Press.

Romaine, Suzanne. 1978. Postvocalic /r/ in Scottish English: Sound change in progress. In Peter Trudgill (ed.), *Sociolinguistic patterns in British English*, 144–157. London: Edward Arnold.

Romaine, Suzanne & Deborah Lange. 1991. The use of *like* as a marker of reported speech and thought: A case of grammaticalization in progress. *American Speech* 66(3). 227–279.

Saville-Troike, Muriel. 1982. *The ethnography of communication: An introduction*. Oxford: Blackwell.

Schilling-Estes, Natalie. 2004. Constructing ethnicity in interaction. *Journal of Sociolinguistics* 8(2). 163–195.

Starks, Donna & Hayley Reffell. 2006. Reading 'TH': Vernacular variants in Pasifika Englishes in South Auckland. *Journal of Sociolinguistics* 10(3). 382–392.

Strand, Elizabeth. 1999. Uncovering the role of gender stereotypes in speech perception. *Journal of Language and Social Psychology* 18(1). 86–99.

Strand, Elizabeth. 2000. *Gender stereotype effects in speech processing*. The Ohio State University PhD thesis.

Strand, Elizabeth & Keith Johnson. 1996. Gradient and visual speaker normalization in the perception of fricatives. In Dafydd Gibbon (ed.), *In natural language processing and speech technology*, 14–26. Berlin: Mouton de Gruyter.

Tagliamonte, Sali & Rachel Hudson. 1999. *Be like* et al. Beyond America: The quotative system in British and Canadian youth. *Journal of Sociolinguistics* 3(2). 147–172.

Traunmüller, Hartmut. 1990. Analytical expressions for the tonotopic sensory scale. *Journal of the Acoustical Society of America* 88(1). 97–100.

Trudgill, Peter. 1972. Sex, covert prestige and linguistic change in the urban British English of Norwich. *Language in Society* 1(2). 179–195.

Urban Dictionary, LLC. 1999-2015. www.urbandictionary.com, Accessed 2008-31-07.

Vitevitch, Michael S. & Paul A. Luce. 1999. Probabilistic phonotactics and neighborhood activation in spoken word recognition. *Journal of Memory and Language* 40. 374–408.

Weinrich, Uriel, William Labov & Marvin Herzog. 1968. Empirical foundations for a theory of language change. In Winfred P. Lehmann & Yakov Malkiel (eds.), *Directions for historical linguistics: A symposium*, 95–195. Austin: University of Texas Press.

Wenger, Etienne. 1998. *Communities of practice: Learning, meaning, and identity*. Cambridge: Cambridge University Press.

Wolfram, Walt. 1974. *Sociolinguistic aspects of assimilation: Puerto Rican English in New York City.* Arlington, VA: Center for Applied Linguistics.

Wouters, Johan & Michael W. Macon. 2002. Effects of prosodic factors on spectral dynamics. I. Analysis. *Journal of the Acoustical Society of America* 111(1). 417–426.

Zhang, Qing. 2005. A Chinese yuppie in Beijing: Phonological variation and the construction of a new professional identity. *Language in Society* 34(3). 431–466.

Zhao, Yuan & Dan Jurafsky. 2007. The effect of lexical frequency on tone production. In Jürgen Trouvain & William J. Barry (eds.), *Proceedings of the 16th International Congress of Phonetic Sciences*, 477–480. Saarbrücken: Universität des Saarlandes.

Zipf, George K. 1929. Relative frequency as a determinant of phonetic change. *Harvard Studies in Classical Philology* 15. 1–95.

Zwicky, Arnold. 1997. Two lavender issues for linguists. In Anna Livia & Kira Hall (eds.), *Queerly phrased: Language, gender, and sexuality*, 21–34. New York: Oxford University Press.

Name index

Agar, Michael H., 66, 69
Anderson, Gisle, 84
Aylett, Matthew, 18

Baayen, R. Harald, 95
Babel, Molly, 155
Bailey, Guy, 31, 73, 120
Baker, Rachel E., 18
Barney, Harold L., 13
Barras, Claude, 75
Bates, Douglas, 130
Bayard, Donn, 138
Beckman, Mary E., 113
Bell, Allan, 5, 18, 19, 29, 106, 108, 153, 155
Bentler, Peter M., 132
Biber, Douglas, 78
Bock, Kathryn, 18
Bod, Rens, 6
Boersma, Paul, 13, 88
Bourdieu, Pierre, 114
Bradlow, Ann R., 18
Breiman, Leo, 86
Bresnan, Joan, 17
Bucholtz, Mary, 110, 166, 167
Buchstaller, Isabelle, 81, 110, 128, 132, 149, 153
Bybee, Joan, 5, 17, 18, 20, 80, 106, 107, 154

Campbell-Kibler, Kathryn, 1, 15, 17, 138

Casasanto, Laura Staum, 15, 152
Cassidy, Steve, 91
Charon, Joel M., 7
Chartres, Laura, 112
Chomsky, Noam, 4
Chun, Elaine, 110
Clifton Jr., Charles, 142
Clopper, Cynthia G., 16
Cole, Jennifer, 113
Conrad, Susan, 78
Coupland, Justine, 29, 155
Coupland, Nikolas, 29, 155, 166
Cukor-Avila, Patricia, 31, 73, 120
Cutler, Anne, 142

D'Arcy, Alexandra, 77, 81, 84, 128, 129, 132, 149, 153
Dailey-O'Cain, Jennifer, 110
Daly, Nicola, 9
Dilley, Laura, 113
Docherty, Gerard, 14, 90, 154
Docherty, Gerard J., 14
Drager, Katie, 15, 156, 157
Drager, Katie, 3, 15, 16, 42, 115, 144, 155, 167, 169, 170
Du Bois, John W., 166

Eckert, Penelope, 7, 10–12, 23, 34, 109, 110, 150, 161, 166
Edwards, Jan, 113

Fix, Sonya, 89

Name index

Fletcher, Janet, 113
Fougeron, Cécile, 113
Foulkes, Paul, 14, 90, 154, 156
Fromont, Robert, 87, 134

Gahl, Susanne, 17–20, 106
Geertz, Clifford, 165
Giles, Howard, 29, 138, 155
Girand, Cynthia, 5, 18, 19, 106, 108, 153
Goffman, Erving, 168
Goldinger, Stephen D., 153
Gordon, Elizabeth, 9, 112
Gordon, Matthew, 8
Gray, Alison, 23
Griffiths, Thomas L., 154

Hall-Lew, Lauren, 89
Harrington, Jonathan, 91
Hay, Jennifer, 6, 9, 14–18, 87, 106, 109, 115, 134, 144, 155–157
Hebdige, Dick, 109
Herzog, Marvin, 2
Holmquist, Jonathan C., 10
Hudson, Rachel, 81
Hymes, Del, 5, 12

Jackson, Douglas N., 132
Jannedy, Stefanie, 6, 18, 106, 109, 155, 157
Johnson, Keith, 3, 145, 147, 154, 156, 157
Jurafsky, Dan, 5, 18
Jurafsky, Daniel, 3, 5, 18, 19, 106, 108, 147, 152, 153

Kattab, Ghada, 166
Keating, Patricia A., 113
Kiesling, Scott F., 166
Kirtley, M. Joelle, 166

Kondo, Dorinne K., 32

Lévi-Strauss, Claude, 150
Labov, William, 2, 4, 5, 7–10, 13, 24, 73, 74, 80, 161
Ladefoged, Peter, 88
Lange, Deborah, 78
Lave, Jean, 11
Lavoie, Lisa M., 91
Levelt, Willem J. M., 121
Lewis, Gillian, 9
Lewis, Stacy, 38
Luce, Paul A., 154

Maclagan, Margaret A., 9, 14
Macon, Michael W., 113
Mani, Lata, 29
McConnell-Ginet, Sally, 11
McNair-Knox, Faye, 120
McQueen, James M., 151, 152
Mendoza-Denton, Norma, 12, 18, 34, 68, 106, 109, 155, 157
Messick, Samuel, 132
Meyer, Antje S., 121
Milroy, James, 10, 73, 109
Milroy, Lesley, 7–10, 66, 109
Munson, Benjamin, 18, 106

Narayan, Kirin, 20, 29
Narayanan, Srini, 3, 147, 152
Niedzielski, Nancy, 15, 16, 156
Nielsen, Kuniko, 152
Nolan, Aaron, 15, 16, 144
Norris, Dennis, 151, 152
Nosofsky, Robert M., 154

Ochs, Elinor, 7, 44
Ostendorf, Mari, 113

Peterson, Gordon E., 13

Name index

Pierrehumbert, Janet, 3, 145, 147, 151, 153, 154, 156, 161
Pisoni, David B., 3, 16, 153
Podesva, Robert J., 12, 166
Pomerantz, Shauna, 1
Powesland, Peter F., 29, 138

Rabinow, Paul, 32
Rampton, Ben, 166
Reffell, Hayley, 9
Reppen, Rani, 78
Rickford, John, 120
Roelofs, Ardi, 121
Romaine, Suzanne, 9, 78

Sarkar, Deepayan, 130
Saussure, Ferdinand de, 4
Saville-Troike, Muriel, 7
Schilling-Estes, Natalie, 166
Shattuck-Hufnagel, Stefanie, 113
Solomon, Nancy Pearl, 18
Starks, Donna, 9
Steiner, Richard, 10
Strand, Elizabeth, 5, 15, 156

Tagliamonte, Sali, 81
Traunmüller, Hartmut, 91
Trudgill, Peter, 9, 24, 154, 155
Turk, Alice, 18

Vitevitch, Michael S., 154

Walker, Abby, 155
Warren, Paul, 15, 156, 157
Warren, Paul, 9
Watt, Dominic J., 14
Weenink, David, 88
Weinrich, Uriel, 2
Wenger, Etienne, 5, 11, 44, 53, 54
Wilson, Colin, 152

Wolfram, Walt, 9
Wouters, Johan, 113

Yaeger, Malcah, 10

Zhang, Qing, 12
Zhao, Yuan, 18
Zipf, George K., 18
Zwicky, Arnold, 113, 150

Subject index

/k/, 74, 86–96, 100, 102, 103, 106–109, 113–119, 123–125, 129, 131, 135, 140, 141, 143, 144, 148, 151, 153, 157, 161, 162, 167, 169
/k/ closure, 89, 102
/k/ release, 88
/l/, 86, 88, 89, 92–94, 96–100, 103, 105–107, 113, 123, 131, 132, 136, 142, 148, 152

activation, 154–156, 158, 161
awareness, 33, 55, 144

Bayesian, 3, 147, 151, 152, 156, 157
bricolage, 109

communicative competence, 5, 12, 165
conforming, 114, 115
constellation of practices, 44
control variables, 97, 98, 101, 104, 107, 108

diphthong, 10, 12, 16, 88, 105, 110, 112, 124, 137, 142, 143

exemplar cloud, 154, 155
exemplar model, 3, 153, 155, 156, 158

F1, 13, 89, 91, 97, 136
F2, 13, 88, 89, 91, 97, 104–107, 123, 130, 133, 135–138, 148, 149
First Wave, 7–9, 12
footing, 168

formant traces, 91

glottalisation, 13, 86, 90, 91

high school, 2, 10, 23, 24, 34, 41, 42, 47, 61, 68, 69, 166
hybrid model, 151, 154, 157, 161

identity, 1–3, 5, 6, 11, 17, 20, 23, 24, 29–32, 34, 47, 50, 60, 67, 74, 112–114, 118, 120, 147, 148, 150, 151, 161, 163, 165
intonation, 95, 99, 100

laboratory phonology, 17, 170
language ideology, 110, 114, 120
lemma, 1–3, 6, 17–20, 121, 123, 132, 136, 138, 140, 142–145, 148, 149, 151–153, 156, 157

mixed effects model, 95, 96, 100, 104, 107, 140
monophthong, 129, 135, 140, 143
multidimensional representations, 147, 158, 160, 161

naturalness, 74
NCR girls, 35, 39, 44, 52, 54–58, 60, 75, 81, 83, 84, 90, 91, 102, 103, 106, 107, 109, 114, 115, 117–121, 123, 141–143, 147, 148, 151, 168

NCR groups, 31, 35, 44, 45, 52–57, 70, 114, 115, 120, 141, 142, 147, 151
New Zealand English, 9, 110, 128, 149, 153
norms, 3, 10, 32, 35, 37, 44, 45, 51, 53, 55, 56, 114, 115, 117–119, 143, 147, 148
NZE, 9, 15, 78, 112, 134

perception, 1–3, 5, 6, 13–17, 19, 20, 30, 54, 61, 63, 65, 68, 75, 105, 110, 111, 117, 121, 123–126, 132, 138, 142–145, 147–149, 151–153, 155–158, 165, 170
pitch, 89, 95–97, 99, 100, 103, 106, 112, 123, 129, 148, 149, 170
probabilistic models, 14, 163
prosody, 105, 113

rapport, 28–30, 47, 48, 63, 64
repetition, 109

salience, 154
Second Wave, 7–10, 54
Shortlist B, 152
social groups, 10, 11, 23, 75, 102, 109, 132, 138, 166, 167
social meaning, 11, 12, 34, 76, 109, 110, 150, 158, 160, 167
sociophonetics, 6, 109
speaker-specific frequency, 81, 85, 108
speech rate, 96, 99, 100, 169, 170
stance, 2, 7, 11, 12, 31, 32, 44, 48, 52–55, 59, 70, 91, 95–100, 107, 114, 119, 121, 136, 144, 147, 148, 150, 157, 166, 167, 169, 170
stress, 87, 112, 142
stylistic resources, 119

The BBs, 26–28, 34, 37–41, 43, 47, 48, 51, 52, 55, 57, 60–62, 67, 76, 93, 125, 126
The Christians, 34, 35, 37, 50, 54–56, 58, 59, 65, 77, 117
The Geeks, 30, 34, 35, 37, 45, 47, 51, 55, 57, 65, 76, 84, 117, 126, 167
The Goths, 34, 37, 42, 46–51, 54, 55, 57, 60, 65, 76, 84, 88, 92, 117, 119, 126, 134, 139, 158, 167
The Pasifika Group, 26, 27, 35, 37, 45, 46, 50, 55, 61, 65, 77, 94, 117, 118
The PCs, 26–28, 33–35, 37–40, 49, 53, 55–57, 63, 76, 77, 88, 111, 114, 120, 126, 128, 134, 139, 157, 167
The Real Teenagers, 26, 27, 34, 35, 37, 45, 47–50, 52, 56, 60, 64, 66, 84, 128
The Relaxed Group, 1, 26, 27, 34, 41–43, 47, 51, 57, 60, 64, 84, 93, 119
The Sporty Girls, 26, 34, 37, 39, 41, 45, 56, 57, 63, 65, 117, 118, 158
The Trendy Alternatives, 26, 27, 34, 37, 40, 41, 43, 57, 62, 84
Third Wave, 7, 8, 11, 12, 55, 157
token frequency, 5, 6, 17–19, 80, 106
token probability, 80

usage-based model, 147

velar pinch, 91
vernacular, 73

youth culture, 1, 76, 110

Subject index